A MURDER OF CROWS, SALVATION

By Tony Crowe

Published by New Generation Publishing in 2014

www.newgeneration-publishing.com

New Generation Publishing

Dedication

Thank you to all the people who helped by reading the
manuscript.
Thank you to Rita for the foreword.
For her diary notes and for putting up with hours of
looking at the back of my head
As I wrote the book on our computer.
I Love you Rita.

I dedicate this book to my Mother.
For all the times she came to where ever I was being
held.
And just for being my mother.
Love you Mum.
God Bless You.

Kevin J Commons my solicitor went the extra mile for
me.
He was a great friend who never stopped believing in
me.
Even whilst in jail he never failed me when I needed
his help.
The free work he did was motivated by his kindness.
A true gentleman.
On June 2nd 2010 Kevin was shot and killed at his
home in Frizington.
I am compelled by emotions to dedicate this work to
him also.
R.I.P. Good friend.
You will awake again.

A Murder of Crows
Salvation
By Tony Crowe

PK 111 Varna 9003 Bulgaria
www.ritanightingale.org

This is a true account to the best of my knowledge.
The real names of the people in this story have been
changed to protect the guilty.
All living people have been given new names apart
from those who have given their permission.

Contents

Foreword

"You have to get rid of that anger, give it over to God and let him deal with it." Words I spoke to Tony on many occasions.

I knew only too well of that burning anger and the pain of being unjustly convicted. Many years before I had been sentenced to 20 years in a prison in Bangkok Thailand.

Lots of people think and often say 'Oh everyone in prison says they are innocent', but in fact that is very far from the truth and I feel with over 20 years of visiting prisons and 15 of those working in the chaplaincy I do have some experience. No, not all people say they are innocent but every once in a while you come across those individuals who truly are. Tony Crowe is one of those people. One of the difficulties of this is that most people who work in prison and I include many chaplains too, don't know how to deal with this. They may come to accept that an injustice has been done but what can they do about it? Sadly many find it easier not to talk about it with the individual. They just don't know how to handle it. They sometimes feel they have to take sides or do something. From my own personal experience I used to say, they don't want you to get them out they just want to have a voice and be listened to.

Tony Crowe is a larger than life character, very intelligent these were two obvious characteristics when I first met Tony at Garth prison in 2001. Over the months so much more was to be discovered about this remarkable man. It's true he had a fearsome reputation and many staff members only go by the prisoners file. I in fact never looked at an inmate's file unless I had to; to write reports etc. Even then I would much rather a person tell me about who they are and their journey through life. Some would say that is naive, but as a Christian who came to faith from a prison cell, I believe that God loves every sinner but he hates the sin! That's not to say I believed all I heard either!

Tony was greatly respected by other inmates and he never compromised his faith, he " walked the walk' whether he was in chapel, on the wing, or in the gym. He was always ready to encourage or sometimes challenge. As I got to know the man behind the number, I have to say I was impressed by his integrity and his great sense of humour. I also saw the pain in his eyes and the deep hurt which so often is stored up as anger. I had no doubt about the sincerity of his faith but I knew unless he got rid of the anger he would not truly be free even after his release from prison, that's why I challenged him on many occasions. He knew my story that it was only after being set free from anger that God would release me from that prison cell.

After serving only 3 years of that 20 year sentence. That's why I could write a book with the title 'Freed for Life' and that was my deep desire for Tony. To be free.

So prepare yourself for a great read! Tony's honesty humour and at times despair will keep you wanting more. God used prison to reverse the course of Tony Crowe's life.

Be prepared as you read on. For the One who called this remarkable man may put a call on your life too.

By Rita Nightingale.

Into despair

The smell of fresh paint from recent renovation fills the air. A middle-aged guy dressed in a dark blue uniform stands tapping a pen on the high counter. His belly hanging over his belt.

"Stand on the yellow line, give me your name," says the officer. His fingernails carry soil from last weekend's exploits at the allotment.

"Tony."

"Last name son?" instantly "Crowe," I answer.

"Right - Crowe, you will be given a number, CP3703, that's you now, son - What's your number?"

"CP -3703."

"Sir! Or Boss will do son." His muddy brown eyes widen. "Do you know why you're here son?" my thought is, the best way to get through this is say as little as possible.

I say "No."

"You," he starts "have been remanded into the custody of HMP Durham by the courts till next week, that's – let me see – the twentieth of November - All right?" A question needing no answer. I give it none. Next for the charms of the fat-faced controller at the desk are The Six men who came on the bus with me, not a real bus, a van. With a small box regulation size. 900mm high; just taller than me, with 810mm between plastic moulded seat and front wall. 650mm from the door to the side wall; and window of dark tinted plastic.

For journeys of more than two and a half hours the seat is suppose to have a full-seat-cushion. We'd been on there for over three hours by the time we reached HMP Durham; no cushion. Three hours, of what for me was an eternity. The six others on the bus are all friends of Swindles. The slag I'm in this situation for. Imagine the abuse I've had to put up with.

I got to the police station on Friday night. The Six pals of "Dangerous" Swindles' had been on their committal hearing all week. They missed the deadline for getting back to Durham jail. A lockout. Overnighting in Whitehaven cop-shop. I was put into the first cell, number one, so as not to pass the others. I asked the desk officer not to tell them the new inmate was me. I was respected enough by the police to be able to make some requests and get them granted. First thing I needed was a walk in the small yard. Second, a cigarette. I had been travelling for days without washing, smoking, eating although I got a good breakfast at the police station in Gatwick airport. After my walk I was back in the cell ready to get my head down on the wooden bed with its wooden pillow when it started. One of the six shouted.

"Who's in one?" I ignored the question. Again it came. From the other cells it came. I kept my anonymity. Then one said to the other.

"It's Tony Crowe." I couldn't believe it. When my hot sweet mug of tea came, courtesy of the desk officer, I asked him. "How do they know it's me? I asked you not to tell them."

"I didn't Tony. They have a radio. It's been on all day about you coming back from Malta. Your arrest by Interpol is big news," he said. All that night I had them in my ear. Then on the road trip in the van they told me how they would do me in when we got to the jail.

"Next." The desk officer shouts in his distinct Geordie twang. As I sit in the reception waiting room I can see them. I know two of them; not the one doing the mouthing-off. He's not that big with a Scouse accent. Perhaps Skelmersdale just outside Liverpool. As long as I can keep away from them until I can work out how to handle the gobby one, I might stand a chance.

"Crowe." Someone out of sight is shouting. Although I don't know why. The door is locked from the outside I can't go to the call even if I want to. I can tell you – I don't. Someone gets the message; I'm let out and led into the next room of this warren. There is an equally stern red-faced man sitting behind his desk.

"Stand on that board," he points at the floor, "Put your feet on the marks." He gets impatient, I look down to my feet, there, painted in black are two foot-marks, I stand on the marks and wait for whatever is to come.

"Height, five foot seven – Strip."

"What." I say in an instant reaction to the order.

"Strip off." His voice more forceful. I start with my top, looking around, there's nowhere to hang my clothes. Another officer, the one who opened the door, grabs my top.

"Put all your stuff on the table."

"I've just come from the police station; all my stuff – was taken off me there - I've got nothing."

"You just take off your clothes, I'll tell you if you have or haven't got anything lad." I'm standing completely naked, still with my feet on the black marks.

"Lift your arms, turn round, now squat. Open your mouth, now get a shower then you can get your clothes on and go in that room." It's as if I'm being deloused in case I take some infectious disease into their prison. I'd forgotten about The Six would-be assassins. In the room I'm given something to eat. Not up to the standard of Gatwick. But I suppose you can live on it, I wouldn't recommend it. I'm doing okay up till now in avoiding a confrontation with The Six.

"Crowe,' I'm still eating, "Come on, you have to see the Doctor."

"I don't need to see a Doctor now." I had asked for one when I got off the aeroplane at Gatwick. I was ill

11

with what I think was decompression sickness. The bends. Interpol put me on a plane before it was safe after I had been scuba diving for a full year.

"Everybody sees the Doc for a full check up, come on." I'm led to another room and locked in. After a short time the door opens. I get up to go and see this Doctor. To my horror in comes The Six, now what? Time to face up to them. If I take out the gobby-one first, maybe the others – what am I thinking? No way will they watch as I take out their mate. This is neither the time nor place; I'll have to go for plan B. what is plan B?

"You're in for cutting up me mate Lar – Dangerous."

"Yeah that's me, what's that to do with you?" Attack said to be the best means of defence. My heart rises up into my throat so far if I reach into my mouth I could touch it." Dangerous is me mate Lar." A whole circus trapeze act is going on inside my stomach.

I give a long look around the small cell; I'm out numbered six-to-one. But I have one weapon left. Reputation. He doesn't know me. He will know my reputation. It was said I was the one who took a shotgun and shot up a house that one of the six was sitting in at the time. I don't wish to comment on that now. Here goes.

"Look – it's got nothing to do with you, I don't even know you mate, but if you want to have a go, well that's up to you. And I'm not you lad." Or lar as he puts it.

"When you get in there you're getting cut-up lar."

The door opens. I pick up my bed pack and leave. Saved by the Doctor.

"How are you?"

"I'm okay."

"Stand on the scales; eighty-six kilos. Right that's it; next." Two minutes, one question, now back to the cell and The Six?

"This way Crowe you're going to the wing." It looks like I've survived today. I walk through the labyrinth. Locked door after locked door. The silence is a dark cloak hanging over the prison. We arrive on B wing. I can see one cell door secured with a large padlock; it has scene of crime tape over the handle.

"What's that all about then?" I ask the officer.

"Suicide, young lad hung himself last night." He doesn't bat an eye as he tells me all the gory details of how this lad made a hang-man's noose out of a sheet. A thought comes to me – a thought that makes me shiver from top to toe.

"Don't put me in with anyone from Whitehaven or Cumbria," I say, he looks puzzled, "I don't have a very good reputation in my old town. I'm charged with chopping the hands and feet off one of the drug dealers in the area. Prison's full of drug users, I'm sure you get my point." Now he thinks I'm off my head, I can tell by the look in his old grey eyes.

"Just put me with someone who won't give me any grief; a Geordie; you Newcastle boys are just fine." Off he goes to the wing office to sort out my cell. I look round at the row upon row of blue steel doors with their white handles. From the first floor all the way up through the Victorian ornate wrought iron work to the third floor, blue doors. I can't help but wonder who; what is lurking behind all these doors.

"Two-twenty-seven; come on." Time to find out. I pick up me bundle of old torn and bedraggled bedding, two sheets, two blankets, one pillowcase. I climb the iron stairway, leading to the cell opposite the suicide cell. The door is opened; I wonder. Who will greet me on the other side?

"All right mate?" A voice comes out of the gloom. The cell is eight-foot by twelve; there's a tin toilet a tin sink, and two iron beds. Although the sink and toilet are stainless steel they show years of use; red rust erupting from the surface at the water level. The smell is nothing I can compare it to. A hole in the wall is where a window once was. Now a rusty sheet of metal drilled with rows of small holes takes its place. Bang: the door slams behind me.

"Darrel's me name mate, what's yours?"

"Crowe," I say.

"No ya first name?"

"Or, Tony; Tony's my name." I throw my things onto the empty bed and sit down on the edge with a heavy sigh.

"Just come in mate?"

"Yeah, I've been travelling for the last five days, I'm worn-out."

"What ya in for?"

"I've got about twenty-nine charges where do you want to start?" He looks worried his face blank.

"I'm in for an eighteen me-self." I sense him trying to impress me with his charge of wounding with intent.

"I've got that one," I tell him with no great fuss, "And attempted murder." Then comes all the legal advice. "Listen mate I'm a bit knackered I just need to get my head down. What's the score with the window?" I ask.

"I never bother, the fresh air's good for ya."

"Not for me it's not, I've just come back from the Med, I'm freezing."

"Med mate? You mean the Mediterranean? What were you doing there?"

"Hiding from the Law. Later if you don't mind."

"No problemo mate we'll have plenty of time later." It's the middle of November and cold. I make a

14

blackout curtain from my oldest blanket, to cover the hole in the wall, keeping the best one for my bed. The mattress has more stains on it than there are dots of white on the blue walls. The dots are toothpaste, a primitive form of glue. I don't want to think of what the stains are. My mattress is two inch thick on the edge, half inch in the middle, and the rusty pattern of the bed frame imprinted on the under-side; it's a mess. I'll ask for a new one in the morning. Darrel's bed's no better and he doesn't have a pillow.

"What about a pillow?" I ask him.

"Ya must be joking mate." He chuckles. "Ya don't get a pillow unless you're a long-termer." He laughs.

"So what's the pillowcase for?" I hold it up to show him.

"That's just to wind ya up, I'll bet they give ya a toothbrush but no toothpaste and a towel but no soap?" he's right.

I didn't sleep all night; the police station was red-hot, just right. But this place! I am sure I'll die of cold.

Bang – I jump up with a start, the door swings open.

"What time is it?" my first question.

"Breakfast time." It's eight in the morning and not a lot warmer, time to face the world of prison and The Six. I step out onto the landing; the stench of body-odour hits me like the exhaust of a jet engine. A foul sweet sickly smell of rotting flesh makes my nostrils flare. The noise is that of one hundred and fifty men moving up and down iron stairs in a military procession. No sign of The Six. Maybe they went to another wing! As I stand in line waiting for my breakfast I see one, the one I know, Baggy. He is the one from the house destroyed by the shooting. He's on his way back to his cell on the third landing. I pick up a food tray and move with the flow of half-asleep men. I'm far from half-asleep. I'm ready for whatever they try; the tray is a heavy stainless steel thing with a good sharp corner.

"Cornflakes or porridge?" The server asks me.

"What? Oh, Cornflakes." I push my would-be weapon out in front of me. The Cornflakes barely cover the bottom of my tray; but there's more than enough to soak up all the milk the next guy puts on. It's a production line with a conveyor belt of people moving past white clad cons tattooed with homemade designs from a pin and Indian ink. I make my way back to cell twenty-seven on the twos, looking for signs of normality; there is none.

The cell door bangs behind me. Darrel's already sitting on his bed eating the sticky grey goo slopped into a kidney shaped indent in his tray.

"Porridge." He says sensing my interest in it. I finish in no time and go to the tin sink to wash, and to clean my teeth. Remembering I've got nothing to wash with. Apart from of course; my toothbrush!

"Do ya want some soap and toothpaste?"

'If you've got some."

"In the bag on the table." He points to a brown paper bag sitting on a small table over in the corner. I start to wash, Darrel climbs into bed.

"What happens now?"

"What do ya mean?" The question puzzles him.

"What I mean is what goes on now?"

"Nothing goes on, nothing ever goes on."

I can't believe I'm going to be locked up for a week in this hole in the ground. The door opens. This is my chance.

"I need a new mattress and a pillow..."

"Trays – get that off the window or I'll nick you son." Putting the trays on the floor outside the door I try to speak again. Before I can say anything more the

16

door slams shut. From outside I can hear the slag laughing.

"He wants a pillow." Having finished washing and making my bed. It's looking like I'm not going to get a new matters or pillow. I sit on the bed wondering what to do. There's a magazine under the bed. I pick it out of the dust and green fluff that covers the floor, cars, great that's all I need right now. The price guide in the back doesn't look right. A closer look at the small print on the inside cover tells me why. It's only out of date by four years. May 1993 the date on the cover. A thought! If a magazine can't get out I've got no chance.

In two days I've read every word, after a week I could tell you what page to look at for what car you wanted. I'm at the end of the magazine for the first time when the door opens. I know it's not the norm. Darrel lifts his head.

"What's happening mate?" he asks.

"Induction Crowe." The officer calls out.

"Good luck." Darrel says, "You'll need it." The Officer or screw as they are known by the cons, takes me to an office just off the wing. A guy in a suit of drab dark grey with worn collar and tired cuffs sits behind a desk. He greets me.

"CP3703 Crowe?" there's a seat about two yards from the desk, "Sit down. Now - I'm the Governor do you know why you're here?" Again I think say nothing, no was as good an answer as any so that's what I give him. It turns out he knows even less than I do. Believe me that isn't easy I know nothing.

"Do you have any dogs or other animals that need looking after or feeding?" I resisted the obvious answer to his somewhat unconvincing concern for another creature's well being. I just stick to the same answer.

"No."

"Do you want anyone told of your whereabouts?" My arrest was all over the radio and on TV. This must be the only person in the UK who didn't see it. Again the answer is.

"No." The next question is by far the best.

"Have you left a fire on in your house or flat?" The questions are too ridiculous to answer.

"Is there anything you would like to ask me?" now is my chance.

"Well as you're asking, there is. I need a mattress, a pillow and a window would be nice…." On and on I go with my questions. I'm not wasting this chance, when I finish the Governor says.

"No, as far as the pillow's concerned every cell has two pillows." His pre-rehearsed way is obvious. This man doesn't know or care what day it is let alone whether or not CP3703 has a pillow. Next on the list of must-sees is the probation.

"What are you here for?" Great, she must be trying out their system to see if the rest of the mindless morons are doing their jobs right. It's worked up to now so I answer.

"I have no idea." Like a drone she goes into the spiel, now I understand why Darrel said "good luck" he knew it was a waste of time and of no use to anyone. I take the opportunity to ask anyone I speak to for soap and anything else I can think of. It works. On my way to cell, twenty-seven on the twos, I'm given a small brown paper bag of toiletries; there's even a razor in there. This induction is nothing like the time I was inducted into a Hells Angel Gang at the age of seventeen. It sure isn't induction into any hall of fame either. When I get back Darrel's out of bed.

"Cup of tea mate?"

"Yes go on."

"Have ya got a cup mate?"

"They never gave me a cup."

"They never give ya anything; he' ya are mate; I'll use this." He picks a marvel tin out of the plastic bucket under the small table. The bin. It's plastic so you can't light a fire in it and make toast after evening lock-up. I think of saying I'll use that, then I think again– I say nothing other than thanks when he gives me a nice hot cup of tea in a blue plastic mug.

"How come you're up?"

"Exercise, I've been out on exercise man, ya missed it. How did ya get on with the Governor mate? Did he offer to feed your dog and all that shit?"

"Yeah, how long have you been here Darrel?"

"Six month now – six month," he repeats it, as if it's been all his life, "I'm up at court next week; I'll get two to three." He says without a hint of emotion.

"Two to three what?" I ask.

"Years."

"What for?"

"I hit some lads with a bottle, outside a chippy in Newcastle." He then goes on to tell me the whole story. How a gang of lads set about him and his wife when they were eating chips in the car with their kids, sounds like self-preservation to me but there you go. Taking this opportunity I tell him about The Six. Just in case they come in the cell and try anything. He should know if he's in with me.

Next time the door opens is dinner time, Darrel sits up on his bed, and waits with plastic cup in hand, white plastic knife and fork in his cup. Just before the door opens. It's as if he has been programmed like some computer, or lab rat, to the door opening. Right out of the blue he says.

"I'll watch ya back mate in the queue down stairs if ya like."

19

"Sounds good to me." So off we go for something they say is food. Day turns to night, peace and quiet to noise and shouting. I've been in for over a full day now; and the only other inmate I've talked to is Darrel. Apart from meal times I've been locked up for twenty-four hours, this is going to send me mad.

That night I sleep well, not because the bed has a new mattress or a pillow. I am just worn out with all the travelling back from Malta. Monday I phone Dawn, the mother of my son. I ask her to get in touch with Kevin Commons, solicitors. My faith in Rolly the duty solicitor is nil. Roland Earl (Rolly) came to the police station. With twenty-nine charges Rolly told me.

"Don't worry you'll walk on all these." He didn't know what the evidence was or what half the charges were. That worried me a lot. He had to go. I ask Kevin to be in court on Friday for my next hearing. I make it clear, I want him not some, & Co Muppet, day after day I stay in the cell with nothing but an old car magazine and Darrel. He is true to his word; he watches my back any time we are out of the cell, which isn't that often. If a cloud's in the sky exercise is cancelled. Let's face it, the north-west of England isn't known for its sunny days in November. Kevin's there on the dot.

"Right, I'm Kevin Commons," a portly guy wearing a dark pin-stripe suit. His upper lip supporting a large moustache. Is sitting behind the single table in the small room under the court steps. "All I know about your case is what I've seen on the TV, you'll have to give me some background."

He opens an A4 pad, unscrews the top off a fat fountain pen, rubbing a finger on his greying temple.

"Background? I'm charged with trying to kill someone and loads of drugs shit, and don't be telling me not to worry like Rolly, because that's why you're here not him."

"Rolland's outside, he wants to see you, should I send him in?"

"Yeah but you can tell him you're my solicitor now, and tell him I am worried." Kevin gives my message to Rolly; he sees no point in coming to see me. He knows he has just lost a legal aid cheque of three quarters of a million pounds. I'm in court for a total of two minutes. Just enough time for the prosecuting solicitor to ask for me to be remanded back into custody, this time for twenty-one days. Kevin never asks for bail there's as much chance of them giving me bail as the pope becoming a Jew. You only have two applications for bail so it has to be a good one.

"You will be remanded to Durham for twenty-one days, to prevent you from intimidating any witnesses, do you understand?" Other than I was being locked up for something I might do. To stop me committing further offences, what is there not to understand? What about innocent until proven guilty?

The court is full of police, at the back stands Detective Sergeant Hatwood a tall solemn man in his forties. He has the look of an undertaker. It will be his job to make the charges stick and bury me. Mine to make sure they don't. Not a very worthy adversary, but he has all his brother officers to help him weave his tangled web of deceit. I once had the pleasure of throwing him and four of his brothers out of a house they were searching. The warrant had the wrong date on it. We'll see just how far he'll go for The Job. He came to Malta as my escort. I don't think he likes me. Back in the court cell waiting for the end of the court day my time is spent reading the local newspaper and drinking tea. Lunch time I set about the microwave meal served up in its plastic tray. Added to my one room restaurant, with on call service, is a young fellow who is too drunk to stand, let alone stand in court. He's put in the cells until he is sober. He takes no notice of me and I likewise pay him no heed. The cell officer starts feeding him with hot coffee by the mug full. After the first mug he sits down on the wooden bench next to me.

"All right mate. What you up for then?"

"I've been up young'en. I'm waiting for the van back to Jail."

"Are ya on remand mate?"

"I sure am. What you doing here then?"

"Before I come like I downed a bottle of cider so now they won't let me in."

"Get that coffee down ya and get yourself away home son."

"What ya on remand for mate?"

"Attempted murder." The blood drains out of his face all the way down to his feet.

"You're not Tony Crowe are you?"

"I am indeed son. Pleased to meet you."

"Wait till I tell me mates tonight. I can't believe they put me in with you. You're in for cutting up Swindles. O man I can't believe it. You made a right mess of him mate. He's just a dick-head he slapped me mate around the other week. Ya should have finished him off mate. Wait till I tell me mates about this."

"You look a lot better now son call the jailer and get yourself back up stairs. I don't want to burst your bubble but I didn't cut Swindles up."

"Whatever you say big fellow." He calls the jailer who can't understand the boy's sobriety. Off he goes with the story of how he was in with the mad axe man of Distington.

Seven o'clock the van pulls into the prison grounds. The big sliding door slips open slowly. Screeching, revealing an old dark wooded inner door. We go into the air lock's deep void where a screw examines the van inside and out. Mirrors show him the underneath. I can never understand why they think anyone would want to sneak into a prison. When they're happy with the van and its contents. The inner-door opens with the sound a schoolboy makes dragging his fingernails down a blackboard. It reaches its full extent as if it's for the last time in its long life. Inside the prison courtyard the small cell door is opened. From the van door to the caged walkway leading into the reception building is one step.

"Stand on the line." here we go again. "Crowe CP3703."

"Yeah that's me." I answer with a, can't be bothered voice.

"Did you leave here this morning?"

"You know I did you were the one that put me on the van." You moron, I add under my breath. I don't get a chance to say any more.

"Wait in the next room." I can see him pass a file through the hole in the wall to another mindless moron, so he can ask me the same questions all over again. It takes him half an hour to finish his coffee and come for me.

"Empty your pockets onto the desk."

"I've got nothing in my pockets, just like I had nothing in them when you searched them this morning on my way out."

"Strip off, stand on the marks painted on the floor." He says it without even looking up to see if I've complied. After the obligatory degrading strip search I go to the room where I get fed. All day I've had a microwave massacre, two frozen sandwiches, cheese, a packet of crisps and two biscuits, this food's not for enjoyment but necessity. Three hours I'm sat in the waiting room before I'm taken to two twenty-seven on B wing. Darrel's keen to know what went on, not

23

because of any interest he may have in my case but because he's bored out of his head.

"Twenty-one days remand." keeping it as brief as I can.

"They always do that, seven days then it's twenty-ones after that." He tells me as a matter-of-fact.

"Has anything happened here?" Not expecting anything exciting or of great importance to have upset the day-to-day drudgery of prison life. Thinking hard to make sure he hasn't missed anything.

"No; someone was stabbed on the yard but he was just a sex-case, I think. Other than that no nothing's gone on." It's not unusual for sex-offenders to be stabbed or even cutup with a razor blade melted onto a toothbrush. So that's why they gave me a toothbrush when I came in? Sex-cases are usually kept on a wing with other scum bags in for crimes not found to be acceptable to decent cons. The term for this in prison is "on the numbers" because the prison rule that's used to protect sex-cases is rule 45, some of the slags try to mix in with us but are soon found out and stabbed or cut. Vulnerable Prisoners or VP's the prison calls them. Not as vulnerable as the children they abused. It's not the overwhelming desire for justice that drives this violence but sheer boredom. As in all walks of life there are the strong and the weak, prisoners on the numbers are the weak. The problem is, on remand no one is guilty of anything. One guy was hit in the face with a house brick. It smashed his face into five pieces. His left eye was on his cheek. He went to trial and was found not guilty of child assault.

For the next twenty-one days I'm opened up for breakfast at eight o'clock then again at eleven-thirty for lunch, then at four in the afternoon for dinner. Every week's the same as the last one. Monday is shopping day. Food and sweets. Tobacco and twenty unit phone cards. The currency of jail. Whatever you want for your ten pound allowance. Every two-week I can have a visit from family and friends; these are for two hours and in the afternoon. My first visit is from Dawn. It left me with some hope of a good outcome.

On the day of my visit I manage to get a shower and a shave. I take off my own clothes that are not permitted on visits. Put on prison clothing, and I'm ready. The door opens.

"Crowe visit."The call comes. I go out onto the landing and wait with everybody else who has a visit. We're all taken to the visits waiting room together. As I go past the row of DST officers (Designated Search Team) I can see the clean, well-kept room that is the visits. A bit different from the squalor we have to live in.

"Number twenty." The woman says. None of the small low tables have numbers on them. She has a floor plan on her desk.

"Where's number twenty?"

With the wave of her hand, "down there," she answers me. I wander off in the general direction of her waved hand hoping to see Dawn, as I get closer to the tuck-shop I see her sitting at the corner table. She's a welcome sight. The time goes faster than a full week behind the cell door. With our good-bye said the visit is over, now a thing of the past a memory. On the way out I find out why the DST are so called. They search like no one else. Even they can't look inside the body; most drugs are brought in by screws. Or in the anal cavity of a paid addict.

Back on the wing in my cell, it's as if the visit never happened.

The next big thing is association, this is when they let me outside the cell to shower and watch, an old film on an old T.V. it's also the time you can stab a sex-case, if that's your thing in life. The most popular thing to do is use the phone. It's not as easy as you may imagine. At the dinner time unlock you've to put your name on a list. You get five-minute slots, if you're fast. There's a saying in prison, if you're not fast you're last. In this case you aren't last; you do without. Imagine the fight to get your name on the phone list.

When the door is unlocked at a quarter to six it's like opening cages of lab rats. All trained to come out on demand, that stench hits me. People come and go. No one seems to stay long, thank God. When the screw calls my name I go to the phone. There are only six phones; they're on the end of the wing. The noise is deafening, everybody not on the phones are talking to people they're not locked up with. The screws are shouting out orders at the top of their voices. Five minutes and it's all over for another four long days, then I'll go through it all again; just for five minutes on a noise phone. The best five minutes of the four days.

After the phone I sit on the floor, keeping me back to the wall. There's still the small matter of The Six. One is working as a wing cleaner, Tommo the gobby one. That means he's open all day and every association time. I know he won't do anything on his own so I'm safe. Safe for now.

I use my time making alliances with the top of the tree in the criminal underworld. I very soon become someone people keep on the right side of. On association I talk to the right people. On the yard I stand with the same right people. I soon don't have to get into the melee at the phone queue. I just pay a queuer to do it for me. I don't queue for anything. I pay someone to do it for me.

The yard is surrounded by four high walls festooned with strands of green string torn from the bedding, used as fishing lines to pass items one cell to another. A ticker-tape parade in some other place or time. Over the yard, from my wall to the one opposite there are wires with orange balls on them the size of grapefruit, helicopter wire. Stretched out like tight ropes in a high-wire act. The once red sandstone walls are now black with vertical white lines of pigeon faeces cascading from the window openings, feculent mist drifts from the holes in the walls that mark out a cell.

Poem CP3703

CP3703, that's me!
I once had a name,
It was given by my Mother.
When I came to jail,
It was taken away by another.
CP3703, that's me!
Sometimes even that's reduced,
To. "Last three?"
No-one knows my given name.
When asked I tell them. (Tony; I Say)
They don't listen,
They always repeat with.
"Antony? Or is that Anthony?
I don't know.
Do they honestly think
I don't know my name?
They only ask it so as,
To take it away.
They lock it in a file.
Only to be taken out,
At the end of my,
"Rehabilitation"
My long mile.
Until then it's, Crowe!
Or, CP3703.
Whenever they call me.
I feel like a man with no name.
There's nobody to,
Call me by my name.
I feel like a man with no name.
Because without using my name,
It's forgotten;
Not just by me, but by we.

Kevin comes to jail

Out of the blue my spy-hole opens, a voice, a Scouse voice.

"Tony; Tony Lar."

"Who's that?" I can't make him out but only one person on this wing has a Liverpool accent.

"Tommo it's me Lar Tommo," the gobby one of The Six.

"What d'ya want," I ask with a voice full of contempt.

"Listen Lar, I want to tell ya, we've decided to forget about what we said in reception."

"We; is it? I only heard you say anything LAR, listen." I say because that's what you always say in prison before you tell anybody anything. "You just do what you think you should, don't bother 'bout me, "LAR" I have him and his mates on the run, I've suffered all this time, now is my hour, I love it. "You said it, now do it." I tell him. I can't watch a man grovel too much though, the next week he comes back; I let him off the hook. Funny, but he can't do enough for me now. He is now my queuer for the phone.

I'm sitting on association watching Clint Eastwood saying make my day, when at the gate to the wing there stands a lad; I notice him looking at me as if he knows me. My mate, Vinnie, sitting next to me says.

"D'ya know him?" pointing to the lad.

"No I've never seen him before in me life - why?"

"He keeps looking over here as if he knows ya," says Vinnie. Not long after the screw lets him in, he has his bed-pack, it's obvious by the bundle he's a new recruit to our happy family. After the screw's taken him to his cell he makes straight for me. As he gets closer I get out of my seat. I face him. Eastwood's words fresh in my mind. It's clear he is going to say something to me, I don't know what.

"Are you Tony Crowe?"

"Who are you?"

"Garry Porter," he says it as if I should know. The name turns on a dim light in my thoughts, but I can't put my finger on it.

"I'm from Distington." My heart sinks faster than the Titanic; this must be a friend of Swindles', right away I get on the defensive. Vinnie is up in a shot. Porter takes a step back.

"It's nothing to do with me."

"What's nothing to do with you then?"

"All this with you and Dangerous, I haven't said nowt, neither has Dangerous. I've got nothing against ya."

I know as much as the police told me. Nothing. I wasn't asked any questions. I haven't been given the depositions, the papers that would tell me what was going on.

"Well somebody's said something, or I wouldn't have been dragged onto a plane and brought back from Malta by Interpol. I wouldn't have been charged with attempted murder on your mate Danger – would I?" I spit the words into his face.

He's speechless his face a deathly pallor, I look him in the eye. I see fear. A bead of sweat erupts from his forehead and rolls down his cheek. I break the silence.

"I'm going to court on Friday, I'll get the deps, your name better not be in them." Off he goes to his cell. I sit back down watching him go. I realise why he's worried. He is in the same cell as Vinnie. Outside the cell is a card with the name of the occupant. Vinnie's name is Crowe. Porter saw it thinking he was in with me. A smile comes on my face, I tell Vinnie the joke.

"I'll do him in for ya."

"No, I don't know if he even had anything to do with any of this shit."

"Well when you come back on Friday night, if his name's in your deps he's getting it."

Friday my day in court; at seven o'clock in the morning the door opens and the ritual of going to court begins again. I'm taken to the other end of the jail, locked into a holding cell with fifty other soon to be criminals. See, what you may not realise is all the people on remand waiting to go to court are not guilty of anything yet. Everybody is smoking farting; there's some that have been in the same clothes for a week. In short it stinks. Breakfast is a bowl of Cornflakes and a mug of sweet tea. I'm sure that's so you'll need the toilet on the way.

"Crowe, Whitehaven." One thing about having to travel so far is you're the first out.

"Stand on the line and strip off." Here we go again. The senior officer (S.O) comes with a file, which has my photo on it, taken on that first day.

"Crowe CP3703, is that you son?" It's not fun anymore so he gets a.

"Yes."

"Where are you going?" It's not easy to resist saying something that fits the stupid question. After weeks of saying things like; Disney world, just down the shop, I answer.

"Whitehaven."

Downstairs Group Four Security wait; from being stripped I've walked down stairs with a screw so how I can have something I didn't have before is beyond me. The van is right outside the door. Inside the prison but before they open the door I'm put into handcuffs, searched, and asked who I am; then where I'm going. The van has cells inside that stink. Mucus stains up the walls, urine stains on the floor; some have dry blood in

31

them. The only thing in the cell is a one-way window I can see out but no one can see in.

Three hours I'm in the van. Halfway there the tea does its job, there's only one way to relieve yourself, if you don't want to just piss on the floor. I ask for a plastic bag from the woman guard. If you moved animals like this you would be put in jail. Ironic isn't it?

The van pulls up in the yard of Whitehaven police station at 10:00 A.M. A reception committee of police and Group Four greet me. The first thing they do is search me. I've never been out of the van. I'm taken into the court cells, I ask for my solicitor Kevin J Commons. After a short while Kevin comes. He and I go to the small room under the stairs for a conference.

"Right Mr Crowe, I have the depositions, for twenty-nine charges they amount to thirty-nine pages of weak evidence." He watches for my reaction and I don't disappoint him.

"I can't believe I've been brought all this way on the strength of statements from police and drug addicts."

"It's not that Mr Crowe..."

"Me dad's Mr Crowe, Call me Tony," I tell him.

"I expected the papers to be reams and reams thick Tony. Where are all the photos? all the phone records? Where are the logs of comings and goings?"

"What does all this mean to my case?"

"Well – as far as I can see they haven't even got your fingerprints on the drugs; without the drugs you have five charges. I think we can concentrate on those for now."

"That sounds good to me." Already twenty-four charges gone, then comes the bad news.

"If you get a guilty on the attempted murder the rest won't matter." He says with a note of doom in his voice. He knows how to cheer a guy up, that's why I asked for him. I need the best; he is it. I want the truth. A rare thing where solicitors are concerned.

"Time for court," the gaoler says.

Kevin goes up; when they're ready they call me. I'm handcuffed; taken from the small cell, up the seven stone steps to the courtroom door. Just before the call to bring in the prisoner, the cuffs are taken off. The court's full of reporters, vultures who I would soon come to hate with a passion. I don't know why they even bother coming to the court; nothing written was ever said in any court I was in. It's amazing; the first and last question I'm asked is my name. Two minutes later I'm back down in the cell having another cup of tea for the trip back to Durham jail. Three hours with a full bladder and a cold seat to sit on.

4:00 P.M. the transport arrives; I'm taken through the police station and put back on the van. It still stinks, with an undertone of cheap disinfectant brown stains adorn the walls yellow ones on the floor. The length of the van runs a gutter with holes in it leading to the road below so it can be swilled out, or so the piss can run out onto the road. This time I'm double cuffed, once to myself once to a screw. 7.30 PM the van pulls up outside Durham. The well kept flower beds in front of the Jail gives nothing away about the darkness within. Twelve hours for two minutes in court. I'm not even aloud to read the papers from my case on the journey back.

In my cell I read the paperwork, my deps. Page twenty – what do you know? A statement signed by one G. Porter, the same G. Porter that only yesterday didn't know me from shit; "I've known Tony Crowe for years. I've even bought drugs off him...." In the beat of a hummingbird's wing I'm at the window.

"Vinnie – Vinnie, listen, that toe-rag made a statement. It's a load of bullshit. Ask him what he's

33

playing at Vinnie." When you shout from a window it's not exactly private. The whole prison is now at their windows shouting for blood.

"Who's the slag?"

"Give us his name we'll do him in."

"Hang the grassing bastard." Another calls out.

"Tony he's not here, he's gone onto "A" wing."

"Tony I'm on "A" wing." A voice from the row of holes in the wall opposite. 'I'll do him for ya, what's his name?'

Then another, and another, all the wing want the pay day. Nothing like a grass or a nonce; of course many would say it's the same thing. To excite the thugs. I pick out one of the voices that I recognise.

"I'll see you tomorrow on exercise." Best not to shout out of the windows for all the jail to hear.

I read the papers; there are statements from half the lowlife in the village. Some like Porter I don't know, some I know only too well. There's only one thing for me to do. I'll have an old-style committal hearing, that way the witnesses will have to turn up at court and give their evidence. That, as the saying goes should sort the men from the boys.

As the name suggests old-style committals are not the norm. My case started pre 1997 when the rule changed, so I can make them run one. Two months and this is my first move. Now I can sleep a bit sweeter.

On exercise with Vinnie the whole hour is taken up talking about Porter. I pick out a guy on "A" wing who volunteered from the night before. For a price the deal is done. I could have him killed for half an oz of smack, heroin is the big money of jail. Known by many names. But it's not the time for that.

January, the first visit from my solicitor. The visit with anyone who isn't family or a friend is called a special visit. That's what this is. I have to go through the jail to a small room above the main gate. Waiting to be called. But not for long.

"Crowe, your solicitor's here." Kevin and I are put into a room, glass half way up the walls so we can be seen by the screw sitting at the desk. When we open the door the light comes on, one of those sensors up in the corner of the room. Kevin sits behind the square table; I sit on the only other seat.

"Cup of coffee?" he asks.

"Coffee? Where are you going to get coffee from?"

"There's a machine in the corridor." A puzzled look on his face shows his lack of knowledge; he's never been an intern.

"Coffee no sugar please," off he goes. He's gone for two or three minutes, returning with the hot cups of instant brown water.

"Right then; where do we start Tony?" not really asking, more setting up the routine that he must have gone through a million times before. Out comes that big fat fountain pen and a clean A4 book of writing paper.

"Have you read the paperwork?"

"I've read nothing else; I can't believe what's in them."

"Let us just concentrate on the attempted murder for now; we'll come back to the drugs later." He has a hidden dialect, Yorkshire perhaps. "I have some more paperwork for your delectation, but they can wait till you are back in your cell." He slides across the table a bundle of A4 papers, secured with a blue rubber band.

"What do you need to know?"

"We can start at the beginning Tony."

"Well before we go any further I want an old-style committal."

"We'll get to that later as well, what I need to know is what you are saying about the attempt' murder on Swindles?"

"What's there...? – I didn't take any part in that. From the deps I can't see how they can expect a guilty."

"Do you have an alibi?"

"I was in bed, I was in bed with Dawn, it was three in the morning where were you? Everyone I know would have been in bed at three in the morning. Prostitutes and coppers. That's who aren't."

"Do you have anyone who can give evidence to that affect?"

"I was in bed. How can I prove that? I was in bed with Dawn. I can't call her as a witness; the police got her to make a statement. Have ya seen it?"

"Yes I have, it does not do you any favours."

"Well that doesn't matter, she won't be going to court. They made her sign it. They made threats, jail. They said they'd take her kids off her and she would go to jail. It's not worth the paper it's written on."

"Did they tape Dawn's interview?"

"Tape? – She just signed what they put in front of her. From ten in the morning till five they kept her; threatening her, in the police station. The baby was only five weeks old. They told her if she signed the statement she could go home to be with McCauley. If I'd been there I'd have told her to sign it. Tape it? They wouldn't want that on tape. She's not going to court. She wants to make a new statement, the police won't take one."

"I will see if I can interview her, on tape, I will have to tell the police. Tell me why your car was seen leaving Hinnings Road on the night of the assault."

"I'll tell you everything from the start, let me tell you Kevin I will never lie to you so if you can't live with the truth don't ask the question."

36

"That night, the twenty fourth November 1996 was the night after McCauley's baptism. He was five-weeks-old. Being born four week premature he was weak and would feed every two hours or so. I had asked a friend of mine to be Godfather; Dawn's friend was to be Godmother. Billy, the Godfather, lived at Runcorn in Cheshire. On the Saturday I drove to his house to pick him up; with his partner, Linda. He doesn't have a driving licence – I got to his house and someone else was there. Billy asked if he could come as well. I couldn't see why not. I was on the spot a bit; he was standing there waiting for an answer. "Yeah no problem" I said. We all got into the car and went to pick up this guy's partner, Leslie, and his Sunday best. Now there was Billy Linda, Jimmy and Leslie. We all took-off up the M6 for Distington, a small village outside Whitehaven.'

"I know Distington, is that where the baptism was?"

"No Whitehaven. We got home about 4:00 P.M. After a wash and change of clothes we all went out for a meal, then on to a pub.

The children were farmed out for the night. We got home around midnight and went to bed. Dawn didn't know Jimmy was coming so they had to sleep on the living-room floor. In the morning we got ready for church. We all went in a minibus. The ceremony went well and the food was in the church rooms next door. We had a drink, wetting the baby's head and all that. Things were great; the day was a great success, apart from Dawn moaning about the two extra guests. She was a bit under the weather with having to undergo a caesarean section, baby blues, you know?" Not waiting for an answer I go on.

Billy and the others went to the pub; The Castle Inn. It was Monday night. I took them in the car then I came back home. The pub wasn't far but I took them so they would see the way back. As they got out of the car I gave Billy a key for Dawn's house.

Ann was there when I got back. Dawn's aunt, she went home about half eleven, she lives round the corner, two doors off Swindles. I went to bed. I never heard a thing till McCauley woke. We took it in turns feeding him. I let Dawn down the night before, being a bit drunk and all. I jumped out of bed, put on the kettle; it was next to the bed. A bottle was made ready, all two ounce of it. McCauley hadn't been eating, he had lost weight so we had to try and get as much into him as we could. We kept a list."

"Tony is that the list of weights the police say is a drugs list?"

"Yes. The health worker has a copy of the same list.

Anyway; when the bottle was warm I started to feed him. I hadn't been at it long when Jimmy shouted up.

'The dog's got out.'

"We had a white German shepherd, Casper. Said to be the name of one of the three wise men. We had two but Casper got sick and we had to find Sultan, our other dog, a good home.

I thought if he goes on the road he could be in danger of being hit by a boy-racer. They're always speeding around Distington's' narrow roads. I pulled on my pants and ran down. When I was in the sitting room I saw the dog flash past the window. It was dark but he's white. I went to the door. Casper was skipping off up the road.

'I thought he wanted out so I let him out the back.' Jimmy told me, but the back gate was open and he trotted off down the passage between the houses.

I didn't have time to listen. The dog was an epileptic, on large doses of tamazepam. In short he wasn't safe to be out. He had just spent a week in intensive care. One time he had a fit and bit me. There

38

was no way I could leave him out there. I put on my shoes, grabbed the car keys for Dawn's Astra. It was a hatchback the dog would go in the back. That was the car in front, easy to get out quickly. I rubbed my hand on the windows to clear the frost - it wasn't bad. Off I went. The dog was out of sight but I knew which way he had gone.

'On the road there were parked cars both sides leaving room for one car up the centre. When I left the house the car was cold, sluggish. I put my foot down. At the junction were I needed to turn there was an ambulance. Sitting at the white stop line facing my way. At three in the morning I thought they must be in a hurry. I got out of their way by driving round them. There was a silver car right behind them. The light from a full moon lit it up the way sun light bounces off the surface of a still pond. I saw the dog coming out of a garden. Pulling up I walked over to him. He just looked up. I took hold of his neck – he never had a collar on – in the back of the car there's always a lead with a choker on it. I opened the back door. There looking at me from the boot was the wheels of McCauley's pram, not a buggy, this was the biggest thing you've ever seen. The dog couldn't go in there. No worries the most important thing was I had the dog. I closed the boot and decided to walk back with Casper. I could go back for the car later. It was in a bad place, boy-racers and that. I pulled it off the road onto the pub car park, out of sight behind the wall. Then I walked back with Casper."

"Where was the dog when you parked the car?" Kevin make a note.

"Tied to a gate, I put the lead on him and dropped the loop over the gatepost. Anyway, I walked back. When I got home the ambulance was outside Swindles' house – He takes bad now and then – drugs usually – I never saw anyone. I just went in the house. Strange thing..."

"What?"

"When I looked out the window I..."

"What Tony? Did you see something?"

"...When I was looking out the window to see where the dog had gone I saw someone running past the house..."

"Away from Swindles' house?"

"No he was running toward his house. It was his brother."

"Who's Swindles'?"

"It was Swindles' brother" I sit up, lean forward. "Why is there no statement from him? – He was first there – he saw me. He saw me looking out the window – he must know I was in the house. Get his statement – it must be good or it would be in the deps bundle. We need the phone records from Swindles' house. How did he know to go there? We need to hear the phone call to the emergency operator." Kevin turns over the page of his pad.

"Why what are you getting at Tony?"

"What would you ask someone who told you they had just been chopped up? Who did it that's what I would ask."

"What if they did ask and the answer he gives is your name?"

"Then it would be in the deps already. It isn't."

"Did he see you before the dog got out?"

"That's what I'm telling you. I was in the house when he went passed; after his brother had been done-in. If I had been in Swindles' there would be evidence in Dawn's house. There isn't anything."

"The blood?"

"It's not in the house it's on the front door frame. The police were all over the house, I'll bet we can show they were at both houses."

"What happened after the dog thing Tony?"

"Nowt. We were all in the house. I was up now, wide-awake. Dawn was in bed. The baby was quiet. Billy was in bed with Linda. Jimmy and Leslie were in the sitting room with me. We were watching all the action over the road. The police were there. There were people screaming. I suppose it was exciting. The ambulance went and the police were all over the road. Cars came and went. One time there were five police cars outside."

"What about your car? the Astra!"

"That was still on the pub car park. There was no way I was going out. Missing all the action. Lots of police about told me this wasn't just a drugs overdose.

School was 9:15 A.M. Runcorn is two hours in the BM. Billy got up at six. Thanks to McCauley. They all packed and put their things in the boot. Dawn was still pissed-off. Jimmy came in from putting the bags in the car. Then went out with water. He cleaned the windows. It was frosty. Just on the windows. On the cars. Six-forty-five we all got in the BM and set off"

"What about the Astra?"

"Still on the Globe car park, I told Dawn where it was and why it was there when she came down stairs. She said something, that's when I thought it best to exit quickly. It was Billy who said "Ya can't leave it there she'll not get it out" 'The car was in bonnet first and the exit was narrow. I remember Linda said about Dawn's section. How she would have to twist round. I reluctantly drove the car off the Globe car park. Onto the road, I even faced it the right way. I remember Jimmy cleared the windows. With the spray can from the BMW. It wasn't bad. With being next to the wall –

Jimmy wanted to take it round home. I'd had enough. Dawn I mean. Her mood. We were already going to have to hurry if we were to get there for school time.

When we got to Runcorn Billy asked if I was staying for a drink. I didn't want any more drink. I could have eaten something though. I stopped at a phone-box to tell Dawn I'd be late back, and to see if she was in a better mood. There was no answer. I remembered she said she was going out with Ann. Her aunt from round the corner. I phoned Ann.

"Is Dawn there?"

'Dangerous as been cut up in his bed. Last night.' She said.

"I saw all the police this morning," I told her, "where's Dawn?"

'The village is swarming with cops....'

"Tell Dawn I'll be late I'm...."

'The coppers are searching Dawn's house, they think you did it. They say it was you cut him up.'

"I'll phone ya back Ann. Later."

"I went to tell Billy I had to go. I told him what Ann had said."

'Wait here a bit. Phone her back later.'

"That's what he said. That's what I did. I didn't know why they thought it was me. I remember thinking. I'll just front it. I've done nothing – they won't find anything – I'd front it. I thought. I phoned Ann."

'Dawn's been arrested. The police are looking for you.' she told me. 'Drugs have been found in Dawn's house and they're looking for you.' That's what she told me on the phone.

"Did she say anything about the cutting up of Swindles?"

"Yeah – she did. She told me I was the number one suspect. I was in it up to my neck for the drugs anyway.

42

Why would I have drugs in my house and have no alibi then go round the corner and chop up a guy in his bed? It just doesn't make any sense."

"Go on Tony time is getting on."

"I jumped in the car and drove back as fast as I could. If Dawn was in the police station I needed to go there and get her out. She's never been locked up."

"Did you go to the police station Tony?"

"No I needed to know what had gone on with Swindles. What the drugs were all about. I saw Colin Wright; he lived opposite Dawn. He's nosy so if anyone would know he would. From what he told me I didn't think I was in the frame for Swindles. He knew nothing about the drugs. Most of his knowledge came from his fair paying customers, he drove a taxi. If Dawn wasn't out for five I was going to tell them the drugs were mine. That's what I decided to do. It was four-thirty. I still couldn't understand why the police thought Swindles' attack was down to me. I could only think of the ambulance. The police saw me drive from the house in the BMW. They didn't stop me! I was confused. I phoned Ann."

'Dawn's at her mother's the police are outside and they want you.'

"Dawn hadn't been charged with anything. I knew why. There could only be one reason. You can't charge a witness with the crime or they then become a co-defendant who then have the choice of giving evidence or not."

"That is indeed true Tony."

"I needed to think. I couldn't do that there. I phoned Jeff Simms, Ann's husband; asked him to pick me up. He told me what was being said. What the police had said to Dawn. It was worse than I thought, they told Dawn when they found me I was going to jail for fifteen years. Well hey. No way. What chance did I have? This is not even twenty-four hours later and the police have it all worked out up to my sentence.

Simmo took me to a friend's house. Where I tried to think. I felt the police were just outside. I had to move. He moved me to Sandra's, Dawn's other aunt. As soon as I walked through the door I was greeted with."

"Tony what have ya done?"

"Bad news travels fast, now it was all round. It was me who did Swindles in. Cut him up. People were coming just to see me. This was no good. I moved again. This time to someone who wouldn't shout about it. Someone the police wouldn't look at. Chris was the answer. He lived in a good spot. Close to the town. Chris was at work when Simmo and I turned up on his door step. We went to see him there and he gave me a key to his flat. He already knew the stories. He told me he was going to his girlfriend's. I had the place to myself. "Tell no one I'm here," I told him. Just to make sure I told him he'd be in bother. Charged with helping me. I remember Simmo went and bought a radio scanner so I could hear what was going on, what the police knew. Thought they knew. My scanner was now in the hands of the police. Would I not have taken it with me if I had fled the crime? It was now a game of cat and mouse. I was the mouse. Every house I went to got turned over after I left. No coincidence someone was dropping me in it. Chris's flat was on the main road; Whitehaven to Workington. It gave me a good sight of the police going to and fro. I could monitor their radios with the scanner. For the first time I felt safe. I slept that night. In the morning Simmo brought me some clothes. That's when I got my passport; it was in the bag with the clothes. I got news of Dawn. She was under surveillance twenty-four-seven. All day I listened to the scanner and watched the road. The flat had one door and it was on the first floor of a four story building. I was like a rat in a trap. I didn't like what I was hearing, too many codes. Too many references to the target. I couldn't phone Simmo. The police would know I was getting help from somewhere. Phones aren't the safest of things. I waited. I waited till he came as arranged the day before."

"Things are too hot' I told him 'does anyone know I'm here?"

'No just me, Chris and Ann.'

"Four people with me, that's three too many for my liking. Time to move on. I went there and then. Now only Simmo and I knew where I was. We drove round trying to think of where I could go. I had it; there was someone who no one knew. He owed me. Irish John was his name; he lived out of town and alone. Simmo took me there and I told him not to tell anyone. Not even Ann. Someone was telling the police. It wasn't me and it wasn't in Simmo's best interest to tell them, he could have just set me up. Had the car pulled. No it had to be someone else. When we got to John's I prayed for him to be home. The house was set back from the road. Tucked out of the way. The lights were on in the front room. I walked down the path and up the three steps to his front door. Knock knock, I banged on the door. Someone was coming to answer from within. I hoped he was alone. The door opened.'

"Hi John how are you?"

'Come in Tony; come in.'

"He knew nothing about the two days I'd spent dodging the police. I told him only what he needed to know."

"I need somewhere to stay for a day or two. Could you put me up?"

'That'll be no problem. You'll be on your own I'm on manoeuvres with the T.A.'

"When are ya going?"

'Tonight; now - you're lucky ya come now, ya'd have missed me any later,' a car pulled up. 'That's me ride now. I'll be goin' now.'

"Don't tell anyone I'm here John..."

Tony lock the door when ya go. I haven't seen ya right?'

"He closed the door and went off into the night. Now there is only me and Simmo knows I'm there."

"Don't tell anyone I'm here Simmo. Not even Ann. Do ya hear?" I tell him.

'Yeah. No one'll know.'

"I had a hot shower and something to eat. I hadn't eaten for God-knows how long. I had all the lights turned off. A car came down the road. I didn't recognise it as any I knew. It wasn't the police. It stopped outside and Simmo got out. I went to the door and let him in. My thought was he must have news or something."

'Here ya are a pizza.'

"Be careful coming here." I said.

'The police are all over me. I keep losing them.'

"Don't play with them. I can't afford it Simmo. Come back tomorrow. Tell Dawn to go to the phone box at the end of her road; 10:00 pm. I'll phone her. I've got the number.

It's harder to get the number if it's incoming. I watched Simmo drive off. I knew then I had to get away. That meant leaving Dawn and the kids. Not something I looked forward to. I didn't sleep well that night. I had to make the biggest decision of my life. Trying to see Dawn by hiding in the boot of a taxi didn't work. Simmo went on a recce he told me the place was covertly swarming with police. No way was I going to get near her. The last resort was to phone her. I wouldn't be able to tell her anything. Her phone was red hot. Bugged. I had to hear her voice before I left.

Simmo filled up the car with juice and picked me up. I was on the move for the last time. Ann was with him."

'Where we going?' she asked.

"Just let's get out of here. I'll tell you on the way." I told her.

"I didn't trust Ann."

"Do you know Tony, the police have asked for a P.P.I.?" Kevin informs me.

"What's a P.P.I.?"

"It's a public protection immunity request. It's to protect an informant's identification."

"Ann?"

"Could be Tony. Anyway go on with the story."

"I got into the car. Where did you get the car Simmo?' I asked him

'The police were all over. I went to the pizza shop where Carol works, parked outside. Out the front so they could watch the car. Then I slipped out the back into Carol's car.' He told me. That's Ann's daughter.

"Do they know what car you're driving now?"

'No – I don't think so; where we going?'

"Just drive, head out of town by the back way. Not where the CCTV cameras are."

"We made for the motorway. M6 south."

'Are we going to Liverpool?' Simmo asked.

"I didn't know myself where I was going. I just needed to get as far away as I could.

No the police wouldn't be long in picking up Billy and Jimmy. Billy's address is in the church records as Godfather. That would be the last place I'd be safe. Dover. We're going to Dover. I told him right off the top of my head. Simmo went to Dover. The booze run. To France. The car was new and would have no trouble making the trip. I'd run round selling all I could. I had about two grand, plenty for petrol and something to eat."

'Chris's flat was busted this morning. He was locked up,' said Ann.

"The only one who knew I had been there and didn't have a good reason not to tell the police was Ann. I was worried. We wouldn't be stopping on the way to Dover. Not now. I didn't want to give her the chance to drop me in it. I asked Simmo to drive. We got to Dover at 7:00 A.M. Simmo went inside for our tickets. Party of three, no names ask for. I was bursting for the toilet."

"Is there any cameras in the toilet area?"

'No none, just on the desk.'

"I need to go, don't phone anyone. Stay in the car till I get back." I told him.

"I went inside the large hall. It was empty. The toilets were in the corner. I couldn't see any cameras watching them. As I put my hand on the handle I noticed, right up near the roof, a small camera set to watch the toilet door. I didn't hesitate, I went on in. I had looked up at the thing giving it a full face shot. The best thing to do was acknowledge it on my way out. I walked out, looked right at it and touched my finger to my forehead, smiling. This later confused the police. When they saw the pictures they thought I'd gone out of the country just to come back in the boot of the car. To make them think I'd gone. They give me too much credit. I got back in the car and we set off to board.

"Where do we show our passports?"

'Don't bother 'bout it, you just hold it up, the guy doesn't even take it off ya.'

"Right enough when we got to the booth we just got waived through. I learned later there are cameras in the over-head signs on the way to board. It was too late for that now. Obviously the ports hadn't been notified. I wasn't that important.

Once on the boat I was getting more relaxed. Buying a big teddy for McCauley and cigs for Dawn made me feel better. Simmo took them back to help break the news of where I'd gone. She had no idea. It was a sad day for me. France was out of reach for the police but that was me in exile."

'Where're you going?' asked Ann. "I couldn't tell her, not because I didn't trust her, because I had no idea myself. We went to the booze shops so Simmo got something out of the trip; my decision was to hitch a lift in a wagon to Spain. My brother lived in Jib. One flaw put my plan out of action. It was November, like other Novembers round then the wagon drivers had the roads blocked. There was a strike on, an embargo. Quickly I went to plan B. That was made up as I went along. With my good-byes said to Simmo and Ann in Calais train station off to Paris I went.

I've never felt so all-alone in my life. Exiled in a country where I knew no one. The language was alien to me. I knew no one but no one knew me. That's when I thought of Malta. There were people there who I knew. There were jobs I could get scuba diving. They spoke English and drove on the right side of the road, home from home. The train stopped at Paris North. The Metro took me from there to the airport. Flying was a chance I had to take. I found the desk of Air France. I knew where I was going and I had a plan. My schoolboy French got me as far as finding out I was at the wrong airport."

'Oley South.' The woman said. "I had no idea where that was. Visions of a long train ride flashed through my thoughts. Somewhere well south of Paris. The Metro journey I'd just made was fifteen minutes of smelly hot standing up, in a train packed with what I took to be the lower end of the Parisian proletariat."

'If you fly to Gatwick England you will get a flight direct to Malta.' "I thanked her very much and left. Outside there were airport buses, on the front of the first bus it said Oley sud. I hopped on and paid eight franks; a quid. The bus took me all of one stop. Round the corner and up a bit. There in full view was the airport, large glass doors keeping out the cold winter weather. There was a melee around the many cafe-bars and shops. People thronged to and fro with luggage piled up on trolleys which seemed to have a mind of their own. The time was now getting on for 6:00 P.M. My flight to Malta was the next day, 8:00 P.M. I had twenty-six hours to fill. Oley airport closed over night but they didn't lock the doors. I bought my ticket and went into one of the many cafe-bars where I was robbed by the lovely looking young woman behind the counter. The airport was full of cameras. I bought a hat from a boutique. It had a wide rim to cover my face from the cameras. I never looked up. I'm a quick learner. When the airport closed down an army of cleaners set about their nocturnal tasks, cleaning the days grime and polishing the marble floor. I found a quiet bench in a siding next to the check in desk. No one would be using it till morning.

The morning brought fear, and breakfast Parisian style, black coffee with a croissant. I felt trapped. I'd been there too long. I spent the day moving invisibly around the airport.

Time to check in for my flight, 6:00 P.M. if I was 'on top' this was the time I'd find out. By on top I mean on top of the list for being arrested. A term used in the world I live in. The term for running like this is On The Lamb, I don't know why! The desk opened and I was first there. It went without as much as a raised eyebrow. The next test would be at the departure gate. I sat where I could see the gate, I watched as the people passed through, so I would know if I was treated differently when it was my turn. The time came to go, my plane was boarding. I'd been on the run for five days. I was getting more on edge by the minute. I put my new hat on and went for it."

'Pass-a-port.' "First thing I thought was why he asked in English? I never said a word. I gave him a smile and my passport. By now I had the beard that was on my passport photo. I was through. I could breathe again. Leaving it to the last minute meant I had to go straight to the boarding gate without stopping at the duty-free shops. In no time I was on the plane – in the air - on my way to Malta.

Two thousand miles away from Distington, the police and Dawn. The flight ended at Malta's International airport; midnight local time. Sitting in the cool air-conditioned airport it was as if the whole of the world had been taken off my back. From there on it would be easy. That's what I thought. I remember the feeling. I was home and dry it would be a breeze.

The first of December, Christmas twenty-four days away and I'm in a country two and a half thousand miles from my family. I hate Christmas.

The flight to Gozo was 2:00 A.M. I was sitting waiting – thinking – A man in a blue suit sat next to me. I remember him from the plane. He had gotten off the same plane from Paris. We talked. He was a farmer who had been to Holland to buy cows."

'Where are you staying? Are you looking for work on Gozo?' "He asked me in the distinct Maltese lilt; single syllable with an up and down rhythm. I knew it wasn't permitted on a tourist's visa to work. I thought for a minute. But I quickly put it out of my mind.

"Do you have a business card?" I asked him. "I could see if he was who he said he was; without hesitation.

'Here is my card. Phone me. Salvo is my name. I will help you.'

"Farmer was on the card. That was good enough for me. I was worn out all I wanted to do was go to bed for what was left of the night. I had the phone number of an old friend in Gozo, from my past diving trips there. He had apartments for rent, being December I didn't think he'd be busy.

All the phones in Malta use cards, at midnight it's not the best time to find a shop open. I bought one from the airport bank. The Mid Med bank. I knew Victor my mate wouldn't mind me calling him. There was no answer on the number I had. It was for his garage, I thought he maybe lived there. I asked the operator for his home number but I needed the full details. I didn't have them. Salvo the farmer asked."

'Did you get an answer for your friend?'

"I don't have his address. There's no answer at his garage."

'Where are you going to stay tonight?'

"I didn't want him to think I'd just dropped from the sky. I suppose I had really." So I told him.

"I'll stay at a hotel tonight and phone Victor in the morning."

'I will give you a ride from the Gozo heliport. My wife Mary will be there to meet me.'

"An offer I couldn't refuse. The flight took ten minutes in an old Russian thing left over from World War II. (Did they have them then?) It had the comfort of a tank in the desert. The only other way to get to Gozo was the ferry. In winter there's no service after 10:00 P.M. When we landed Mary, Salvo's wife was there waiting in a bright red 4X4 pick-up. It shone like a mirror in sunlight even thought it was only lit by a waning moon. It had all the chromium plating Japan could fit onto one car. Just as Salvo had said Mary took me to the St Patrick's hotel, Xlendi bay. (Shlendy) The large glass doors set in marble stood on top of four shiny black marble steps. They were locked. There wasn't a call bell that I could see so I went to the car park phone-box just outside the hotel. The operator gave me the number and I rang it. That single syllable wave of original Maltese accent flowed from the phone."

'Hello.' There's no Maltese word for hello so they use the English word.

"Is that the St Patrick's hotel?"

'Yes this is the St Patrick's hotel. How may I help you sir?'

"Could you please come and open the door I need a room for the night?"

'That will be no problem sir I will open the door now. Are you at the front door sir?'

"I'm on the car park side."

'Of course you are sir one moment and I will be there. Goodbye sir.' "The phone went dead and I could see movement inside the hotel reception area. The door opened before I had put down the phone. A stocky man in his twenties, although he looked older, aged by the Maltese sun, invited me inside. To my left stood a high counter made of dark red mahogany the slight hum of an air-conditioning unit was the only noise to break the silence of the night."

"Single room with a bathroom please."

'No problem sir all our rooms have a bathroom.'

"Breakfast?" I added.

'Just for tonight sir?'

"Yes I think so."

'That will be...... thirty five Maltese pounds sir.'

"After a hot shower I fell into the soft bed and slept like a bear in winter."

"Finish off." The screw shouts from his desk. Our visit is over.

"Just one more thing before we finish off Tony."

53

"What?"

"Tell me all your pre-cons."

"What?"

"Your previous convictions," turning his A4 pad to a clean page.

"When I was twelve I…"

"No just the recent stuff, only the violence."

"Nothing," he looks at me in disbelief.

"Nothing? I thought you had… you have a fearsome reputation Tony. Did you not nail someone's foot to the floor? Did you not shoot up a house with a shotgun? People talk about you being wild, not someone you should cross."

"Don't worry Kevin the police won't find anyone to put in the witness box that can say I've hurt them. Don't believe all you hear." I smile at him.

"That's it can you finish off please?" the screw getting more impatient.

"One last thing Tony; don't talk to anyone about the case. They've got nothing on you. They'll try anything to get you. From putting an informer with you to bugging your cell. Don't use the telephones. Don't write anything in letters."

"Now I'm worried." Kevin takes my hand. I can see sincerity in his weary washed out blue eyes. "Stay strong." He says.

Back in the pad I look at Darrel in a different light. Who is he? How much did I tell him? My mind is in a mess. The door opens.

"Pack your kit son you're moving." It's Darrel not me they're talking to.

"Where ma gone like?"

"A. wing." The words Darrel most dreaded.

"I've got bother on there boss."

"Ya know the score son. Give us the names, we'll sort it." I know he won't do that. You just don't do that. One of the screws goes for the S.O.

"If ya don't move you're goin' down the block son." The dungeons. He picks up his kit and off he goes to the segregation unit below B. wing. To walk the red line whenever you're out your cell. The line that runs around the floor of the room two foot from the wall. That's the last I see of him. The cell is all mine now, no one to worry about. I remove the blue rubber band from round the papers Kevin gave to me on the visit. Scene of the crime photos, Swindles' bedroom. The mattress is awash with blood. The A4 colour photos show me a sight I thought could only exist in a Hollywood blockbuster movie. The quilt lies at the foot of the bed revealing a once blue sheet, now red, so red it looks almost black. A broken ball-pain hammer lays steeped in clotted blood on the bed. The pillow has a dark circle the size of a football. Bringing to mind a mishap with a football and a bed sheet hung out to dry on the washing line. The poster looking down from the wall above the pillow has tracks of liberated blood spattered up its length. The Mona Lisa holding a reefer. Globules of human tissue adhere themselves to the walls and to the ceiling. The light switch in the bedroom shows clawing finger marks in blood frantically searching it out. A trail of blood leads from the bedroom along the landing and down the stairs. Only to be matched in nature by the silvery paths of a snail on its night-time foray. The sitting-room mirrors the bedroom. Pools of life-sustaining liquid, now coagulated into a gel, lay where the Paramedics tended his wounds. The phone only giving away its true colour by the small cream patches devoid of blood; sitting on a table in the corner of the room. Bandage wrappings lay strewn amidst the carnage. The injures to his body are the last five pages.

Head opened up from front to back with a baseball bat, His hand cut in half with a sharp enough weapon to do the job in one swipe. His legs have cuts down to the bone, both broken, his feet severed from the ankle bone, forearms cut like a side of pork ready for the Sunday roast. The contents of my stomach hits the bowl of the toilet, my eyes straining as the involuntary action goes on until the lining of my stomach is all that's left. Then comes the horror of the reality of what I'm said to have done. This is the work of a madman. Someone not fit to walk the streets with normal people. This is what they think I did!

Old style committal

Nothing lasts for long in prison, apart from the loneliness. That same night, about 8:00 P.M. the door opens and pushed in through it is a guy in a suit with a black tie hung round the neck of a dirty white shirt. Short and fat with two days of stubble. There is no way this guy is a criminal. Now I'm Darrel and this guy is me. Just come in is a stupid question. I ask it anyway.

"Yeah, I'm Timmy." I grill him.

"What ya in for lad?"

"Armed robbery."

"Armed robbery? Where did ya rob? You look like a waiter from the Savoy." I wasn't having it, this guy couldn't rob an ice-cream cone from a two year old on the beach.

"Me an me brother robbed the chippy in the toon."

"Where ya from? What do ya do? Who do ya know?" Questions just keep coming out. It turns out he's brother's down on the ones. Timmy's a first timer with a job. A rare thing in the criminal world. Timmy is a bingo caller at the biggest place in town. Or toon as he says it. I ask you is that the profession of an armed robber? His story amazing as it is checks out. He and his brother, who is a criminal had been out on the toon, on their way home they stopped off at the chippy and robbed it. They got no money and the whole building was camera heaven. All he talks about is bingo and calling numbers. Do you know they hold bingo calling competitions? I kid you not. He's with me for two week. I write him a letter to give to the Judge begging for bail and he never comes back. He was a funny sight around the wing in his silky suit for two weeks. I think he got community service. His brother got jail. Remand prisons are full of people who are getting life, but don't. Next to share my home is John Weston a pill head from Sunderland. Making him a mackam in this part of the world. Well known to the walls of HMP Durham. A waste of skin but a good lad to show me the tricks of jail. He's in for kicking his girlfriend's door in and taking her mate's Hi-Fi. He was off his head on pills, couldn't remember doing it. He got caught by the fact he was still there when she got home from work. He was asleep on her settee. But he was no Goldie Locks. John is well known by everyone, even the screws. He has a deft art of getting the door open and when he gets out he's last to be caught by the screws. He flies around the wing like a bird freed from its cage till they lock him back up. Using the suicide netting strung over the landing as a trampoline to bounce from one side to the other. He knows when the library is open and uses it to get unlocked. Even though it's only a large walk-in cupboard with about one hundred books total. And the Rule book lives there but you can't take it out. You have to look at it there. It gives you a walk and five minutes out time.

Monday, Dawn is coming to visit. I get out for a shower, put on my best prison rags, I have to wear them on visits. When I get to the waiting room Porter is there, sitting in the other waiting room. I can see him through the open door.

"Crowe CP3703 visit." I go in after I've been searched.

"Table twenty-two," says the desk screw. It's down the other end near the tuck-shop. Porter comes into the room and his visitor is only Swindles. Garry David Swindles. He doesn't look too bad for a cripple. On walking sticks with a prominent limp. No doubt from one leg now being shorter than the other; according to the medical records; that tell every detail of his wounds. He's wearing a bright yellow T-shirt, he looks over at me. His face full of dread trying to hide the fear

58

he's feeling inside. Dawn is gutted we decide it best if we finish first so she can get out before him. I get up to go. I haven't got to my feet before I'm surrounded by DST screws. I think they know who he is. He's sat with his back to the walkway. I pass him and he goes to stand, a feeble attempt at intimidation.

"Sit down ya cripple." I go passed. He sinks his six foot frame back into the plastic moulded seat saying nothing. Never again do I have a visit at the same time as Porter, the jail sees to that. I go back to my cell and fill the rest of the day with talk of my visit. Prison life by now is somewhat mundane, repetitive.

The door only opens for meals and twice a week for one hour to phone home and shower. Every twenty-one days I have to give a sample of pee to be tested for drugs. With charges for drugs and the reputation of being the number one dealer in the county I get the VIP treatment. They don't know I don't take drugs and I have nothing to do with those who do. Until, that is now. Sitting in a small room watching the clock tick.

Poem Tick Tock

Tick-tock goes the clock on the wall.
Every tic a second so small.
Tick-tock the second hand hurries round so fast.
Never stopping while making that sound.
Tick-tock the minutes follow on to that now familiar song.
Slower but not as not to show.
Tick-tock, does the hour hand move at all?
For every tic it seems not to move.
If it does, it's so small you would never know.
Tick-tock as day turns to night another day done.
I've won that fight for life.
Tick-tock; tick-tock goes the clock on the wall.

Every twenty-one days I'm taken the three hours' drive to court for more remand. I spend my first Christmas in jail. I have my fortieth birthday in cell two-twenty-seven. My home. March comes and with it comes Flapper. A new companion.

Flapper got his name from ears that must have plagued him all his life. He's not big enough to complain about it though. Flapper's no stranger to life behind prison bars. He's well known by the screws and cons alike. With his two weeks job seekers allowance he stocks up on goodies from the prison shop; tobacco, phone cards, and food. Flapper had been with me one week when the next shopping day came round and the money he had the week before spent was there for him to spend again. A rare mistake made by the jail. So he did just that and we lived like kings for another week. Walking around the yard some young lad comes up to me and gives me one ounce of tobacco. Then another one gives me two phone cards. It must be my birthday.

"Flapper when I was out on the yard some kid said thanks and gave me this." I show him the burn and the cards. "Why do you think that was?"

"Are, well that'll be... that'll be what he owed me from last week I gave him some burn. Double bubble." High interest rates in prison two back for one given.

"The cards?"

"The cards? Yea the cards... same thing."

"Why did they give them to me and not you?"

"Don't go mad big feller. Look at me. Four stone wet through. They'd have just had me off."

"And?"

"Well I told everyone it was yours and that if they didn't pay ya back ya'd do 'em in. Cut 'em up like."

"Thanks a lot Flapper. Did it not occur to ya someone might just stab me in the neck or throw me name in for dealing? And I knew nothing 'bout it?"

He steps away from me in case I punch his face in for not telling me of his little scam. How can I stay mad with him? I lay down the rules. My rules and we laugh about his cheek. That week he gets no canteen and the jail wants their money back. Ten pounds a week but Flapper's scam is up and running. Made for life. Prison life.

"Crowe CP3703?"

"That's me what'd ya want?" The figure of a screw is silhouetted by the morning light streaming though the open door, lighting up our dingy cell.

"Court, you're at court this morning son." I get out of bed. I'm ready in no time. Keswick; my committal hearing is today. I never know when I'm going to court, they only tell me on the morning of the hearing, something to do with having the van, the sweat-box, held up and escaping. It wouldn't be difficult to work it out. After the usual routine I leave the jail for Keswick court in the Lake District. The sweat-box hasn't gone far before in turns off the main road.

"Where we going?" I ask.

"Low Newton, we're going to pick up someone for Workington." Low Newton is for women. Two young girls who I would say had bigger drug problems than I ever seen in Durham board. It's a different trip with the local girls entertaining me for the three hour journey. My fame had reached into their prison. That's when I found out I was going to Whitehaven. Keswick was shut for something or other. We pulled into Workington at 10:30 A.M. By 11:00 A.M. I'm at Whitehaven. I'm not expected. It seems no one knows where I'm supposed to be. Apart that is, me. A few phone calls later and I'm off to Keswick, even then the driver can't find the court building. As a small boy, maybe about eleven or twelve years old I was arrested in Keswick for robbing money out of the town wishing well. The bus fare home was all I needed but it was the biggest crime of the week for this one-horse-town, so I know where the police station is and the court is in the same building. As we round the corner the court comes into view. Four police squad cars stand on the car park, white Volvo's with a wide red, orange, stripe down the entire length. The same as when I was driven back from London Gatwick in the back of a fiat bravo, hand-cuffed to the grab-handle in the roof. We stopped for a paw-wow in Kendal; two of the same cars were there then.

"What's going on? What's with all the coppers?"

"You – It's for you. This is only a small court it's no security." I feel like one of Briton's most wanted yet again. Once I'm off the sweat-box and in my small cell with its half-inch thick solid steel door Kevin comes. We sit on the wooded coffin-like box that I think is the bed and talk.

"How many did you say would turn up?"

"Well I hoped none. How many Kevin?"

"Well you thought one or two didn't you?"

"Yeah. How many? - More? - Four, no more than four."

"No not four, Tony. Not any, none. Not one witness that is not a police officer has turned up."

"Great the plan's going well. How many charges are there now?"

"Thirteen charges have gone. When we get in I'll kill them off for good."

"Never to be resurrected?"

"Gone forever, dead and buried."

"Kevin that's great news."

"What do you want to do with the attempted murder?"

"If we ask them questions that'll help us, we'll confuse the plod. When we come to the questions about my defence we'll give in, tell them nothing."

"The police will try and deduce your defence from the questions we ask."

"That's why we won't ask any. We have what we wanted. No witnesses have turned up and the charges are gone, this is just for fun Kevin. We always knew we would not beat the committal. Let them have it."

We go into court number one, the only one in the building. The door leads me straight into the dock. A small wooden box with a single seat in it where I sit. Armed police in bullet-proof uniforms guard the exits. Facing me is the witness box. Kevin stands up from his position in front of me. He's facing the witness box and the Magistrate is slightly to his right. Let the games commence.

Kevin is great the plod know nothing of what we're about. For the drugs charges Kevin asks questions relevant to the attempt murder. We can use the answers in our trial. I love it. How easy it is to tie them in knots. Kevin makes it look easy. A true master of his art. The questions aren't the ones they expected. Now for my genius, Kevin's last question.

"Is there anything else you want to ask Tony?"

"Ask Hatwood if he searched the garden shed."

"Detective Hatwood, were you the officer in charge?"

"Yes I was the officer in charge."

"Did you search the house?"

"The house was searched."

"Did you search the demesne?" Good word.

"Yes the gardens were searched."

"Did you search the garden shed?" I wait for his answer. I know he won't want to look like he hasn't carried out his duties to the fullest of his ability. My turn to do the burying. He answers with a strong voice, his hands clasped behind his back pushing out his absent chest.

"I can state the garden shed was searched."

"What was the significance of that? None of the exhibits came from the shed." I raise myself up in the wooden chair, lift my head high, this is my crowning moment not to be missed.

"Well there is no garden shed. Detective Sergeant Hatwood is a liar." I announce it to the whole court. Silence fills the room, an awkward tension broken only by the sound of the stenographer typing out the answer on her typewriter, located under the Stipendiary Magistrate's position to my right. Hatwood looks ill, he's rambling about seeing the exhibits log to be sure what was taken from the shed. Digging himself deeper into the grave. There are photos of the garden taken by the scenes of crime officer, a policeman just like Hatwood. They show to all there is no garden shed. DC Hutton is the exhibits officer and now standing in the witness box. Hatwood and he passed in the doorway. No chance to conspire.

"Did you receive any exhibits from the garden shed, Detective Constable Hutton?"

"Garden shed?' he knows there is no shed and he's confused by the question.

"Yes the garden shed Mr Hutton. Were you given any exhibits from the garden shed?"

"There is no garden shed – as I can remember." Bingo.

The day is a great success, thirteen charges gone, the head of the investigation (I use the words loosely) told lies under oath. How will he get out of that? I can't wait to see. Then there's the questions Kevin asked. Totally confusing the plod, not a big achievement I know, but sweet at the time. We gave nothing away about my defence. I'm committed for trial on four drugs charges. Kevin does the business with the legal stuff and I'm committed on the attempted murder charge. More important Kevin secures the Legal Aid for all the charges. A QC, Queen's Council. Or silk, named after the small jerkin they wear will be appointed for my trial. Things are looking up.

Kevin Tells me the police couldn't understand his questions, they even said none of the questions they prepared for were asked. I'm further remanded to jail starting my hundred and twelfth day in prison.

I should tell you how remand is supposed to work. The courts remand someone to prison in blocks of twenty-one days, however. There is a limit of seventy-two days, by which time the prisoner has to be committed for trial, or given bail. It's called The Bail Act. From committal the clock starts again. This time they have up to one hundred and twelve days to start the trial. How can I have been on remand for so long? I hear you ask. Over the seventy-two days? There's an important point to mention here. The Crown Prosecution Service can ask for an extension to the time limits. If the Judge thinks it's valid he'll grant the extension, usually two weeks, it's always valid. Everybody is over their time limits at some point. It's more of a time suggestion. I have to be on trial somewhere at the end of June 1998. Time for more applications for bail. Every time there's a change in circumstances I can ask a high court Judge for bail, I do just that at every opportunity. The police say I have no chance of being granted bail. Even if I put up one hundred thousand pounds. With the help of my Uncle I make the application. One hundred and ten thousand pounds I offer just to show the police one hundred grand in nothing. I can't be the one with the money so my uncle stands the bond. The high court Judge says no.

Too Dangerous

Back in Durham jail life goes on, time is slow. Days are filled with jail news, talk of who's a nonce, sex-case. Who's had their head smashed in for it. The nonces are kept on their own wing away from proper criminals, there is always the odd one who thinks, wrongly, I might add, can hide amongst the general population.

I have a trial to prepare for. After weeks of legal wrangling I get a typewriter sent in, an old finger-numbing thing that could have been used to write the Magna Carta. Every piece of paper I can get my hands on I go over with the eye of a man whose life depends on it. It does.

I find references to details I can't find in my meagre depositions. A picture is appearing. One that looks good. Even the extradition papers are wrong from page one. It says my name is Anthony. I can only imagine that is why I wasn't put in front of a court in Malta. Kevin thinks it best not to mention the extradition. We don't want them thinking I didn't want to come back to clear my name! I have one problem. Dawn and her statement, she was taken to the police station and threatened with losing the children if she didn't sign the statement. I have to stop it from going in front of the jury. Not a complicated thing, all I have to do is marry Dawn. A wife can't be compelled to give evidence against her husband. The next morning I put in an application to marry. Dawn knows the plan and will do anything not to stand in court. Sometime Later, I get a note under my door; they don't open the door for such trivial things. 'The Governor agrees in principle to the marriage.' I tell Dawn to sort out the paperwork and her days of worry are over. She couldn't be happier. A week passes and the form needed hasn't been sent out to Dawn. I put in another application and wait. The crown isn't happy therefore I can't get married to Dawn. Let the fight begin. Time to look at what the Law says. Kevin isn't keen to get involved, even though it's all legal. I figure if the police can use the rules so can I. If the Governor says no to my request to marry he is breaking the Law. I need to get him to say no and I need it in writing. I need my no. I ask them "Can I marry Dawn?" and wait for the no. weeks pass. No answer to my request to marry comes. I force a reply. 'It's under review' not my no. I can't use the courts till I get my no. They've done nothing wrong till they say no.

Back to the rest of my defence. I write to everybody for information. Interpol, the Maltese police, the British police, and the Crown Prosecution. British Airways tell me my ticket was paid for by one of the police officers that came to Malta for me. A private credit card from a private citizen. They had no power in Malta. If you did the same thing you would be in court for kidnapping. Where is the statement from the brother? I read points of law, case law. I'm learning how bent the system is. I'm told truth is not the point. Hard to understand nevertheless fact. Evidence and the defence of it is all that matters. Will my small victory at committal become nothing? I've come to the conclusion, without Dawn's statement I can explain everything. My story will be new. I've never been interviewed by the police. The evidence isn't enough to put me in jail. But I am in jail!

From the day I entered Durham I've attended chapel on Sunday mornings. It's always a full turnout, a pleasant change from the four walls of my prison cell. The Chaplain is an ex teacher with a commanding disposition, a woman with experience in handling small boys who have been naughty. It's a small building with a high balcony at the back. Old and church like, the long Gothic windows lit by the morning sun risen just high enough to clear the wall. A screw stands in every window like a guard in his sentry-box, quick to remove anyone who would offend religious protocol. This is where cons go to see their mates from other wings, or if they want to deal in drugs. Not unlike the temple courtyard that Jesus went mad in when he turned over the tables of the money changers. Some just want out of their cell for the hour. This is where I find out who this week has killed themselves, or tried to. The Chaplain reads out the month's list of dead. Why do I come? – Well I think I find some form of normality. Strange as that sounds. The words spoken seem to be directed at me. The Prodigal Son and my first job in Malta feeding pigs on Salvo's farm. I get solutions to questions I've asked myself over the week. I'm just drawn here.

Wednesday evenings there's a class run in the Chapel. Videos and some Bible reading and no doubt peace, sounds good, something is speaking to me. Something telling me where to look. Where to go with my case. I give my name and number to the Chaplain along with the others. The week after, the names of those who can attend on Wednesday evening are read out. At the end, just after the list of the dead and dying. My name isn't one of them.

"What about my application to attend?"

"You've been refused. – security." I feel like the most dangerous prisoner in the jail, everyone is looking at me. They are thinking what is he? I can see it in their eyes and in their silence. I'm gutted. – Too dangerous to attend – I don't remember going to my cell. Shock fills me up. One screw asks me if I'm going to be made a cat A. That used for the most dangerous of prisoners. May be because I escaped from Interpol in Malta I am to be made an E man. E standing for escapee. To be housed behind the wall on G wing. In the far corner of

69

the jail. The lost wing where the sound of a helicopter means someone from your small number is going to court or to a maximum security jail. Bob with the nick-name Hannibal lives there. He never sees anyone who isn't a screw. Numbness, - empty. I can't think. I go into my cell with the first understanding of how I'm thought of. The cell is smaller, colder and darker than I've ever seen it before. I'm more removed from the outside world. More in prison. Loneliness is guilty of many a death. When you have to look at yourself you don't always like what you see. Reputation.

Time for my answer off the Governor. Kevin has put loads of pressure on. There's no way out for the Governor. Any day now I will have my No.

Off To Preston

The day is the ninth of April 1998. It's 7:00 A.M. My cell door opens and Flapper looks at me. I look at him. Who will be going to court? I've had no word from Kevin about any hearings today.

"Crowe, court lad." I get on with the process now normal to me.

"See ya later Flapper."

"No you won't, you're goin' to Preston for pleas and directions. So you'll 'ave to pack ya kit." Going to court usually means leaving all my property in the cell ready for my inevitable return later the same day. I pack all my belongings and carry bags of stuff to reception. I've to go in front of a High Court Judge, the clock's ticking.

All day I'm on a prison sweat-box. One stop on route for dinner, an apple with a bowl of soup in the reception waiting room of Home House prison, a crossroads in the national movement of prisoners, known as The Grand National.

Preston gaol is a dark sandstone built Victorian institution, much like HMP Durham. Reception is small and filth covers the floor, cigarette ends and plastic plates, plastic knives and forks. Old teabags stain the white walls yellow. The same dog screws shouting out orders. Different dialect. Same orders. The routine is the same except for one thing, the bags. The heavy-duty plastic bags I have my property in are taken off me and all my kit is transferred into black bin-bags. Sifting out anything that Preston prison doesn't permit you to have. One Home Office set of rules, but every Governor has his own rules. No typewriter permitted, first thing to go. Hi-Fi has more rules. Size, speakers, power lead. My small radio passes all the rules. A disappointment to the overzealous screw. The bags are an utter waste of time if I'm going more than ten yards. I don't reach the wing gate before the bottom falls out of my world and the bin-bags give up their fight, property strewn all around my feet, the screw gawking. They never help with bags of property "If ya can't carry it ya shouldn't 'ave it." They say. These are no different why would they be? I do my best to get to the cell helped by a fellow con. C. wing is my new home, a single cell for the night. The same cells as Durham with the luxury of a radiator for warmth and a window of white PVC high up the wall. Breakfast is served before getting ready for the hearing. The court house is just round the corner I'll be back on the sweat-box in no time at all.

"Crowe CP3703? Court son." I go to close the door behind me leaving my kit in the cell.

"Get your stuff together son."

"I'm only going for pleas and ds; I'll be back for dinner."

"If ya go't court ya take' all ya kit son, so come on and pack it up. Come on." I fill new bin-bags, carry them to reception and go through the process of leaving for court. If it's a joke I don't find it amusing. What is the point? What's the point of saying anything when I'm only here for one day? When I come back I won't have to unpack. I'll be on my way home in no time. At court I'm met by my wig and gown.

"I am Mr C.J. Cornwall, your council for today's hearing." His hand comes out as he smiles at me with tight clenched teeth, a false grin that says, let's get this over. I take his bony hand.

"Who are you then?"

"Your council – for the hearing. Tim asked me if I would be so good; he has some other engagement that has kept him from fulfilment..."

"Are you a silk?"

72

"No. I am a Barrister. The Judge will be his honour justice Sachs. The whole thing will be over in no time. You will be asked how you plead to the charges; those will be read out to you. You say, "Not Guilty" got that then?"

"I'm more worried about you knowing what to say."

"Can't go wrong Mr Crone, I do this all the time okay? Anything else? No?"

"Crowe. – My name is Mr Crowe, C.R.O.W.E." I spell it out for him.

"Quite, see you in court Mr Crowe." He gathers up his other briefs for the day; all tied up with pink and red ribbons, tucks them under his right arm and leaves. His black robes swirling in his slipstream. I'm in court before dinner ready for the question, "how do you plead?" I've been practising in the cell. NOT - guilty. NOT GUILTY your Honour. Do I call him your honour? What do I call him? - My Lud? I try it softly but with sureness in my tone. I emphasise the, not. This is my moment, the first time anyone has asked if I did it. All the days spent in jail never to be asked. I stand up as the Judge enters from a door to the right, behind the wooden counter opposite. Waiting for him to bow and take up his position in the high ornate chair before I'm told to sit. There's a guy stood at his shoulder holding white gloves and a sword. The judge wears a purple robe with a silk sash. My man in the wig and gown says his bit, small as it is. I wait for my turn.

"I can't take a plea. I'm not a high court Judge. I'll give it a mention, that'll do for now. You are charged with; on the night of 26th November 1996 you did attempt to murder one Garry David Swindles at sixty-nine Hinnings road Distington. How do you plead?"

"Not guilty."

"You are charged with; on the 26th of November 1996 being in possession, without lawful reason of a quantity of class A. drugs. Heroin, how do you plead?" all the charges are read out.

"Not guilty." I'm here for a high court Judge. I don't understand. I must have misunderstood. It all went so fast.

"Right. Date to be set. Take him down." I'm taken back down the stone steps to the cells and my wig and gown.

"Well I thought that went very well Mr – Crowe."

"What went well? What exactly went on in there?"

"Well Mr Crowe the Judge wasn't a high court Judge; he could not set a date for trial."

"But I've put in my plea?"

"Well no – he can't take your plea." I sit up in the seat and lean forward. "What's just happened in there?"

"A mention."

"A what? A mention? What'd you mean? A mention?"

"You will have to come back on another occasion so as a high court Judge can take your plea. Might I say you did very well Mr Crowe?"

"Very well? As I see it I – we did nothing." I can't believe it, another night in Preston. I go back to jail where I'm put in with a guy doing nine years for armed robbery on a jeweller.

My Mate Frank

Frank's okay, he is a true Liverpool scaly from break road under the shadow of the great Liverpool FC football ground. Another old head and a good teacher in the ways of prison life. His main purpose in life is the gym; Frank's what's called a gym-head. He spends all his time in the Gymnasium lifting weights that I can't help thinking would be best left to some mechanical aid to lift. And playing football.

The cell door opens and Frank comes in from his gym session, five-a-side football. He's ranting and raving about a gym-screw.

"What's the matter with ya?" I ask him.

"You won't believe it lad. I'm playing footy. I kicked the ball after the whistle lad. The screw only calls me over; "put up your hand" he says so I did lad, then he says, "wave goodbye fella." He sent us off. I was fucking raging lad, I lost it, treat me like a fucking mug? I told the prick to get in the showers lad. I'd batter him, the shit-house." He's just finished telling me when the door opens, it's the gym screw. All chest and no legs, his nose was once long and pointed now it's wide and flat, understandable; five-foot-six of attitude. Inside he's a much bigger man. A failed applicant for the SAS.

"You're fucking barred for a month Mahoney." Frank's speechless; the screw doesn't need, or wait for an answer. I get the feeling he's not liked much in the jail, by the screws that is. Every time the door opens the screws want to fight. Frank's lying on his bed in his shorts after just finishing a cell workout when the door opens.

"Put your pants on son," says the screw.

"What?"

"Put your pants on, you've to be fully dressed throughout the day son."

"Why's that then?"

"Rules."

"What rules is that then?"

"Prison rules, you've to be dressed..."

"Go and bring the rule."

"It's a wing rule; just get your clothes on son.' Frank sits up and starts to put on his pants while I'm sat on the wooden seat in a state of disbelief. The screw starts to close the door and I ask. "Why did you open the door?"

"What?"

"What was the reason for opening the door? What'd ya want?"

"I don't want ought son."

"You never opened the door just to tell Frank to put on his pants. Did ya?" Lost and beaten for an answer he closes the door. Frank looks at me and we both laugh so loud he must hear it on the other side of that blue shield.

At 7:00 P.M. The doors are opened for hot water. Two cleaners with an old tea urn filled with warm water, on a wheeled trolley, move from door to door. The last cells to be served are mine and Frank's. The water is all gone. We are told to go to the boiler mounted on the wall. So I go and start to fill my flask. The one thing I managed to get past the reception screw.

"Hey son," someone getting grief. I look round to see who the unfortunate is. "You son – you." There's a screw standing way down the wing looking at me filling my flask. He's all of twenty odd years old.

"Are you talking to me?"

"Tuck ya shirt in son."

"Ya what? Tuck me shirt in? – Son? They're my clothes and I'll wear them how I want and I'm not your son." I say, walking back to the cell. Soon it's in my face, 8:00A.M. Breakfast and the door opens. We don't want any so I close the door from my position on the top bunk. It opens once more with a screw saying.

"Get out of bed."

"We don't want breakfast shut the door."

"Get up lads. Come on."

"We don't want it, close the door."

"Ya still have to get up. - Rules."

"It's not a rule that you have to get out of bed and sit on a wooden seat all day so close the f***ing door will ya?"

"If ya don't get up I'll give ya a warning."

"A warning? And then what? Go and get your warning and then ya can shut the door." By now half the screws on the wing are at my door. One of them goes away for the dreaded warning.

"Here you're son that's a written warning."

"Great now close the f***ing door." I drop off the end of the bed into the bin.

"Get up."

"If I was getting up I'd 'ave done it before the warning. What's the point now?"

"You'll get another warning. Two and ya on basics."

"Basics? Look around ya fella it doesn't get much more basic than this. Twenty-four hour bang-up and a shower once a week. Do what ya like but close the door."

6:00P.M. the same day I'm on the bell. A screw comes to answer the call. He talks to me through the closed door.

"What's ya light on for son?" A red light outside my cell tells them I pushed the button.

"Can I go to bed?"

"What?"

"Bed."

"What about it?"

"Can I get in it?"

"Yeah."

"Well could I've gone to bed at – four o'clock?"

"Yeah – go when ya like."

"What about eight in the morning?"

"Ya 'ave to be out of bed at breakfast."

"So when can I get into bed after I've got up?"

"Ya 'ave to be out of bed through the day."

"And fully dressed?" I add.

"Yeah and dressed."

"Sitting on that seat?" I ask.

"If ya like."

"Tar."

On my way back from the food hatch, dinner in hand, a dog-screw takes the piss out of the slop on my tray. The mash potato has more eyes than a spider with glasses and they're black. Normal jail food. I've had enough and my top blows off.

"You eat it." I send the tray and contents his way. It misses its target. Must be the heavy mash on one side throwing it off line. Name and number son?" Comes the cry. I can only think of Mac Vicar's immortal words.

"Ya no' me f***ing name and ya gave me the f***ing namber." Word perfect. I walk to my cell, twenty-eight on the twos. The screws in tow all the way to my door. Soon all his mates are outside my door. Frank's sitting in the chair eating his food; he looks up at all the heads round the door and says.

"Look, why don't ya's all just f*** off?"

"I'll nick you son."

"Do what the f*** ya want, ya gob-shite."

"He's just called you a gob-shite Tom," says one of the heads.

"I know - I heard him." This is a big thing. "Right son ya nicked," says the gob-shite. I look up at big Tom.

"What ya gonna do? Lock us up?" but he's nicked Frank not me. Like I've said they don't like Frank too much.

"Where's ya food lad?" asks Frank.

"I'm on hunger strike. And I don't give a shit."

"When did ya decide that lad?"

"Just now, I've had enough of this jail, I want out." My one day has now been three weeks of shit. Frank got his nicking sheet that night. In the morning they come to take him down the block for his trial. Not a real trial, you're guilty before you give your name; and number. I tell him to call me as a witness; I'd tell them about the shit we're getting.

"Ya wanted down the block son. Witness." Fun and a break in the mundane routine. I've never been down the seg. It's under the jail like all dungeons. The screws are the big boys of the job.

"In there, strip off son. Search." The cell's devoid of furnishings, a concrete box with a blue door. I do what he orders and he gives me sewn together rags that are a prison uniform.

"Put them on son."

"I'm on remand. I don't have to wear the rags of prison."

"You're in the block so you do as you're told son."

"I'm not putting them old washed out rags on so you can do what ya want. Lock me up." He sees sense and gives me my own clothes to wear; he's get out being I was just a witness and not on a nicking. At the end of the long landing, blue doors each side, is a half-glass door revealing a suited man wearing spectacles. He's sitting in the centre of a long table perusing files. My position is evident by the chair placed at the cell-like table situated some way from the suited guy facing it. A gulf of ten feet between the two. I stand facing the long table. The two screws stand shoulder to shoulder facing me making me stretch my neck to see between their melon heads.

"Give ya name and number to the Governor."

"Crowe CP3703."

"Sir." Says the screw on my right. I ignore his command.

"You are here as a witness for your pad mate is that right?"

"Yeah."

"Have you come here of your own choosing?"

"Yeah I have."

"What can you tell me about this case?"

"I'll tell ya this. I'm sick of being in a cell with someone who the screws have it in for. All hours of the night they come in and give Frank stick."

"What do you mean when you say, 'they'."

"The screws that's who; they wear gym T-shirts and trainers but they're screws. They've got keys."

"What time of night do you say this happens?"

"I say? – It does and it's late on, I'm shitting it all night. Just get me out of here."

"I'm stopping these proceedings and handing it over to the Area Manager. These are serious allegations needing an independent investigation." Independent? The area manager works for the prison service. It's as worthwhile as asking someone's mother for a reference. He writes in the file. "Will you give a statement to the officer?"

"Yeah I'd be glad to – sir." The plan is going great.

"Is there anything else you would like to tell me?"

"Well as you're asking, get me out of your shite jail, send me back to Durham." I can't believe what I'm saying. Durham is bad.

"You're going nowhere."

"Look. There's two ways to get out of a prison, one is to ask nicely, I've just done that, the other's to attack the Governor." The threat hasn't travelled through the ethos before the two screws leap into action, like bodyguards averting an assassination attempt on a head of state. My face hits the table with the ferocity meant to leave an in-print of it on the surface. My wrists are bent to their fullest extent and held against my shoulder blades. I'm carried out and dumped unceremoniously on the floor of a cell where I'm watched over by a camera situated in the corner to cover the whole cell. The cell contains a table and chair made from cardboard, and the steel prison bed, no mattress. When they thought I'd calmed down, and I'd written the statement, the ordeal is over and my taste of life in the lower depths of prison culture ends. Frank and I laugh for the rest of the day.

Walking round the exercise yard. Thinking of how to get to Durham. My mind is not taking any notice of the hundred or so others walking. Round and round we walk in an effort to keep leg muscles in good order. One of the faces comes out of the crowd.

"Are you Tony Crowe mate?"

"That all depends on who you are son."

"I'm a mate of a friend of yours. Mick from Tocky Lad."

"Don't know you son. What's your name?"

"Alan from Speke lad. I've just come from Haverigg prison up in your patch, Cumbria."

"So if I ask about you, people I know from Liverpool will know you?"

81

"Sound lad. They all know me. I was asked to ask ya if you want that fellow, who's goner stand in court against ya, Topped. Danger isn't it? The lads want to send a sorter up to your town and finish him off lar."

"Finish him off?"

"Yeah. 4x4 shogun. Hit and run he won't know what hit him."

"I'm waiting to go to court for attempted murder and you want to change it to murder?"

"You can't be on top for it. You're in here."

"Have you heard of conspiracy to murder?"

"What ya saying then?"

"I'm saying, to you someone I've never seen before in me life, don't be so stupid."

"The boys are only trying to help. What about if they snatch him on your court day then?"

"Don't say any more kid. Every time you say something I get another ten years."

I have to get out of here before I go mad. Letters to Kevin. Letters to my MP. Requests for transfer to Durham stating visits as a good reason.

Escape Plan

"Crowe? Visit son." Who could this be? The visits take place in a port-a-cabin secreted in one corner of the prison grounds. They last for half-an-hour and there's no tuck shop to buy food for munching on. A far cry from Durham's two hours and food to munch on. I put on a green bib and sit at the four-foot wide table. It's my uncle Derrick from Preston. The one who put up my bail money. He lives in the more affluent up-market side of town. Once an employee of a food packaging firm now retired.

In his youth he served in the RAF overseas, Palestine. I had no idea he was coming to visit me.

The drug dog indicates him, so we're on a non-contact visit. There's a plastic seven-inch high screen down the centre of the four-foot wide table stopping us touching each other. I ask him to find the address of the slag screw that's on my case. Big Tom. I know his name, his first name. Not usually given for this very reason. I was waiting outside the wing office for my turn on the phone when I overheard someone call him Tom, the same as at my cell when he nicked Frank. That was all I needed to have my fun. My poor old uncle who has never been in any bother in his life was given all the treatment befitting a drug-dealing gangster, right down to the strip search. The visit goes well; soon our half hour is up. I leave the long narrow port-a-cabin and give the green bib to the screw waiting by the doorway back into the jail.

"Go in there son. Strip search."

"I've been on a no-contact visit, are ya mad?"

"I don't give a flying fuck son. Get in there and strip off." I was once told, "Just part of prison life son" by a screw with just the same zeal. Five times in one week he turned me over. I go into the small room and go through the familiar routine. On the wing things are hotting up. Mick, another unhappy member of our Preston family had gone out on exercise and climbed a lamp post in the corner of the yard. He is sitting on a large sodium light and using another as his backrest. He had tried everything to get shipped back to Walton Liverpool. He barricaded his cell. Piled all the furnishing up behind the door. He refused to bang-up. He had sat out on the yard. Nothing worked. This time it was looking good for him, he has three layers of clothing on, all his burn, skins, even a packed lunch. He is well prepared for a long standoff, he thinks. Mick has been there for half-an–hour when he takes out a skin (cigarette Paper) and fills it with burn (tobacco) to make a smoke. Rummaged through his pockets for a match, Preston being a no lighter jail, and finds himself wanting. A definite flaw in his grand plan. Oh the best laid plans of mice and men. It takes the jail all day and half the night to get Mick down onto Terra-firma, from his lamp post throne. The local fire brigade came with their Trumpton ladder. The next day Mick was shipped-out to Walton.

I don't fancy the lamp post. My plan is to go over the wall, with the help of the tubular handrail bolted to the concrete road outside my window. Three bolts hold down the posts set at two foot intervals. Perfect for a ladder. All I need is a five mm key to loosen the bolts. A visit will fill that need. Frank and I plan the escape time by watching the screw passing our window, dog in tow. A wet towel used to twist around the old cast iron bars will snap them easily. You may say it's a work in progress. For now my hope is in my hunger strike. Every meal I get I leave on the tray and put it outside the door. The flaw in my plan is Frank, he's a gym-head, food is too much for Frank to pass up. Soon I start giving him my food at the hot-plate in front of the screws. They don't like it.

One time the dog-screw takes my food off Frank and puts it back on the hot-plate.

"Why have ya taken that off Frank?"

"Prison rules son, one man one meal."

"If I want to give him my food that's up to me."

"Prison rules son, you can't give your food away. One man one meal." I go to the hot-plate again, get my food, it's a see-through plastic boxed sandwich, go to my cell and give it to Frank right under Big Tom's nose. Uncle comes up with the goods on Big Tom, home address. When I ask him how his wife is, by name, he just about dies of a heart attack. On the spot. I made sure he saw the photos from my deps. He never gives me any more grief.

There's drugs; smack, on the wing and Frank has his eye on securing some for the night but he's got no items, phone cards or burn, the currency of jail. I have phone cards but I don't do drugs and I don't lend for drugs. Frank has a plan. First he smashes up a Bic razor extracting from it the blade. With the blade he scrapes the wooden seat till he has a small heap of varnish dust, the dust amounts to the equivalent of a bag of heroin. Time to call for a cleaner, the wing runners. With me showing him the cards he's off for the bag of smack, with the hope of commission filling his immediate thoughts. He returns and slips it under the door for Frank to check out; he can't see him switch the contents as he's stooped at the foot of the door. Not good enough for the fee asked, four cards. Frank's decision is to refuse the bag and give it back, the bag of dust that is not the brown morsel of smack mixed with whatever could be found in the confines of prison. All seemingly fair in drugs under the door.

Poem A room with a view

A room with a view, eight-foot wide by ten-foot-two.

A bed of iron welded to the floor. A solid steel shield they call a door.

One cupboard one chair, a table in the corner where I sit to eat, like little Jack Horner.

There's a sink stuck to the wall, just below a button marked with the word call.

Sometimes it's cold sometimes it's hot, whatever it is you get what you've got.

This is where I sit to think, this is where I eat and drink.

This is where I sleep at night, this is where I have to shite.

Home Again

Kevin comes through after six-weeks of hard times.

"Crowe, pack your kit son you're at court." I know I've got no hearings due. I don't waste a second getting to reception and out of the dump. In the prison yard stands a small white van, a Ford Galaxy, down the side running front to back there's a foot wide red strip. My transport to court awaits. I've seen these vans at Durham, they're used to transport category A prisoners and are accompanied by the sound of a helicopter hovering over head.

"Why am I going in that?" I point at the van with both my shackled hands. "It's a cat A bus."

"You're going to Carlisle and you're going in this van." I just want to get out before they change their minds. Standing on the first step of the three leading into the cage, I remember a verse from my Bible. "If you are not made welcome knock the dust from your sandals." I reach down with my handcuffed hands and remove my left shoe; ritualistically I knock the dust of Preston jail from the sole then repeat the symbolic act with the right one. It makes me feel better and brings an end to my misery. I hope never to see this place again.

The single seat stands alone in the centre of the van, enclosed within a cage of inch-square steel mesh. There's heavy chains to fasten me into the seat. The same as the strapping that holds a condemned man in Old Smoky, the electric chair. Hannibal Lector comes to mind! I'm on my way north. At Carlisle there's no hearing just good old Kevin for a legal conference after which I head for HMP Durham.

The same screws with the same augustness greet me. One thing's changed. All the screws in reception are wearing dark green polo shirts with the prison legend embroidered tastefully over the heart. The black uniform trousers are gone, replaced with Royal blue pants; a draw-string tied in a neat bow around the belly holds them up. An initiative to address the high suicide rate of the jail. There's at least one attempt per week and every week a name is added to the long list of lost souls that stretches back to the foundations of the prison. However, clothes do not make the man.

"Where've you come from?" First question from the newly garbed officer.

"Carlisle Crown Court."

"Did ya leave here?"

"Yeah." He works his way down the pile of files till there's none left.

"I can't find ya file. Did ya leave here this morning?"

"No, I left here six weeks ago. Now I'm back."

"How come you're here? Where did you come from?"

"Preston, shit-hole, prison."

"Well ya didn't leave here – did ya?" A rhetorical question delivered with pious discord.

"Yeah – six-weeks ago I did. You didn't say "did you leave this morning?""

"If I find you've got here through the back door you'll be sent back."

"I didn't know jails had back doors." I smile as I continue. "Bring your pals coz I'll fight ya."

"Stand on the black footprints and strip."

Back on B wing I'm put in cell eighteen on the ones. My compeer for the night is a one-eyed gentleman of the road who's in my company for working as a tarmacker in the employ of an Irish gypsy whose car of choice is a seven series BMW. New. It gets better. He was paid with bottles of cider and fish and chips from the local chippy. He's pleased to see me. I've teabags and a flask of hot water. He's more pleased to see them.

I filled my flask from the water boiler on the landing when the screw went to the wing office to sort out my cell. The one-eyed paver tells me how he, along with four other equally impoverished mates come to find themselves with three hot meals a day and a dry bed at the expense of our good Queen. Bless her. His boss, Mr BMW, got the drive-laying work quoting good prices then did a bad job and demanded exorbitant payments. The usual scam of migrant workers of the travelling people. Not that they're all at it. Why this guy's in jail is beyond me. Time for some supper with a cupper. Tuna from a tin. First I have to open the tin without the aid of a tin opener. They're not permitted. Can't have it too easy. Every cell has a bed. Every bed a corner bracket with a sharp edge. The bracket puts a hole in the tin when I give it a short sharp strike with the heal of my hand. Once I've got a hole the plastic knife removes the lid. Plastic cutting tin? Only in jail. When we've had our tea and tuna sandwich I make my bed, cover the hole in the wall and set myself for a good night's sleep. My one-eyed pal gets ready too. He pops out his left eye places it on top of the cupboard, then jumps under the worn-out green blanket that's hung over the worn-out mattress. I suppose he's use to sleeping in all he owns. Apart from his eye that is. When he came through reception he'll have been given his razor and a shower would have been a must, clean if not new clothes in place of his day-to-day street attire. Like I said, clothes don't make the man. He still looks the tramp he is. He brings to mind Billy on E wing. Billy The Brick spends more time in prison than out. Whenever he gets to the end of his short prison term the routine's the same, choreographed. He gets out of HMP Durham with £47.50, gets drunk, walks round to Woolworth department store with a brick and throws it through the window. Then sits on the pavement till the police arrive. Billy The Brick. – He holds the record of two hours between discharge and return. That's reception to reception with a court appearance in the middle. Back on the twos Tommy is my new pad mate. Blond hair with blue eyes and his boyish face is not the look of a bank robber. He just can't get bank staff to take him seriously enough to hand over the money. One woman even told him to go to the other window. The proceeds of his criminal exploits amounts to zero. His charge is the result of one bank saying twenty pounds was missing from a two thousand pound bundle Tommy dropped on his way out the door. Never has he succeeded as a robber. When Tommy tells me about his master plan to stab the woman on the van when she opens his door at Newcastle court, I can't help thinking he is going to mess up big style. For his well-being I drop his name in the box, something I would never have thought I would do. The jail-made weapon Tommy fashioned from a toothbrush fell from his buttocks in reception when he was asked to squat as part of his search. I need to get on my own and away from all this.

I would never work in prison workshops; noddy shops. Folding one plastic bag to put it into another is not my idea of a job'. £5.00 a week is not a wage. Cell number three on the threes is a single cell. My cell if I were to work. The threes is for those who work, all work up there; I can't go up without a job. They'd asked me for months to work and I'd always said no. They stopped my £2.50 bang-up money, only allowed me one night time association per week and put every type of junky in with me, I still held out. I don't like to move cells; that's one reason I refused. Now I would have to move, the ones are for short-stay or new recruits. The two's are for people who can't or won't work. The next day I take a job in the net making shop and move up to my single pad. Every man has his price, not every man gets to choose when to cash in. This one's much the same as my old cell with the one exception, the hole in the wall has a window that closes. I can see over the prison wall. The Cathedral stands high on the hill over the river. I can see the sunset shining in through my new west-facing window. Durham City lays to the right, roof-tops of shops with the odd tall, out of kilter; glass government building catches the light of the orange glow before it melts into the horizon. I always watch as it falls lower into the morro of a distant landscape. I know it's sinking into the sea at Whitehaven and Xlendi Bay. Gozo. So far away now, I ask myself was it ever real? The sunny days spent swimming with exotic fish and beautiful women. The nights of love without having to say I love you.

My new net-making job consists of knitting sports nets for a myriad of uses, football eighteen-foot long by eight-foot wide to snooker pockets. All the same knot. All the same finger-numbing twists and turns of the wrist. The same way years ago on the shores of the Sea of Galilee fishermen made their nets. For them it was living; for me its fifteen pounds a week. That's to say, once I attained the enviable position of number one. Not that I place a number on another prisoner. I leave such things to those who carry keys. The workshop's a world of trouble. In one year one guy's stabbed in the neck, well the underside of his lower jaw. The scissors came through his tongue as they entered his mouth from below. Another smashed in the head with one of the inch-thick round wooden poles the nets hang on during their construction. His head resembled a breakfast boiled egg, its top missing. The blood frothing and flowing bright red from the hairless wound as he runs around aimlessly in the darkness.

Friday afternoon we get to see a movie. Some old video, but better than working. We sit in rows on steel-tubular-wooden-based seats. The lights are off to create cinematic effect. The office light is the only luminance, that's where the two screws sit. They can never see into our dark world from their brightly lit domain. The guy who lost his head weighs sixteen stone and stands five-foot-seven. His sixteen stone is the best steroid induced muscle that bones can hold. He never saw it coming. Who or what hit him was one of life's mysteries to him. A dangerous place if you don't watch your back. When the usual rush is over and we're taken back to B wing, suspicion falls at my door. I had had words with the sted-head only one week earlier. I was in the front row of the would-be cinema, this is not my hand. I have long arms and an even longer memory of those who think they can get away with doing me an injustice.

The Witness

I'm standing in a queue of men all holding stainless-steel food trays. Moving slowly past the array of once frozen food left over from some supermarket mishap, where their stock has thawed out and needs eaten now. Or even yesterday. A voice from behind me calls out.

"Tony." I start to turn "Tony man it's me, Henry." There four or five places behind me is one Henry Hudson Forest. The same Henry Hudson Forest who made a statement to the police saying I was a smack dealer and that I'd asked him to sell smack for me. The same Henry Hudson Forest who's a dirty stinking smack-head. – Who for a wrap of heroin would sell out his own mother's soul to the devil. My eyes flash left to the S.O. whose keeping order. The uniform with its shiny silver pips on epaulette shoulders catches my eye. He opens his arms, palms up-turned, as he hears the exchange, pulls his shoulders to his red, high blood-pressured ears. His body language saying "there you go. What?" I can't believe Forest's there facing me. I'm in here to stop me intimidating this sort of person. He's a witness against me. I'm held in prison so I can't intimidate witnesses and they put them in with me. On the very same wing at that. I watch him to see what cell he's housed in. twenty-two on the two's. All over tea I walk up and down my small cell like an animal in a cage. Boiling up at the thought of this slag just over the landing on the floor below. Questions fill my head, who's his pad-mate? Would he do him in? When my door opens for trays to be put out I'm off. Making straight for pad twenty-two on the two's. The door's closed by the time I arrive and two trays lay on the floor outside. Most of the stew still filling one of them. Opening the steel flap covering the cell viewing window in the door, known as the Judas hole, the spectacled thin body of Forest sitting on the bottom of two bunks meets my bulging eyes. He's thinner, more drawn than I remember from eighteen months ago. The ravages of heroin has taken its toll. There's no doubt, it's the same person whose name's on the statement in my depositions.

"You slag, I've a statement with your name on it – tell me why that is –," giving him his full title, "Henry Hudson Forest?"

"Who's that?" He looks confused making my blood boil even more.

"Who's that? You shit, you know who this is. Why did ya put your name to the crock of shit that's a statement in my cell?"

"I've never said owt. – honest Tony."

"Honest you say? What do I have then? A f***ing forgery is it? Did the police forge it? No it's your signed statement. You are dead meat my friend Hudson. You hear me?' spelling it out. 'D-e-a-d dead meat."

"Crowe get back up here now." The screw that opened my door stands waiting to bang it shut again.

"Coming boss, just seeing me old pal. Just come in and he's got nothing, you know the score."

"I know you just said you'd kill him. Who is he? Has he put a statement in against ya lad?"

"No he's me mate from my town. He's doing his rattle, you know? I told him to get off the smack or it would kill him. That's all."

He has his hell to go through first. The next week will be his cold turkey period. Coming off heroin is not a nice experience. I have sat up night after night with guys doing their rattle. First hot, then cold, uncontrolled shaking with a smell like nothing to compare it to. The scratching of itchy skin results in lesions. The last thing you want in a filthy prison.

In the morning I go to show him his statement, there's only one person in the pad.

"Where's Forest lad?"

"Gone mate. Are you the lad who came to the door last night?" The kid's smoking a dog-end that's burnt down to his yellow fingers.

"That's right lad. What did he say?"

"When you went he was on the call-bell. He told the screws you'd cut him up and that he'd grassed ya up mate...." I cut him short.

"Why didn't you do the grass in then?" I pounce.

"He ya are mate. Not my problem. I'm only in for two week, I can't be doing that."

"Where's the slag now...." He cuts me short this time.

"A Wing. They took him over before breakfast."

Another time will have to do. I make my plan.

"Crowe visit lad." The rest of the lads are waiting by the wing gate. I join them. Together we walk the long corridors to the visits waiting room. The gate opens, revealing a small room furnishing one wooden bench adorning the three walls of prison-blue uniformity. There sitting on the bench is my old friend.

"Now then Forest remember me?" A right foot lands on the side of his head sending him flying from the bench. He lies on the red shiny floor and his glasses lay in the corner. His body contorted in a painful heap. A heel feels the soft tissue and then hard bone of his ribs as it comes down in a crushing stomp. My eyes follow his crawling body as it moves between the legs of the other fifty, or so, smartly dressed men waiting for the call of their name. Expelling its life's breath, reminding me of the sound a balloon makes when you untie the knot around its neck. Burying a foot left then right into his legs and arms. I stand back watching him. Leaving his face for another day. Another time. Another place.

One of the screws approaches the small waiting room from within the visits. I can see him through the crowded room; all dressed in the black uniform of the DST.

"You tell them Forest and I'll suck your eyes out of your head. Do you hear me Forest?" The con who administered the jail-justice must remain anonymous.

"Yeah," he moves his head "I know." He says as he slides up the wall onto the end of the bench. Nursing his broken body.

"What's wrong with your glasses son?"

"I'm okay boss, honest I am." The screw turns round glaring at everybody in the room. He can't do anything but go back into the visits room. Closing the half panelled door behind him. I've said nowt Tony honest, I said nothing."

"I've a statement man, your statement. You've not got a visit so you can go back to the wing. You're here because I want you here, do ya understand? I got ya here." I arranged for his fictitious visit to be on the same day as mine to show him how I could get to him whenever I wanted. He's on remand like me. No V.O. is needed for a remand prisoner, just a phone call. Can I help it if other cons don't like scumbags?

"Why did Forest get a kicking?" The black uniform asks.

"If you want to see me wait till after my visit. Now get away from me table." I tell the DST guy.

"Is he a nonce?"

"Look – I'm on a visit with me girlfriend just leave us will ya?"

"Do ya know who gave him the kicking?"

"I've nothing to say to you or your pals in black. Okay?" As the DST screw walks away from my table Dawn's wide eyes show her disapproval. Her mouth follows.

"Have you beaten up Forest?"

"Just let's have our visit should we?"

"I knew you were up to no good, you told me you only needed to talk to him."

"I did only talk to him. Whilst I was talking to him he fell on the floor."

"You mean you knocked him onto the floor?"

"I don't do the knocking, I leave that to others. Now leave it will ya before the whole jail gets to know?" As I walk through the wing gate I can see a screw at my door. The two pips on his epaulettes show his rank of Principal Officer (P.O.) nearly a Governor.

"Afternoon. Open the door please."

"Crowe?"

"What number?" I ask.

"Crowe CP3703?"

"That'll be me then. Do ya want something?"

"Come down to my office son."

"I'm not your son. What do ya want?"

"I'll tell you all about it in my office s..." He hesitates.

"No problem. Lead the way." He sits down on the only chair, behind the only table. Another P.O. stands behind me in the doorway. His large body filling the frame that the door should occupy.

"I have a statement here that says you assaulted another inmate on your visit. What do you say?"

"Can I see the statement?"

"No, the lad needs to remain anonymous."

"Did you assault anyone on your visit?"

"If I did it'll be on camera, just look."

"This was in the waiting room, not in the visits room."

"O' I see. You said on my visit. Not in the waiting room – who are ya asking about?"

"I've already said I can't tell you."

"If you think I've committed an offence call the police. But if there's no victim I don't see the point."

"There is a victim; he says he's a witness in your case and that you beat him up."

"Henry Hudson Forest?"

"How do you know who I mean if you didn't do it?"

"For one. I didn't say I didn't do it. Secondly I know its Forest because he is the only witness in this jail since Porter went to HMP Haverigg last month."

"Does that mean you did beat him up then?"

"No."

"What then?"

"One statement from fifty cons that were there is not an investigation. Take statements from all the witnesses then get back to me. Okay?"

"That's up to the Governor and you know good and well them inmates will back you up."

"Forest should not be on a visit the same day as me. You know he's a witness in my case. Tell that to the Governor."

"He says you arranged his visit, to have him where you could get at him."

"How's that then? I don't know if you have noticed but I'm in jail! The onus probandi is on you, on the governor, to see to it we are kept apart."

"Forest's on remand and he doesn't need a visiting order to book a visit, so you got someone to phone the prison and book a visit for him on the same day as yours."

"I'll leave it with you then?"

"You'll be put onto the anti-bullying register and I'll be watching you Crowe."

"Don't forget to spell my name with an E in it. And its first name Tony."

"Take him back to his cell Mr Hudson." Mr Hudson, the P.O. standing in the doorway has a face as red as his wiry hair from drinking to forget. He leads the way to my cell and without a word unlocks my door, stands back and waits while I step over the threshold. The door bangs shut. Forest's given a new job as block orderly. He lives in the segregation unit and cleans the cells when they've been shit-up by prisoners on dirty protests. He washes the walls when somehow blood from a con has found its way onto them. He cleans the toilets down there and the infamous red line, but most of all he keeps his mouth shut to the abuse carried out by the bullies of the prison service. Rob is one who was a victim of the Durham block. They kicked him in the chest that hard and that much his ribcage slit in two. When his family came to visit the prison told them he was too violent to be let out. Too broken at the feet of bullies he was. One holding each arm outstretched with a third booting him in the sternum. Rob was on remand and was granted bail so they had to release him into the custody of his lawyer. He spent the next three weeks in a Newcastle hospital. Hudson never comes out without a screw to look after him. The block steps leading down from B wing are enclosed in a cage of steel mesh. He's a rat in a trap. He'll wait. The charge resulting from his statement of lies was one of the thirteen dropped at Keswick so he can go on to my grievance list and the back-burner for when I get out.

Rules

Cell time, or bang-up is spent with my one speaker three battery two band transistor radio. Bought from the prison shop at twice the price of a high street store on the outside. Every week I renew the batteries. My Olivetti typewriter serves me well. All day and most nights I thump away at the white plastic keys. Not easy since I never before found a need or had the inclination to write anything. I couldn't write. I have to learn if I stand any chance in this fight for freedom. Every word I type that's more than two letters, yes two letters, I have to look up in my pocket dictionary for the correct spelling. A letter takes all day to compile then I retype it correcting any mistakes. No carbon paper in jail means I have to type another copy for my file. One letter usually takes two days in total. But I have lots of time to learn. How hard can it be? Children do it every day.

"Request and complaint form please."

"What's it about son?"

"Why?"

"I can maybe sort it out for ya."

"I want to get married to the mother of my son."

"Put in an app to the Governor."

"Done that."

"What was the answer?"

"I've never been given an answer."

"When did you put the app in?"

"Four months ago."

"And you've had no answer?"

"No."

"Put in another application to the Governor."

"Can I have a request and complaint form please?"

"I'll put you down for one son."

"Thank you very much."

Time to complain – complain about everything and anything I can think of. Bombard the Governor with paperwork. Every form is a black mark against the jail. Hence the screw asking if he could sort it out. Good practice for my typing skills and spelling. Every morning at breakfast I approach the S.O. taking applications and order my daily request/complaint forms. If I'm asked what I want to complain about I utter the words they both loath and dread. "Make that confidential access." Now he can't ask. Soon they don't ask. I complain about food, milk rations, my marriage, wet floors and anything I see throughout my boring day. I write to HMP Head Quarters to find out rules. Then I complain at the lack of compliance. I even make up new rules when I find out the prison has so many no one really knows even half of them. It's a trick I learned when I was a health-and-safety-come-union-man in my youth. I find a rule. Prison rule ten paragraph six. "The Governor will hold daily oral Request and Complaint hearing every day except bank holidays." How better to wind up the Governor than to have him face-to-face whilst I complain about no salt at food times. Time to make an application for an oral hearing. I give the app to the S.O. at breakfast. And wait. Eleven-thirty my app, along with my mail, comes under the door. Wrote on the bottom of my app in red pen,

"You know full well we don't hold oral request and complaint hearings in this jail." Time to submit a request/complaint complaining about the non compliance of prison rules. The sound of keys outside and my door opens.

"Did ya get your app?"

"Yeah – I did indeed. Was it you who answered it?"

"Yeah."

"May I point out prison rule ten – paragraph six?"

"What's that then?"

"That's the rule you're breaking. That's the rule that says you're supposed to hold oral hearings every day. Conducted by a Governor. What I'll do is write to prison HQ at Cleland House and ask why Governor Mr Ford thinks he has no need to conform to prison rules."

"Wait."

"For what?"

"I'll ask the Governor if he'll see you."

"You mean have an oral hearing?"

"Well I don't know about that."

"Go and ask him but I've got my answer right here." I wave my app in his face.

"That's what I was told by the Governor."

"Just a minute S.O."

"What?"

"This letter – I posted this letter out and I've got it back under my door. Hang on. There's a note."

"What's it say?"

"It's in red pen. It's from one of you lot – it's from the Censers office." I read it out loud.

"You cannot send this letter. It's against prison rules to write to the press."

"There's no name, it just says Censers. Aren't they all civvies?"

"Yeah. They're right though..."

"How dare they tell me who I can write to." I'm so incensed. "Only a Governor can stop mail. I demand to see the letters book." It has to be signed by a Governor to stop mail.

"I'll have to see if you're entitled..."

"If I'm entitled?"

"I'll get back to ya after lunch."

"And I'll sit and write a letter – or two."

'Well I'll...' I stop his mumbling.

102

"Close the door on your way out." How can an office worker say who I can write to? They can't in truth. Only a Governor can and only with good reason. All letters are posted open so they can be searched. The days of censorship are long gone. The rule covering correspondence with the press is so no one can write about prison business or prisoners. My letter does neither. I know the rule well.

"The Governor will see you in the wing office."

"Great. You found the rule then?"

"We never looked. He just said you could see him if you have a problem."

"Really? – changed his mind since this morning?"

"I didn't ask him this morning. You know we don't hold oral R/C hearings."

"Seems you do now." The office is down the three flights of iron stairs. At the end of the wing. When I enter, the unfamiliar heat of a central-heating radiator takes the moist breath from my throat. New carpet smells drift past my nostrils. A far cry from my one-bed-penthouse-suite.

"You asked to see me?"

"You a Governor?"

"I am; what can I do for you Crowe?" Never mind the salt that can wait. I have my letter now and an attentive Governor. Walking the six yards from my seat, no table, to the Governor's seat, behind a big desk, I ask.

"Can you explain that?" I drop my letter and the red pen note onto his desk.

"Can you sit in the seat and not approach the desk." Not a request but an order to establish his authority. "If you need to give me something you can give it to the S.O. okay?"

"Sorry." I return to my allotted position. 'I've never been on an oral hearing before. From what the S.O. told me – neither have you."

"This letter is addressed to a newspaper."

"Yeah."

"You're not permitted to write to the press."

"Why?"

"Prison rules."

"What rule's that then?"

"Standing Orders."

"So when my daughter has her twenty-first I can't wish her happy birthday by way of the press?"

"Yes you can do that."

"Wouldn't I have to write to them?"

"Yes..." I stop him dead.

"Isn't that prohibited under Standing Orders?"

"You can't send this letter with anything in it about the prison."

"You've now read the letter? What part do you think offends prison rules?"

"I'd need to go away and read the rule."

"I know the rule. I know that letter," pointing at the brushed aside paper on his desk. "Doesn't offend any rule."

"It attacks the police."

"That's not the rule."

"You say the police are liars."

"Yeah. The last line in the letter says "in my opinion" I can hold an opinion. Human Rights Act."

"You can't slag off the police."

"Who are you to protect the name of the police?"

"They're a public body and the rule says..."

"So now you know the rule?" I jump in.

"They have no way of answering your allegation."

"Open letter to the same newspaper. Like me. Freedom of speech they call it."

"I'll have to go and look up the rule."

"You do that Governor. Find out why I was told by a censor, and show me the letter's book with the Governor's name who signed it. You can keep that letter. I have a copy."

"I have no doubt."

"I'll leave it with you." I make a point of leaving before I'm dismissed. Back in my cell I write to my Solicitor, Kevin. In the letter I put a copy of the newspaper letter that was so controversial and a note asking him to forward it on. Legal mail is protected from censers by law and can be sealed in my cell. Prison Rule 37A. Rules, Rules, Rules. After dinner my letter, with a note from the Governor, is pushed under my door. I pick it from the floor and rip it in two then drop the two halves into my bucket-bin. I know his answer. The object is to have him look for it. I win every time I get an answer.

New Job

"Do ya want to be a wing cleaner son?"

"No." I tell the screw standing in the cell doorway. "I go to the gym Monday, Wednesday and Friday mornings ten till eleven."

"You can still go the gym. That'll be no problem."

"Will I have to move into a cleaner's cell on the twos?"

"Yeah. All the cleaners live on the twos. You'll be out all the time. You're only banged-up at 8:00pm."

"Double cell?" my next question.

"I –." He hesitates. "You're only in there at night."

"Okay I'll take it. Do I start now?"

"Tomorrow. When I've sorted your job change, I'll move you then." After breakfast the next morning true to his word I'm moved. Padded up with mister tarmacker. The one-eyed tramp's Boss. Mister BMW.

I can touch both walls at the same time by stretching out my arms. Swing a cat? You couldn't swing one of the mice that scurry across the floor during the night by its tail without smashing its head in on the wall. John, mister BMW, takes the top bunk. I the more favoured bottom bunk. At meal times Mister BMW takes the chair, I sit on the toilet with the black plastic lid closed to take my bum. My steel tray on my lap. The only toilets on the wing are in the cells, stuck to the wall in full view of the door. In full view of the person not using it. Before prison I'd never had to be in a toilet when it wasn't me using it. The sign on the wall in reception on the way in said "Dignity and Respect" Where is the dignity in sitting on the toilet with someone in the room? Where is the respect? Making me eat food sitting on the toilet. Dignity and respect. Words. Hollow empty words on a blue board nailed to a prison wall.

106

Every day Mister BMW looks at his Holy Bible. The gold lettering stands out against the white leather cover. He looks but can't read one word. He never learned. His youthful days spent in a caravan moving from town to town only taught him block-paving, tarmacking, and ripping off old people who didn't know the whole thing was a scam. I wonder how the Lord God will look on his life when it's over. I have to read out his letters, usually sent by Misses BMW. She can't write either. I have to work out what she's saying. My own imaginative spelling helps me to decipher her message of love and foreboding. One time I wrote a letter to Misses BMW. His words dictated to me. 'I love you, I miss you, God will help us, soon I'll be with you, I love the kids, I miss them.' The letters I read out were written in an Irish phonetic dialect. Mister BMW, who I doubt was ever in Dublin, spoke with the same lilt. "I've not done no'thin', I'm just a poor man lookin' out for me family." He would tell me. "Jesus knows I'm a good man, I pray to The Lord bless him." When Mister BMW tries to climb onto the top bunk his short legs let him down. The chair is a stepping stool.

His black hair is slicked back with oil or gel. When he shaves he leaves a thin line of black hair down each cheek converging in the clef of his chin. Please sir. Yes sir. No sir he would say to the screws, no problem sir. Three bags full sir. Grovel grovel grovel. My spine froze every time he said sir. He tells lies all the time. I have to move out or kill him. Two weeks it takes before someone is sacked and an opening comes up. I move out.

Baggy, one of The Six is a cleaner. He lives in number twelve on the twos. He lives alone now and the way it works is one of the two living in the dog kennel, John or myself, is upgraded. Baggy doesn't much like the idea of living with John so I move in at his request.

He has no problem now and the hollow words spewed out on that first day seem a lifetime away. To be fair Baggy kept a discreet silence. It turns out he is also the reason Tommo's ass fell out, Baggy told him I would kill him and think nothing of it. It would seem I do have a fearsome reputation. Two weeks we last together before Baggy gets the sack, you could say he got the boot for booting. He was caught smoking smack, tooting, having a boot, chasing the dragon, many names describe the act of sucking up the heroin smoke through a pen sheath as the black slug slithers down the tinfoil hotplate. The screw caught him and another cleaner banged to rights. Tube in mouth sitting on the bed during association. My duties are now serving food and cleaning up after meal times dressed in my white uniform. The screw whose job it is to order us around is a right dog. The one who's responsible for Baggy's demise. He drinks on his dinner break, most days he's pissed when he comes in from lunch. Over weight, over stressed, and over paid. All the way a boss. A piss-head with years of abusing prisoners under his fat belt. During my short employ as a cleaner he's been off work. Now he's back. He takes an immediate dislike to me, nothing I've done. Just because he can.

There's a new recruit in number seven on the ones. Ricky Daniels. Another mate of Swindles'; I don't know him but he knows me. I've got to see if he's going to give me any trouble. At six-foot-three and seventeen stone he's not someone I want to fight. I open his door-flap and look in on him. His enormous bulk fills the iron-framed bed. He's just come from G wing where the Cat A prisoners live. Max security.

"All right mate?" my voice wobbles.

"I."

"Listen, are you a mate of Swindles'?"

"Well a know him like."

"I'm Tony Crowe and." I don't know what to say. I'm pleased for his interruption.

"A know ya are." He sits up. "It's nowt to do with me."

"Well I don't want any bother with you mate. I don't even know ya lad."

"A know him like but it's between you and him like. A want nowt to do with it." He now sounds like an ally of mine.

"Have ya got smokes and that? Is there out ya need?"

"A job. I've been locked up for eight weeks and it's doing me head in like.- I don't smoke lad."

"I'll see if I can get ya on this job you're open all day. - The wing cleaners."

"Great stuff." After closing his flap, I make my way to the food-service line and take up my post. Dressed in our off-white garb sleeves turned up to show off the skills of the wing tattooist we wait for the procession of hungry cons. The order in which they come changes every day so the same ones don't always get just whatever is left. Who says jail isn't a fair place? Today it's twos, ones then threes. Seven cells at a time are opened with timing of a military procession until the last door bangs shut with the cry of "threes clear sir" from the screw standing high up in the roof space.

On my right is a six-foot two kick boxer from Hartlepool called wolf. Standing at the entrance waiting to move along the line is a young angry man who is new to our happy home. Wolf loads his tin try with the half dozen chips deemed to be The Kings Ration.

"More chips," he pushes his try forward, "and stop taking the piss pal."

"You've got all ya getting mate so move on."

"Give us some more chips you fat twat."

109

"Listen mate just fuck off, move on. Next." Wolf calls. The young angry man walks off chuntering threats at Wolf.

The eagle-eye of the boss-screw watched his every move. The most common reason for cleaners getting the sack is for running out of chips and making it necessary for the fat screw to walk the twenty yards to the kitchen for more. Chip servers are an endangered species and make enemies of everyone. Drugs come in a close second for upsetting the boat. Violence is an everyday thing, if not from the cons from screws. But some is beyond belief even for in here. The next day the disgruntled guy comes for his Kings allotted, with one aim in mind. I can imagine him sitting in his cell all night and festering in the thought of how some screw's boy had dissed him at the expense of all those watching. Revenge is a cancer. As the angry man passes through it becomes more and more apparent to me he is not here for food, he has no tray. What he does have is a two litre plastic jug full of water, taken from the boiler outside. In the boiling water is sugar, lots of sugar. When the angry young man unleashes his weapon of choice on Wolf, the result is horrific, the skin falls from his face and his ear is gone.

You cannot defend yourself against madness. My new job is over before it really began. I'm not one for putting up with dog screws who, most likely, were bullied at school. One good thing comes from my sacking. Ricky gets to have a go on the chip scoop. My old job is given back to me in the net shop and I am happy to have a cell all of my own once more.

My great plan to stop Dawn from going to court is going nowhere, time to up the ante. When I came from Preston my application to marry had to start again. So it did just that. I make a new one every day till at last the Governor says yes.

However, he did not send the paperwork out to Dawn. He was saying yes but doing nothing, I can only use the court if he says no. Hunger Strike # 2. I am without food for forty two days. Three times a day I go for my food; three times I put out a full tray when the door opens with the call for trays. I am on hunger strike for seven days before the screw asks me why I haven't eaten my food. He then informs me the seven days won't count. Thanking him for the weeks extra life, before I die of hunger, doesn't make any sense to him. My body weight falls by seven pounds a week and I am sent to the prison Doctor once a week for assessment. Sometimes, mental assessment. I am taken off work duty and housed back on the twos. Stopped from attending the gym deemed to be unfit. Then the day comes when the P.O says.

"The Governor will let you marry if you stop now." Winner. I come off my 'Food Refusal' and in the morning I'm put on the van to Preston prison for my Not Guilty plea. First thing I do at Preston is tell them of my impending wedding.

"Put in an application." I'm told.

"No you don't understand, I have permission to marry already."

"Not from here you don't son, put an app in tomorrow morning." My win has gone in a van ride. While on hunger strike I was not fit to travel, coming off only gave them the chance to move me. When I return to Durham prison I am told to put in another application to marry. For one year I sit on remand waiting for my day in court.

One year of living a life far removed from mine on the outside. In a way my alleged crime is my saving; no one would say a wrong word to me lest they incur my wrath.

Court day

"Crowe, Court."

My big day that would last two weeks is here. New suit sent in by Dawn waiting for me in reception. Six hours a day in the van. But the end is in sight. The whole Jail knows it's my time. First day the jury are picked, Twelve Men good and true. In this case eight men and four women take the oath to judge the case on the evidence given in this court. Second day the case begins with Swindles giving his story. A best-seller if not for the inconsistency. Day after day the prosecuting silk brings police officers and friends of Swindles' to tell the lies they wove between themselves.

The truth will set me free, I know it. The evidence is that weak Tim; my Q.C makes a motion of no case to answer when the case for the prosecution ends. The only thing the Judge says is. "I want to know why the car was seen leaving the village. Motion denied." I give him his answer in my four hours of evidence. Not once did the prosecutor trip me up. There is only one truth. Dawn did not attend another victory for Tim. The photos of the horrendous scene are deemed not of evidential value as we don't dispute the ferocity of the attack. They don't prove who did it just that it was done. The summing up of the case by Tim is great.

"Ladies and Gentlemen of the jury, you often hear it said the evidence fits together like pieces of a jigsaw, well this case is more like a dot to dot and a lot of the dots are missing." The judge told the jury Porter was serving a sentence for fraud and deception. That one witness admitted he would lie for his friend. And that he himself could be a suspect in this very case. The police were confused at best and unclear as to who opened the front door of Dawn's house, where very important evidence was found. There were inaccuracies in their evidence. But it has been two years since the crime. All good things, to my untrained ear.

Down in the court cells we wait for the Jury to come in with their verdict, whatever it is now is the time it will end.

Not quite. Deliberation continues into the next day, leaving me with a sleepless night back in Durham prison. This could be, should be; my last night in prison.

Three O'clock the court officer comes to my cell situated in the belly of the court building.

"They're back Tony."

"Is it a verdict?"

"I don't know, Good luck Tony. There's no way from what I've heard over these weeks you'll get a guilty."

"Thanks for that, I can't believe what I've heard." I tell him.

Upstairs the court is set, the Judge, the Jury, the all important press, not an empty seat there. Two Q.C" Two Barristers, Two Lawyers, and one stenographer tapping out every word.

"Have you reached a verdict on which you all agree?" The Judge asks the Foreman. The silence following that question lasts an age.

"No." He answers.

"Have you reached a verdict that ten, or more, of you are agreed?"

"No Me Lud."

"If given more time is it likely you will reach a verdict?"

"No Me Lud we are deadlocked." A gasp comes from the public gallery.

"Then it only remains for me to declare a hung Jury."

The Q.C prosecutor rises from his seat, quickly putting his motions forward. My Q.C rises equal to him. In a second it's over. What? What is over? Am I free? The prosecutor said at the start of this farce.

"I will prove beyond doubt to you The Jury, by the end of this trial that Tony Crowe is guilty." Well he didn't. Kevin is sitting in the small room down stairs when I get back.

"What just happened Kevin?"

"You will have to do it all again."

"No, I can't go through it again, I'll change me plea to guilty. I need to know when it will all end. I'm going crazy in jail."

"You can't give in now Tony. You have not been found guilty."

"I haven't been found anything, what will they do now? I'll tell ya what; they'll change their story and plug the holes in their case." That's what I tell him.

"They can't, we'll get the transcripts from this trial."

"What about Dawn? She will be back under pressure."

"We'll sort it Tony."

"I'm worn out Kevin, I've given my whole. I'm physicality and mentally bankrupt."

My Q.C. Mr Haywood arrives holding a bundle of briefs under his arm. His right arm extended toward me looking for a handshake.

"What's going on Tim?" I ask him. "What's all that about? We had our trial and we won; is it not for them to prove my guilt?"

"Yes..."

"Well did they do that?"

"It was a hung Jury so..."

"No, Not "SO"; I am not guilty and I should go home now."

"Retrial..." I cut him off again.

"Do they get to keep having trials till they get their Guilty? How many trials can they have?"

"There is no number it's up to the Judge. We can move the trial to Preston court."

"No I'm not living in that shit hole."

"You can change your legal counsel if you would like."

"What, for somebody who knows nothing about this debacle? To have-a-go? I don't think so."

Back to jail

Back to Jail on the longest, loneliest, ride to date.

Nine O'clock I walk into the Jail that is now my home once more. Already the jail knows my fate. The radio gives the news every half hour just in case a potential Juror misses it.

Back to my wedding plan. Dawn is still the prosecution's best hope. That will give me something to do. To take my mind off the next six months of waiting. I can never beat them but I can buzz around their ears. Let them know I will not go away.

Christmas comes once more to the prison. Screws with tinsel on their key-chains and Santa hats on their heads. They even put up a tree with all the trimmings. Two days it lasts before someone, who needs no reminder it is the festive season, sets it alight. A Christmas service is held in the Chapel with songs, cribs, wise men and shepherds. Screws and cons.

The only day in the calendar when you can pick from a menu what you want for dinner. A choice of three items, fish, chicken, or veggie stuff. I don't want to know its Christmas outside. It certainly isn't Christmas in here. The birth of Jesus! I wonder if he knows this place exists. Bed is where I spend it, closing the door whenever it's opened.

A new year but the same old routine. Durham is for people waiting to go to court. Not for serving a sentence. Only the short sentences are served here, like Billy The Brick's. Apart from the women that is. Yes women. They are mostly lifers serving time for murder.

I have been here longer than those sentenced by the courts. Some cons have been in, served their sentence and come back for another go. I'm asked on lots of occasions if I'm back in. "No, I tell them "I'm still here from your last visit" "what did ya get?" Is the next

116

question. "I'm still on remand" I tell them. Hundreds of days locked up without trial, then a trial leading to nothing. I've got a letter from Darrel conveying his sorrow at my receiving a twenty years sentence.

John Watson stopped coming in on his monthly roundabout of drugs, jail, drugs. An overdose of heroin stopped his crime and his heart at the same time.

Stabbings continue day by day, some worse than others all bad. Crazy Ronny opened up his pad mate with a blade from a razor, spilling his guts onto the cell floor. Too big a job for wannabe screw-doctors, an ambulance crew load him ontothe pool table, replace the contents of his abdomen before wrapping him in cling-film so as not to lose any body parts. From the small crack in my cell door I can see them working on him. Ronny's defence is suicide, he did it to himself he tells the screws. I am looked at as the Don of the wing with my long term residence. Nothing that I have done I may add. Only by way of time served. Even the screws think I run the wing. One normal day in bedlam, in the gym two brothers call me over. Nigel Abandon the eldest says.

"Tony we have a problem."

"Really," I say. They are hard core in the world of drugs on the outside.

"I don't do drugs." I tell them.

"We have a friend on B wing that is getting shit off some of the others on the wing."

"Yes. What's that to do with me?"

"If you say to leave him they will. You can say don't do it and it will be so."

"I know who he is and he's a sex-case, no way will I get involved in that, I'll get cut up myself."

"No he's in for his woman it's not rape."

"You can rape your own woman so I..."

117

"No he's innocent bro." Now how can I condemn him if he is innocent like me?

"I will stop the jail justice on him till he has been to court, but if he comes back with a guilty I don't want to know, I will let it be known, I have no interest in him."

"That's all we ask for. Thanks Tony."

I don't know if I have the authority over the others. I do know who is setting up the attack on Nigel's ethnic brother, Campbell.

One word in the ear of the wing thug stops the boys fun for now. They can't believe I even care about him, but they do as I say unquestioningly. Moving their self-styled justice on to someone else. Reputation is a great thing until its put to the test. I know. That's why I test even the biggest reputations up front. Mine is intact only because no one ever fronted it. Well that's not true; one guy did once a long time ago. I was a Hells Angel and the hard man of the moment was all talk, I thought. One night he wanted to fight me. We headed out to the car park for the dual. The time had come for me to be, put down or back down. At the door he stopped, turned, smiled then laughed at me. "I'm only joking with ya, come on I'll buy ya a beer," says he. Front, it's a gift. It doesn't work unless the guy is of sound mind. Don't front a lunatic. Maybe that's why I don't get anyone fronting me!

Dummer

Dummer Dale lives on the twos in a cell with a white door. A single cell with a blue plastic box to the left of the door. The box is for Dummer's clothes. He's what the prison calls an E Man. Someone who in the past has escaped. Even typing the word, escape, now seems wrong for me. The mere mention of the word could put me into clothes of bright yellow. With a police escort on court days. Dummer is the only person I know charged with conspiracy to murder, committed outside, whilst he was in prison. Can you get your head round that?

The white door is for the screws to know he is an E Man. The box is for his clothes. When he is in the cell his clothes are in the box. Food is given to him last. They are moved from cell to cell on a weekly bases; white door to white door. A book is kept by the screws with every move logged down. Every minute of every day is recorded in the book. Often they are referred to as being 'ON THE BOOK' by other cons.

I think Dummer is the least liked prisoner in Durham Jail. Not by other cons. By the establishment. He gets less than nothing. The lowest you can be is basic regime that says it all, Dummer was put on double basics. The only thing the Governor could take away was exercise. Not the whole thing that's a legal right. Dummer had to exercise in the block-yard, alone.

For the last fourteen years he has been in jail. Twelve years in Frankland maximum security prison, of which he did every day, not one day off. He was discharged from the block and out for seven days before he was back inside. A tattooed garland of small flowers adorns his neck, black ink scars his face and arms. He lives in his own drug influenced world of who knows what?

119

Why tell you this? He is one of many lost in the world of prison, dead end lives that all-too-often end in prison cells. Their eyes are empty. If the eyes are the window of the soul these men are soulless. They are already dead.

The suicide rate is no less than last year; in fact Durham holds the record for suicides in 1997. That's why the screws changed their clothes in reception to casual wear. My part is to become a prison listener run by the Samaritans. Listening to the problems of others. Some first time cons, some not guilty, some guilty of common sense. What do I mean? Like Darrel defending his wife and child. Who wouldn't?

Nine O'clock, Friday night; footsteps rattle on the steel landing floor, the key clatters in the lock.

"Crowe come on lad we need a listener."

"Anyone I know?"

"Kid in twenty-four."

"Has he asked for a listener?"

"No but he's kicking off and he says he'll kill himself."

"OK, let's go. What's he in for?"

"Murder."

"Remand?" I ask.

"Yeah." The screw says it like there's no difference.

"We won't lock the door when you're in with him."

"Can I have a jug of hot water? We may need a cup of tea."

"I'll send one up Tony."

Only the P.O. (Principal Officer) has a key after bang-up. He is always called Oscar One whatever the jail. This Oscar One knows he has a problem for the night if I don't talk the guy down. A threatened suicide means every fifteen minutes Oscar One will have to look in on him.

"All right mate? Tony's me name. Can I come in for a talk?"

On the bed, crying like a baby at 2am, with his head in his hands sits David.

"I can't do this anymore."

"You tell me what the most difficult thing for you is."

"All of it."

"Do you want to talk about your problems? I won't tell anyone what you say to me. It stays with me."

"I can't go on like this."

"Do you want to kill yourself?"

"Yes."

"Will you want to kill yourself tomorrow?"

"WHAT?"

"Will you want to kill yourself in the morning. Because you only get to do it one time. No going back."

"I'm going to be lifed off with years of living in places like this, with people like these, with screws shouting." The door opens for the jug of hot water to be handed over.

"Tea David?"

"I've no tea bags left. They're all on the floor." Torn photos, broken picture frames, and tea-bags cover the floor.

"I'll sort that David. P.O. Can you get us some tea-bags please? Are these your family?" I pick up the torn photos from the floor.

"Was."

"Do ya want to tell me?"

"I'm in for murder, I killed a guy."

"You don't look like a man who would go out and kill someone."

"I was out with my girlfriend in Newcastle, shopping, when we saw her ex, she has a restraining order on him. He's been messing with the kids, ya know what I mean?"

"Yeah I know. You mean he's a nonce."

"Well he came over giving us shit so I punched him knocking him down."

"Did you kick him on the ground?"

"No I only hit him once but he hit his head and it killed him, then I got charged with his murder."

"I'm not here to give you advice, but, that is not murder. That's manslaughter at worst. Self-defence is what it is."

"I phoned my girlfriend on association but she wasn't there. The phone just rang and rang. She's got somebody else."

"How do you know that?"

"I just know."

"You don't know that. You don't know if she was with the kids in an emergency. Do ya?"

"No but she knew I was phoning and..."

"And what? She's not said anything to you as she?"

"No."

"I can get you a phone call now if you want. If it's over you need to know. Right?"

"I don't know."

"Drink your tea and we'll see what the P.O. says."

"OK I'm ready now."

"If you get any jail it will be no more than three years. With one year on remand that's it done. Do you believe me David?"

"Yes." His crying is down to a sniffle.

"Come on let's do that phone call." Nothing is too much bother at eleven O'clock if it leads to a quiet night for Oscar One.

"What's his problem?" Oscar One asks.

"Ask him. You know I can't tell you."

"No I only mean is he OK now?"

"Do you mean is he safe to leave?"

"Yeah how is he?"

"Fine, but if he wants to kill himself you know he will. I can't tell you he won't. That's your decision." The call makes all the troubles of the world disappear for David. She was at her sisters when he phoned; looking after her kids while her sister went to the hospital.

Three times a week is normal for listening jobs with all night vigils high amongst them. One week I spend more nights out than in. Most problems come from outside, that's where they have to stay. Leave them in the showers when you come in or they'll drive you mad. That's my advice to the new recruits. Sometimes that can't be done, like when the problems follow you in. I have had to put up with the witnesses coming in after me. Now I find out some twenty one year old drug dealer, who is responsible for my fourteen year old son being admitted to hospital, is on D wing. The story I get is that he beat up my son breaking his jaw. The news is not what I need to hear. Time to have a word with this disrespectful bum. First thing to do is send him a message. My disapproval is carried to his cell by one of the jail messengers. Soon after I make sure we are in the same place at the same time.

A crowd of cons are being moved from the workshops back to the wing. In the crowd is my man Mark, but I don't know what he looks like. The screw walking in front stops to unlock the gate that will give us access into the exercise yard. The one taking up the rear is asked a question of no importance by my co-conspirator. My Judas marks out the quarry for me. When I ask him about my son he tells me.

"Nowt to do with me mate."

"What makes you think I'm ya mate son?"

"Well I just mean..."

"Do you know who you're talking to?"

"Yeah Dom's Dad. I'm just saying it wasn't me that done him like."

"Well you have a problem son, coz I think it was and no one is going to take the piss with my son and not have to pay for it. Do you know what I'm going to do to you?"

"You're in for chopping up that kid aren't you?"

"What do you know? How do you think I'll treat someone who puts my son in hospital? Why are you even knocking around with kids of fourteen? Are you a nonce son?"

"No, no I just know him that's all."

"Drugs is it? Do you give him drugs? I'm going to suck out your eyes and break your jaw. How about that? Then you my get an idea of how much I want you to leave him alone."

"I know now Tony."

"You don't know nothing son. You want to play in the big league? Well welcome to my world."

"What you up to Crowe? Come away from that fence where I can see you." Comes the call from the rear guard screw. My plan is at an end. However, Mark gets the message. The result is he never comes out of his cell without a screw to escort him. Food, association, even when he takes a shower, the most dangerous place in jail, he has a chaperon. I get the usual grilling from the screws. Never to be moved onto that wing while Mark is a guest.

Legal suit!

Visits, letters, phone calls home; court appearances every twenty-one days for my continued remand, waiting for my re-trial date to come. I want it to come, but I don't want it to come, all at the same time. One thing prison can't do is stop the clock. They only slow it down to a pace known as the jail shuffle. No point in rushing when time is something you have lots of. Without anyone telling the interns how to walk the yard, I find it fascinating that in every prison, the direction walked is anticlockwise. I don't know if it's some far forgotten ritualistic protest or an old rule passed on from old lag to newcomer.

Superstition is rife in jail. Always eat your last breakfast or you'll come back for it. Never look back when you leave the jail. Don't bang your own door shut. Never close another man's door. On and on it goes. There must be lots of uneaten breakfasts in Jail going by the number of people who come back to eat them.

June 1999 my retrial has come round. The trips to court are here once more. In reception waiting to leave for court, my suit clean and pressed, shoes polished, matching tie all wrapped in a prison plastic bag, hanging on a hanger. The same as the last time. After the strip search the screw gives me my suit.

"No," I tell him, "I don't need that till I get to court." Assume nothing is a lesson I have yet to learn.

"You have to put it on now if you want to wear it in court."

"For three hours in the van? No way."

"If you're taking it you'll have to wear it."

"Why?"

"You're only allowed one set of clothes, the ones you're wearing, so if you want the suit put it on."

"No. I'll take it on the hanger and put it on in court."

"What will you travel in?"

"I'll go like this." I'm sitting naked, all but for my underwear.

"We can't let you go like that."

"Well I'm not going. Tell the High court Judge why I won't be there."

The door closes with me left bewildered at the stupidity of the situation. Why I can't take my suit and change in court is puzzling. All the tricks available to them are coming out is my only answer. The door opens to reveal the suited figure of a slim man in his forty's. In the background is the P.O.

"Hello I'm Governor Brown." He says.

"And I'm pissed off." I reply.

"What's the problem with getting dressed Crowe?"

"I'm not travelling in me suit. I go like this or I don't go."

"You can take your suit to court. There's no need for all this." I can't believe the change of attitude. Not one word of persuasion. I don't trust them to put it on the van.

"I'll carry it onto the van."

"OK."

"Right let's get going then."

After getting dressed the matter is over. Victories don't come easy in here. My marriage never came off. This is a good day in my fight with the rules of prison. I walk to the van. Suit over my right shoulder. Shoes in my left hand. Handcuffed of course. The trip's the same. Thrown forward when the driver steps on the break. Slammed into the side, left, right, when a corner or roundabout tries to hinder his mission. The small side window giving no indication of imminent changes in motion or direction.

Carlisle Crown Court. The van drives into the air-lock. The roller door lowers slowly from high overhead. Stopping only when it hits the red concrete floor. Walls of dirty white. The van is boarded by court officers. One by one the occupants are taken into the court cells. First job is change into my suit.

"Give us me suit Dave."

"Can't Tony. The prison's been on the phone with instructions not to open any bags."

"You are kidding? Give us me suit. There was no problem last time. You run this place not Durham."

"Can't do it. If we remove the security tag we'll be in bother."

"I'm not going up in these rags. Where's Kevin me solicitor?"

"Not here yet Tony. It's not us."

"Tell the judge..." He stops me.

"Kevin's up stairs, on his way down now. Come on, I'll take you to the interview room." Two aluminium tubular chairs with blue plastic seats and a small desk are the only furnishings. Kevin is sitting in one. I take the other. All round glass walls keeps us in view from outside.

"They won' t give me my suit. I had to fight to bring it and now they won't give us it. It's not on Kevin."

"Don't worry Tony. I'll talk to the Judge. You can wear what you want."

"I can't believe them."

"Let us concentrate on the trial. Today the jury will be sworn in."

"I've done this before Kevin. Without me suit...!"

"I will deal with that Tony. Jury, if you see anyone you want off give me the nod."

"Can I have the nine from last time who said not guilty?"

"No. All new Jury. But you can object without giving a reason to any of them. I'll go and talk to the Judge about your suit."

"I don't like this Kevin. They are doing anything to beat me. I mean! The suit thing?"

"They are going to try and enter the photos into evidence."

"No, I thought we got them thrown out last time."

"This is a new trial. New evidence. Change of tack."

"Same trial. You said. New Jury. Same evidence. There can only be one evidence. Two and a half years and you tell me they can bring in new evidence?"

"We have the transcripts from the first trial. They can't change what they said." Q.C. Haywood dressed in his silk jerkin, buttons running up the cuffs, cream coloured wig set just off to the left, stands in the doorway.

"There's only one truth Kevin." I add.

"Truth has no place in court Tony." The educated accent-less voice comes from behind me.

"Truth is our case. Isn't it?"

"Evidence and the defence of it. They offer evidence, we defend it."

"I'll tell you about evidence Tim. There was forty five items taken from Swindles' house, Evidence. Only one piece of that Evidence is being put to the court. If it doesn't prove me guilty it must prove me innocent. Why can we not tell the Jury about the other evidence? The finger prints, foot prints in the blood, fibres, ball-pain hammer..." Tim stops me mid way.

"Not for us to offer evidence, only to defend the evidence given by the prosecuting counsel, Mr Thwaits. We don't have to prove you innocent; you already are until a jury says otherwise."

"We can't defend against what did not happen, why are the photos back on the list of evidence?"

"We will have to deal with that matter again."

"If they are evidence what do they prove? We don't dispute the extent of his injures, we have the report from the R.V.I (Royal Victoria Infirmary) at Newcastle."

"I will argue the point in court."

"All they do is horrify the crime and are therefore prejudicial to me."

"I will argue the point." Tim tips his wrist, looking at his watch, looking for a reason to end the onslaught aimed at the system. His system. A system failing its duty on the first occasion. Scotland doesn't have retrials. You are proven guilty or let go. I should not need a court to find me not guilty. That is my status until a jury say otherwise. Just as Tim says. Being innocent before the trial with no change after the trial, leaves me still innocent!

I wait in the cell along with four others all with tales of woe. All with knowledge of my long awaited trial. All sympathetic.

Dave comes; clinking keys, stomping boots, as if he knows not to sneak up, for fear of finding his charges indulging in activities not wholly legal. The odd time someone would have drugs to calm them down before their big day. Not Dave's problem. Not worth his time filling in paperwork.

"Tony you're up. Come on."

"Not without me suit."

"Kevin's sorted it Tony."

"All right, give us it then."

"No, we can't open the bag. Kevin's got a new suit for ya."

"What about the Judge...?"

"In there Kevin's on his way down."

The same room with the same two chairs. Locked in till Kevin turns up with a new suit, shirt, tie, but no shoes. A suit with trainers! Old ones at that. I don't think so. Why can't I just put on my suit, my shoes, that aren't even in a prison bag? Dave comes with a pair of black boots in his hand. Trainers on his feet.

"Tony put these on for now."

"Thanks Dave. I don't know why I can't wear my clothes."

"You know now for tomorrow Tony. We've never had this before."

"Just for me this shit. I piss them off so they do all they can to get me a guilty verdict."

"You're not going to get a guilty Tony. I sat in on the last trial. It's all lies. You proved them liars last time you can do it again this time. Good luck Tony."

"It's not about truth Dave it's about evidence. The last jury didn't give me a not guilty."

Round two and we have lost the element of surprise. They now know my evidence and I can't change it. Kevin says neither can the police. I don't agree.

I walk into the court, not even a jury in place, with a deep feeling of loss. The Judge is high up in the chair of power right in front of me. The bright red leather jury seats are all empty. The press seats are all full. In the well of the court there sits two lawyers in front of them sits two Barristers at the front standing, are two Queens Counsel, Tim Haywood my Counsel; Mr Thwaits for the crown. Four times now I have been asked.

"How do you plead? Guilty or not-guilty?"

"Not guilty." I resound from behind the glass wall between me and the court.

"You may sit down Mr Crowe." The judge instructs me.

The court officer leads in the potential jurors, sitting them in the empty seats one by one. When they are all seated the court officer stands in front of the first one.

The one farthest away from me. After giving his name the officer asks if any one has any objection to this juror. Kevin looks at me, Tim looks at Kevin. I nod an approval. Kevin nods the approval onto Tim. Tim says nothing giving a silent agreeable nod to this juror. Two men disqualify themselves with admissions of personal knowledge of me. I think they just want out of jury service. I turn down one guy who I think has got to be a police officer. I now have twelve good and true.

Five women, seven men, all the women on the front row, first and last being a man. I try to pick out the foreman who hasn't even been thought about by the twelve yet. The one who will say the words that will free me from all this, or condemn me to years of prison. The Judge tells the jury that this is a retrial but not to speculate as to why it is a retrial. Why not just tell them I was found neither guilty nor innocent?

Tim told me why. The jury may think I have been found guilty but there was a technicality whereby they have to find me guilty again. Already I'm fighting from a position of guilt. The two adversaries give their opening speech Tim speaking of what the defence will be and how the baseball bat found at the scene of the crime cannot be said to belong to me. The blood on the door of Dawn's house was not put there by me. How the police cannot even say who of their number opened that door. He will ask why the blood on the door lock was not found by the scene of crime officer at 8 O'clock when the door was first opened. Was the blood there then? Or was it put there later by someone who went to that house from Swindles' house? What about the garden shed? The one that Hatwood said was searched? The one that only exists inside his head.

Mr Thwaits tells the jury how my car was seen fleeing the scene. How a baseball bat found inside the house of Garry Swindles belonged to the defendant. He

131

tells them that Swindles and I had a falling out two weeks before this vicious attack on a defenceless man in his own home, in the early hours of that Tuesday morning. The blood DNA found at the house of the defendant. Blood DNA he tells them again. The same DNA that did not convict me at the first trial. He tells them how I was brought back from Malta, where I was hiding from justice.

"We will break for lunch at this point. Reconvene at one O'clock," says the Judge. I know the protocol and stand without any prompt. The door behind me opens and I leave the court. I have to leave before the Judge so he doesn't have to bow to me; it's the same when I enter the dock. The Judge is there in his seat having bowed in my absence. Kevin comes down after ten minutes, gives me fish and chips from the chippy over the road. For two years I've been eating prison food and with the year I spent in Malta on the run this meal is pure nectar. I have to eat it in the small room where we meet for our conference, out of sight of the others.

There's not much to say about the trial. Kevin is a lawyer not a comforter. The two hour interval passes quickly. Time to start the case for real. First in the witness box is Swindles. I know he is well enough to play rugby. He was named in the local news paper as a team member. But now he can't walk without his crutches. He takes every step with a grimace. At the witness box he asks for a chair. This is the same Swindles who one year ago visited Porter in HMP Durham fully able to walk albeit with a limp.

Sitting in the box his head just higher than the stainless steel rail adorning the top edge he looks like a small boy who has been wronged on the school playground. Tim stands up out of turn. It's the turn of the prosecutor first.

"Point of Law Me Lud." He says.

The Judge then asks the jury to leave the court for the point of law. The jury must not act on information not entered into evidence. So they can't hear Tim's point of law.

"My Lud in the statement of Mr Swindles he says." 'I was told Crowe had a meat cleaver to cut off the fingers of the one who had robbed his garage.' I would put it to the court that this is hear say and cannot be entered into evidence. We don't know when this was or if it ever was the case."

"Quite Mr Haywood. Mr Thwaits?"

"No objection Me Lud."

"I will instruct the witness not to mention this. Mr Swindles you must not make any mention of the comment made in your statement relating to this cutting off of fingers. You will not be asked about it and you must not say anything in your evidence about this. If you were to it could mean the dismissing of this jury and the swearing in of a new one. In short we will have to start all over again. Do you understand Mr Swindles?"

"I, a do."

"OK you can bring in the Jury."

The jury shuffle in, taking up the same seating order as they were in before they left. All wondering what they missed.

After giving his name and swearing the oath of truth. The same truth that has no place in a court of law.

He gives his evidence. The first answer he gives is nothing to do with the question asked. Out comes the very thing he was told not to say. Tim jumps to his feet. The jury are sent out. Tim asks the judge for a time out to ask me what I want to do. Out of the door at the rear of the court I go. Tim comes through the dock and the same door.

"Well, what do you want to do Tony?"

"What do you think? Is it really that bad?"

"Yes. I think it is very prejudicial to you."

"Well then we'll have to ask for a new jury. What if we don't get one? Will this be a good reason for an appeal later?"

"Yes but we need to deal with this first; we don't want to have to appeal."

"OK let's go and see if we can get a new jury."

Back in court the motion is put to the Judge, his response is beyond my understanding.

"I have given this matter some thought and I have decided the jury did not hear the comments made by Mr Swindles. Therefore I see no need to dismiss this jury for a new one. You may bring in the jury please. Mr Swindles please do not mention this again."

Just in case the jury didn't hear the comment of cutting off fingers Mr Thwaits asks

"Did you receive any injures to your hands?"

"I, me fingers were cut off." Says Swindles just as he has been coached to.

Twenty four statements he has made to the police. Every one different to the last. The last one was written last week. Over Two years after his attack.

The only thing of importance is his first one. He had no idea who it was. They had masks on their faces. There were two men. Who he did not know.

Now he knows there were three men. One of them was me. He says he recognised my eyes. He couldn't even find the light switch on his own bedroom wall. It was that dark. The emergency operator asked him "Who cut you up"? He said "I don't know" I know all calls to the emergency services are recorded on an audio device. When I told Kevin to get the tape, knowing they must have asked him who did it, Kevin asked me what if he says it was you. Why would he? I wasn't there and he knew it then and he knows it now.

The tape is played by the prosecutor to the jury at full volume, starting with the blood curdling scream of a man bleeding to death. After an apologetic address to the court he plays it again with the volume a little lower. A trick, giving the jury two chances to be horrified. Swindles is trying to plug the holes in his story but he hasn't got the intellect. After an onslaught of cross-examination from Tim he is a gibbering wreck. True to his medical records of, Years of drug abuse, mental illness, violent behaviour. The day over we call it our day even with the suit fiasco. Even with the photos being allowed into evidence. We win more points than the prosecuting counsel, Tim tells me.

On the half-hour every point is reported. Through the radio news in the van.

The next day starts in court with witness number two an old man who lives over the road from Swindles. He tells of two people walking a dog. A white dog past his house at about ten O'clock on the night in question. Nothing that puts me in any danger of prosecution. He does, however, tell the jury, under cross-examination from Tim. How the policeman given the job of guarding the front door of Swindles' house came into his house for a cup of tea. "I never left my post" was his evidence in the last trial.

Garry Porter is next up. Lead into the box by two security officers. Handcuffed to one of them. Porter's evidence is, the bat belongs to me. He knows this because he had seen me walking round the village with the bat on many occasions. This is the Porter who didn't know me when he saw me in prison. Tim asks him if Swindles is a good friend.

"Not really a good friend." He says.

"Well Mr Swindles is a good friend. Good enough to come and see you in prison on five occasions in the last six months. Is that not so?"

135

"Yeah he visits me."

"As your friend would you do anything for him?"

"Yeah is a mate of mine."

"Would you lie for Mr Swindles?"

"No. I don't tell lies. Just because I'm in jail doesn't mean I'm a liar mate."

"You are serving a prison sentence now, are you not Mr Porter?"

"Yeah."

"For lying?"

"No. I'm in for cheque books mate."

"Yes! Is it right you are in prison for fraud and deception?"

"What? I'm in for cheque books."

"Thank you Mr Porter. No further questions."

Mr Porter has not the brains to know what crime he has committed. The prosecuting counsel never even showed Porter the bat. He was never shown the bat from Swindles' house because no one thought to ask him. "Is this the bat you have seen Crowe with?"

His evidence is. The bat from Swindles' house, which I have never been shown. Is the same bat I have seen Crowe, who I had never met till Durham prison, walking around the village with. Is that not a joke if it were another occasion? Next up is Tanner. Just Tanner will do for this witness. He was shown the bat. At 9 O'clock on the morning of the attack Tanner went to the police officer on the door of Swindles' house. He then said.

"The baseball bat you found in there is Tony Crowe's."

How he even knew there was a bat found is a mystery. Unless he knew it was there to be found, It came out in Swindles' evidence the hole in his front door was the result of an incident with Tanner two weeks before the attack. Tanner said to Swindles I'll be back, I'll kill you. Swindles told the jury. But he didn't mean it. He added.

The bat was brought to the front door and Tanner identified it as mine. It was in a clear plastic bag with a tag on it. The one who brought it out was a scene-of-crime officer. Mr Stag. The problem with this is the officer on the door says that no one went in or came out of the house. That is why Mr Stag had to stand at the door while the other, Tanner, stood at the gate. Then there's the 'I never left my post' officer, who went in for a cup of tea. Mr Stag says in response to the showing of the bat at the door to Tanner.

"No that never happened."

"Do you mean you don't remember this happening?" asks Tim.

"No I mean that did not happen, I did not show anything to anyone at the door."

Tanner finishes off by referring to me as that slag in the dock. I don't think he likes me. Could be he is still holding a grudge about the time I had to have one of my meat head associates talk to him about his antisocial behaviour. Police are the only witnesses left to come.

Day by day they stand up one by one; lie by lie they weave their web. All do not lie the same lie. The new police officers called in as replacements for those who messed up on the first trial don't know the story outside their scripted evidence. Our transcripts are no good when the witnesses are new to the case. New witness means new evidence. New lies. One officer, a dog handler made a statement one week ago. I have the log of the police radio traffic on that night. There was no dog man called to attend. He wasn't at the first trial. They must have forgotten about him back then. So must the officer in charge on the night. His evidence is there was no dog man called while he was there. The only thing with any credence is the blood DNA.

The blood sample amounts to twenty percent of the tip of a swab. Too small for a conventional DNA test. The Blood was sent to a London lab to be grown into an amount large enough for the test. We are talking about a small blood spot lifted from the lock-keep of the front door of Dawn's house. They say it got there by me carrying it on my clothing from Swindles' house to ours. We say it did not get there from anyone who was involved in the attack. Was it there at eight O'clock? Why was it not found till eleven forty? Did anyone who went into Swindles house then go into our house? The big question is who opened the door, which had the blood on it? Then there is the age of the blood that could only be seen with lights used to find organic matter. The forensic expert for the prosecuting counsel said. Swindles could have put it there months or even years ago from an old cut. While visiting our house.

Of all the officers who were at our house, none of them would say they were the one who opened the door. Why? The one who obtained the search warrant had been the second person to go into Swindles' house. This officer then picked up Dawn, put her in his car then drove to our house to give the warrant to his brother officers. Dawn's car was taken for examination. This was said to be the get-away-car. Nothing was found in it. But there again no police from Swindles' house had been in the car.

The warrant and the keys from the car, along with the house keys, were in the possession of the officer who had been in Swindles'. At some point the warrant with the keys found their way into the hands of D.S. Hatwood. No one knows how, when, or by what means this took place. The defence of the police is this. 'No one from the crime scene would go anywhere near Dawn's house for fear of contamination. The officer who picked up Dawn. Who had been in the house of

138

Swindles, was named on a warrant to search my garage. The answer from the police is "There was nothing found in the garage" So he could be there with no problem? No. He still is not clean enough to go near a search scene. Dawn sat in the same car as police who had been in the house of blood.

Blood DNA is used to prove the person whose blood it is was where the blood was found. That is not the case here. They now want to say the blood was taken there by the attackers. Not left there by the owner. All the waste-water pipes from Dawn's house, the wash hand basins, the washing machine and the sink traps were taken, all to look for signs of blood from washing hands or clothing. Nothing was found.

No blood anywhere but for a dot smaller than the spot on the wing of a ladybird. Can this be all that is needed to send me to prison for years? They don't know how it got on the door no more than I do. The time has come to stop all the evidence giving. It's my turn to speak. In my first trial I was standing in the box for four hours. Giving an answer to all the questions put to me. Only to be attacked by the prosecutor for having all the answers. I am ready to do it all over again. The walk from my seat in the dock to the small box at the right of the Judge is long. I go over in my mind every question asked in the first trial. Tim asks me to tell the court my story. I keep to the facts. I know I will tell more when my cross examination comes.

After the photos being let into evidence, then the blood DNA with no one opening the front door. The new dog man with Saxon his German Shepherd giving a story equal to a Stephen King best seller I only have the truth. My story.

The prosecuting counsel, Mr Thwaits asks me questions lasting ten minutes. The four hour onslaught of the first trial is not mirrored here. I have left out the things I thought I would be asked about by Mr Thwaits. I have been robbed of my evidence. My defence. My four hour evidence only helped my case in the first trial that is not going to happen this time. Ten minutes is a damage limitation exercise by a counsel well informed. He knows the danger in letting me speak. I have no other witnesses. Dawn did not come. The police tell the court; she was served a summons. She is now in contempt of court.

The two Queen's Counsel give their closing arguments to the jury. This is the last of ten days. I've sat listening to lie after lie. I'm finished. Worn out in body, mind and soul. My spirit is broken whatever the outcome. The only thing left before the Jury decides my fate is the Judge's summing up, New Judge with new insight into the evidence. The first comments from him are about the police's inability, after two and a half years, to tell the story in a unified clear way. My Q.C. Told the Jury.

"You often hear that the evidence is like pieces of a jigsaw, each piece fitting together to reveal the full picture. In this case it is more like a dot-to-dot and a lot of the dots are missing. The prosecuting counsel has filled in the missing dots to make the picture they want you to see."

That just be the bit I was told would be the same from the first trial. The Judge tells the Jury.

"You must understand that this was a long time ago and some of the police were inconsistent in what they remembered. It is your job to determine what is relevant and what is not. You may think who opened the front door where the blood of Mr Swindles was found is not important. You may think the identified baseball bat was not shown to the witness, Tanner, at the front door of Mr Swindles' home. Or that the police officer who showed it forgot about the showing of it that morning. You, and only you, ladies and Gentlemen have to decide whether Mr Crowe went to Malta to work as he says, or he was fleeing justice after committing this heinous crime. It is your job to look at all the evidence and decide what is important and what is not"

The Judge goes on telling the Jury what the law says and what it demands of them. No mention of the first trial. No mention of how the blood may have gotten on the door. No mention of the lack of evidence. I know my prospects are dire. Waiting. Waiting. Waiting for the Jury to come out from their deliberation.

Sitting in the court cells hour-by-hour hoping for the verdict to be against what I know will end in years of prison. Tim comes in with Kevin.

"If this goes wrong I'm looking at fifteen years." I tell him. Then Tim looks at Kevin as if to say "have you not told him?"

"It may not get to that Tony. The Judge was fair in his summing up."

"I don't think so Tim, I think it went bad, the Judge did me no favours in his summing up. So if it goes against me?"

"Well. Maybe twenty years," I can't speak.

Kevin breaks the awkward silence as he clears his throat. His hand smoothes out his moustache while he thinks of some encouraging words to offer me.

"Twenty Years? For what? How can I get twenty years in prison for something I never done? Do I have any grounds for an appeal?"

"I don't think so, don't think of that now."

"What about the Judge not dismissing the jury after the Swindles thing?"

"Let us see what the Jury say first," Kevin says.

The first Jury were out for three days without being able to reach at least a ten two verdict. This Jury is still

141

trying for all twelve to agree. I am resigned to a long wait. Days of going over the evidence piece by piece. Dot by dot in my case. Filling in the dots as they go just like the prosecuting counsel did.

Three and a half hours, Dave's key-clanking din heads toward my cell. Lunch time? No I've had my lunch. I don't want the door to open. I don't want it to be time for the verdict. Not yet, I'm not ready for a twenty year sentence. Time and tide wait for no man. The tides of time are flowing over my life with the force of a tsunami. This is the time, after two-and-a-half-years, to find out if I will spend, what could be the rest of my life in prison.

"The judge wants you up stairs Tony."

"Do you know if it's the verdict?"

"I don't know Tony."

Walking through the lower annals of the court is longer, the stairs are gone before I realise it. In front of me is the court room door. I have to wait for the Judge to take up his lofty position before I can enter. As the door opens my view is filled with faces. All looking my way. As if they know the verdict already. On my left are the twelve empty seats of the Jury box. To my right the press box, full. In front and to the right, Kevin. Beyond him Mr Cunningham, Brief. At the front standing sideways, looking back at me is Tim. To the right the prosecution team. Centre front facing me, the Judge. One by one the Jury take up their seats. The same order as they occupied them on that first day so long ago. For the last time they sit. Not one of them will meet my gaze. Not a good sign for a not guilty verdict. I knew that first day who would be the foreman. Sixty odd year old man, grey hair, glasses with an air of military discipline in his manner. Sitting closest to the Judge's position.

"Would the foreman please stand?" The Judge asks.

"Have you reached a verdict of which you are all agreed?" The foreman turns to face the Judge, stands to attention, hands down his sides. He's back on the square, standing in front of his drill Sergeant, obedient to the authority figure whoever it may be.

"Yes we have Me Lud." He says clear and loud.

I know it's not good. Too soon. They've come back too soon for a not guilty. None of them looked at me.

"Would the defendant please rise?"

An order, not a request. Standing between two court officers I face the court. Like a cuttlefish in a panic, flashing with bands of colour the waves rise up from my feet. On and off my nervous system switches like a lighthouse in the dark.

"Mr Foreman. On the charge of attempted murder what is your verdict? Guilty or not guilty?"

"We find the defendant guilty."

"Tony Crowe you have been found guilty of attempted murder by this court; is there anything you want to say before sentence is passed on you?"

"No. Nothing."

"Mr Haywood?" The Judge addresses Tim.

"Yes Me Lud..." I stop his address.

"No sit down Tim I don't want to say anything."

Tim goes on with his last speech. The one where he tells the Judge how sorry I am, how I have had a bad life. Mitigation. I want no excuses given. No mitigation for a crime I did not commit. Just give me the number of years.

"That man is not speaking for me. Tim you are finished, you don't work for me anymore. Sit down." Fact is he never worked for me. He works for Kevin so I can't sue him for cocking up.

"There is no history of violence Me Lud." Tim ends with. I still hold out some hope for fifteen years.

143

"I have never in all my twenty five years as a high court Judge had the misfortune of sitting on a case where the injuries inflicted on a living human being are such. This is the worst case of attempted murder I have ever seen. If you had killed him, and you very nearly did, I would have no option but to sentence you to life in prison. However, you have no convictions for any violence in the past."

Now I'm thinking my fifteen years has gone up to twenty. Just give it to me so I can get out of here. "This was a very well planned and executed crime that but for one small mistake you would have gotten away with. However, the best laid plans of mice and men often go awry.

Your sentence must be one of many years. Tony Crowe I sentence you to twelve years imprisonment."

Did he say twenty years? Or was it twelve?

"After six years you can ask the parole board to release you. That will be up to them. After eight years you may be released back into the community to serve out the rest of your sentence. You may go. Take him down. Members of the Jury thank you, you are dismissed."

The press box empties before I reach the door. Strange, I now have a peace inside. As Jesus said on the cross 'It is finished.' My mother is in court but the press don't know her. Kevin takes her out the back door to his car. The police haven't got any photos of me so the press at my first trial phoned my sister to ask if she would give them one. She said no.

Six years for parole. Two years done. In four years I can ask for parole. Twice what I've done to-date. Two years waiting for this moment. Two hunger strikes. Four different prisons. Hundreds of miles in the prison van. Two trials with two Judges. Two juries. The fight for the right to marry Dawn. Who now has been given

144

an eight month prison sentence for contempt of court for not answering her summons; Hatwood says he gave her. He lied once more. The fight to keep my mind intact. More stabbings than I could keep count. Pad mates came and went, some dead of drugs some dead inside. Eyes of cold grey. I enter the gates of hell as a convicted man. It looks bigger this time. Darker. Colder, windows look down at me as the moon casts a yellow light over the high prison walls. Quiet greats me stepping from the van. Standing in the prison yard looking up to the night sky I wonder what will become of me.

The prison knows my verdict. Not just the officers on the desk. All the jail knows I'm coming back.

"What happened today Crowe?"

"Convicted. Twelve years." I just want to get to my cell and rest.

"You are the biggest today." The screw says.

"Do I win a prize?"

"No you win a night in the hospital wing son."

"Oh no I don't just put me back in me cell."

"It's prison..."

"Don't be giving me any prison rule shit. Just take me to me pad."

"How do you feel?"

"Ask me in the morning. I'll still be here."

"Is he all right Warren?"

"He'll be fine. Won't you Crowe?"

"I'll do it standing on me head. Just get me to me pad."

Walking through the prison to B wing there isn't one cell that doesn't voice disdain at the lack of justice. They forget about the crimes I'm not going to trial for. All other charges have been put on file. Never to see the light of day. Lies put me in here for a crime I have not committed. What is the point of saying anything if it may or may not be a lie?

From this point on I will never tell a lie. A promise made to myself. I will put on the belt of truth.

Convicted

The morning brings with it a new life for me. The life of a convicted prisoner. I can no longer live with those men waiting to be tried by their peers. Prison uniform is all I can wear. Gone are my own clothes. The work I have to do is paid fifty pence per thousand. Plastic sacks for charity drops. Fold one bag; put it into another bag with a sticker stuck to it. Life just got worse. New life, new wing, new cell complete with pad-mate. The screws on D wing, my new home, don't know me. My knowledge of who to ask for what I want is gone. My pad is to be number fifteen on the three's, my pad-mate greets me at the door. The first question I ask is out of fear not interest in this guy's life.

"How long are you doing?"

"Six month I got mate. I know you're doing a big'en."

"How long have you done lad?" I ask him.

"I'm out next week mate. I've done it. I'm going home mate." He's all ready gate-happy and I don't want an hour of this never mind a full week. Time to meet the wing S.O. I head on back down to the one's and straight for the office with my twelve year attitude.

"Fifteen on the three's is not for me. What else have you got?"

"You're in three fifteen son. Do you have a problem with that?"

"Yes I have. I've just come from B wing and a single cell. I'll go in a double cell but not with, a-week-left-to-go-gate-happy-shoplifter."

"I've nothing else son."

"What about three twenty five? There's only one card on that door. Is that a double?"

"Dummer Dale's in there son. I wouldn't wish him on you."

147

"How long's he doing? Seven or something?"

"Seven years I think but you don't want padded up with Dale."

"He'll do for me. Is he still an E man?"

"No he's out of stripes now and off basics, but you..."

"I'll have that one."

"I wouldn't put me dog in there with him, but if that's what you want son..." he nods with a grin on his face to the landing officer. "Put him in with Dale."

"It'll do for me." How can I miss. I'll be like a bright light in the darkness shining for all to see. Dummer is the only one in the jail who like me has a CP number, he came in forty numbers after me. CP3743 is his number.

"I'm in here mate." He's sitting on the chair wearing only shorts. His drug abused body on show.

"No problem, take that bed mate." The one to the right of the door is empty. This is my new bed. Nothing is new about it. Same old worn out mattress melting through the iron framed bed. No pillow. That can be my first job. It's good to set goals in prison. When I left B wing I left the pillow I had. Not because I felt sorry for the next unfortunate soul to take up residents in my old home. The screws search every one when they move. They don't look for Drugs. They don't look for weapons. There's a weapon in every cell. For toilet cleaning there is a long plastic nylon-bristle brush, it makes a tool that when sharpened will go through a man's body and out the other side. The only thing they are looking for is pillows. I don't have time to waste on such petty games. My first night with Dummer is no different from the five hundred and eighty two nights I have done as an innocent man.

On the morning of the 18th June 1999, two days after my sentencing, a document called. (Release Dates

148

Notification Slip) is slipped under my door. It says Number of DAYS in sentence 4,383. Sentence expiry date 15/11/2011. Even the extra days for leap years are added to the tally. Twelve years isn't enough, they have to tell me how-many days I have to spend in this hell-hole. For something I did not do. I have one day in Malta that is not credited to me on the slip, who would not fight for even one day less to serve? They can have their four and a half thousand days but I want my one day back. Dummer knows all about sentencing from his long time spent in prison over many years. He was out for two weeks from a twelve year sentence before getting locked up for this case. He is doing four different sentences some running together, some running back-to-back. All of them are under four years so none are parole sentences. He only has to do half. The prison service, who hate him with a passion. Say he is doing seven years so, as it is more than four years, it is a parole sentence. I will try to explain. The total years added together come to seven. Dummer says the Judge gave him the years in this order. First for escaping eighteen months. Then for count one he got eighteen months. Then six months. Lastly the Judge gave him three years and six months. Are you with me? The first sentence was done before it was given. On remand. Nine month after Dummer was jailed he had done an eighteen month sentence. After being in prison one year and six month he had done the next sentence. He only needed three months to clear the one of six months. He has done that one too. He is left with the three years and six months to do. That's not a parole sentence; it's less than four years. My day is one thing. Dummer is fighting for four years. He gets out the law book and goes to work. A newspaper comes under my door opened at a story about my attempt to marry Dawn. A prison spokesman is quoted in the story. The

149

spokesman tells the paper private details relating to my application to marry. I can't believe the prison has talked to the press about me. Remember my letter to the press? Not permitted. Time to call the screw. I press the bell button and wait. It's nearly time for food unlock; four o'clock on Friday evening. This won't wait till Monday. Pacing up and down with my rage building, blood rising, knowing they don't want to come all the way up here when they are coming in five minutes to unlock the whole landing, I start to kick the door. A sure way of getting their attention. The flap opens. A fat face fills the glass opening.

"What do ya want son?"

"I'm not your son, your mate, or your any other term of endearment buddy. OK?"

"Why are ya booting the door?"

"Because my light doesn't work."

"Yes it does. I've just turned it off."

"Well why did you not come when I pressed it five minutes ago?"

"We are unlocking soon for meal time. What do you want?"

"A Governor." I demand.

"There is no Governor on. It's Friday night."

"Don't give me that bull. There is a Governor in the jail twenty four hours a day every day. Get me the duty Governor and open this door."

"Can't open the door till meal time. I'll see what I can do about a Governor. What's it all about?"

"'I want to know who has been telling the press my business." The flap closes with a bang. Off he goes to the wing office with my request.

"Don't put up with that Tony. Get the door open and refuse to bang-up. They'll take you down the block and everyone has to be seen by a Governor."

"I will if I have to. This is not on."

"They can't treat you like a dick-head you're doing twelve years. If you lose days now you have years to get them back."

"I don't want to start that way Dummer."

"You have to start off bad so you can get better half way through your sentence. It's all about improvement Tony. You have to get better over time so you have to start as bad as you can."

"You can't be serious! They must know that's not true improvement."

"No they don't. Anyhow what do they care? It's all about ticks in boxes for them. If you do this they tick that."

"That's not me."

"You won't find any one in here who is who they really are. Shit protest."

"What?"

"Shit up, it never fails. It's the only thing in here that works, Shit up and I bet you get whatever you want. But you need to get to the block first. No one shits up on the wing."

"Are you having me on? I can't rub shit over my cell."

"And over yourself. Put it under your pillow first to get use to it then you're off."

"You're off Dummer, off your head."

"I was discharged from Frankland from me twelve off a shit protest. I had one week left to do of the full twelve when the number one Governor came and said 'get out of my fucking jail, Dale' Never even got a shower, the bastards."

"You done every day of a twelve year sentence, bar one week? Then you were back in within two weeks? Now you are doing seven years..."

"Three and a half."

"And I'm listening to your advice? I must be madder than a March hair Dummer."

"It's June"

"What is?"

"It's not March Tony it's June."

"When did you go mad Dummer?"

"After about six years you go a bit funny. If you don't play their games you'll be all right. But you are, aren't you?"

"No I just want to know who the slag is that told the papers about my business."

"Why? What does it matter? You're doing a long time for a bad crime; no one will fuck with you Tony. Let them play their games, you keep your mind. Who is better off? Me on double basics, or the guy with the good job and all the extras prison can give you?"

"Are you asking who is better, the man with everything or the one with nothing?"

"That depends on what everything is."

"More is better that less."

"Not in here it's not, I had nothing for them to take away from me so no head games here."

"You had drugs, still have them."

"So will you given time. You have to get out now and again. Don't condemn those who need to get out of their head to stay in jail."

"Can I say never?"

"No. Don't play their game. You can't win."

"What about the twelve you just done?"

"Was playing their game, just like you're doing now."

After the S.O. telling me I would have to wait till Monday for a Governor. Or I could make a complaint through the Request/Complaint form system on Monday. I found myself saying to him.

"If I don't see a Governor now, before bang-up, I will shit-up my cell. This cell; on your clean wing." I couldn't get out of the cell to refuse to bang-up. I was going to barricade the door so they couldn't open it like my old friend did in Preston but in a double cell you get charged with kidnapping your pad-mate. Fifteen years for kidnapping on top? I don't think so. Within half an hour a Governor is waiting for me in the wing office. Dummer is right all my rage and anger leads to nothing. I'm told it was head office who told the press.

"Who in head office?"

"It will be looked into." Nothing, Nothing, Nothing. That's what I get for all my work. Twice a week we are turned over by the DST. The down side of living with Dummer. Piss tests for drugs fortnightly. He will take any drug any time anywhere. Day and night he has a syringe in the side of his mouth. He can talk, eat, and even open his mouth for the screws to look into it and not give it away.

Once a week he gets a new pin from a diabetic on the wing. By the weekend the old pin wouldn't break through the skin without bending. Whatever the drug it goes in the pin.

He is a bit low on good veins. His favoured one of the moment is in his upper thigh. Each to their own, it's not for me. I tell him. He assures me I will change my mind when it's the only way to have a day out of prison yet still be in. I didn't take them outside, and I hope I don't give in to them inside. Who knows what the years will bring. Where will I go from here? Ricky Daniels has gone to Garth at Leyland with his sixteen years. Maybe I will go there. When he came back with his sixteen years, for cocaine importing from Ecuador, although he tells people it was from Colombia, he was wiped out. On that night; I used my pull on the wing to get something to make him sleep. Funny, Porter was to

153

be the mule but pulled out at the last minute, I told Ricky his friend, Swindles, had informed on him to the police but he wouldn't have it. I have police on my payroll so I know it was so. Dummer knows where is good and where is not. When I say good I don't mean good I mean better than some. Over the landing on the twos is a famous prisoner from years ago, a name that means nothing to me. He was the one who started the Manchester prison riot. He was last off the roof when they gave in. His name is not worth a place in my story so I won't put it in. On the day before his release he starts a fight with a friend of mine on the way to the gym. He doesn't want out. He was in jail for ten years after the riot and that was on top of his four years for a crime not fitting any decent criminal. A big man on the roof of Strangways prison, now a scared nobody who was trying to get a nicking to stave off his release. I can't help thinking what I will be like when my time comes to go home. Will I have a home? I've told Dawn not to wait but she says she will. We will see, three years seems to be the limit to a woman waiting for her man to come back home to her. It's already been two and a half. After that it's one day at a time. No Dear John letters for me just stop coming and I will know I tell her. How can I ask her to wait so long? She has her life to live and twelve years is a long time, even with parole I won't be out for four more years. If I don't admit to the crime I won't get any parole so it looks like I'm here for another six years. Or some other prison just the same as this one. Big crimes carry big sentences, in big jails. No one in Garth is serving less than four years. Life sentence prisoners go there for the second stage of their sentences. Dummer wants to go to Frankland it's just round the corner from Durham but they don't want him. Not after his last stay there. Old friends are on this wing. Some do their entire sentence here if it's not a long one. Remember Dave who was going to get life for the guy he hit and killed? He's here doing the last month of his three years. He nearly killed himself just over a year ago when his woman wasn't in to answer the phone. Now he's smiling and laughing, life couldn't be better for him. All the witnesses in my case have moved on to other jails. Some of the old lags from B wing are dead from drugs. Flapper is on one of his out times. Darrel is out I think but I'm not sure. My visits now need a visiting order, (VO) given to me twice monthly on request. I can only spend ten pounds in the prison shop. No more court trips or days out. There is no reason for me to go outside the jail now. Phone calls and visits are my only contact to the outside world. The real world. Some don't have a visit or any phone calls, they say you can't do your jail on the outside, you have to get your head inside. Cut off all outside things. I don't know if I can do that. My new job as a convict is in the charity bag shop. I fold a plastic bag, put it into a paper sleeve and stick a small label on it. For one thousand I get fifty pence credit for the prison shop. This is not for me. I am a twelve year prisoner. I don't do bags. After the first day I'm given the job as boss of the workshop. No folding bags. No stickers. No fifty pence. I get ten pounds a week. Making my total spends twenty pounds. I have to buy everything I need out of this twenty pounds. I bought a radio with a tape player back in the days I had money from outside. Durham jail cells have no electric. My radio is run by battery. Four C cells. Every four weeks I need four new ones, working helps prolong their life. Phone cards are two pounds each. Tobacco is sold by the half oz. You can buy cigarettes. But no one does. Roll your own is the way in prison. The first time I went to the shop I was told HMP stood for. Half oz, Matches, and Papers. That's what I got. A friend of mine asked for HMP and got H.M. but no P. Not enough money for papers the screw said. At times like that you need a bible. I know a guy who smoked all the way through Revelation in a week and done Jude in on the Sunday. It does say in the Bible; 'fill yourself up with the word.' When Dummer was in Frankland doing his twelve he got into devil worship. He told me how he had killed his budgie, painted a pentagram on the wall of his cell with its blood and set up a satanic alter with black candles and soil smuggled in to the prison from his dead father's grave.

"I've asked God to do things and nothing," he said, "so I thought I would try the other fellow." The other fellow, as he put it was only too pleased to show up. All manner of demons moved in with him. His cell was cold all day. He was set on in his bed by someone. Something. It got that bad Dummer asked the Chaplain to speak the word of God over the cell. He had to swear by pain of death not to tell a soul what Dummer had asked him to do. The cell was soon back to single occupancy. I think without the Chaplain the demons would have gotten sick of Dummer and moved out on their own. Time to meet with the allocation officer. He is the one who finds me a new home for the next six years.

"You're doing a long time so you have to go to a Cat B prison." He tells me.

"OK, Garth. I'll go to Garth prison." I say.

"No you're doing too long for Garth."

"No, me mate; Ricky has gone there and he's doing sixteen years."

"Long Lartin. They have a new wing and need prisoners for it. You're going there."

"Where's Long; whatever you said at?"

"It's in Evesham."

"Which is where exactly? I'm from Whitehaven in Cumbria."

"About forty miles south of Birmingham."

"You need drug testing mate. I am not going all the way down there." Time for my new found twelve years attitude. I want to see the wing S.O. In the wing office I tell the S.O. I will not go to a prison three hundred miles from my home town. I'm playing their game again.

"No problem," he says, "where would you like to go?" so I tell him.

"Garth prison."

"OK," he says, "I'll sort it for you." I'm over the moon. Looks like my twelve year sentence is going to serve me well. When there is room in Garth I'll be off. My time here has come to an end and I need to move on as soon as I can. In Garth I will have a TV and a single cell; heating and electric. No more money for batteries. Own clothes most of the time. Get me there now. Two weeks pass then at lock-up the wing S.O. gives me the news.

"In the morning you're going. Ship out. Pack your bags tonight ready." This is it my big move. Ricky says life in Garth is one hundred percent better than Durham. It would be hard not to be. In the morning, after a restless night, I'm ready. I clear reception before seven o'clock. Only two for the van this time. The other transportee? a Lawyer who got caught with his hand in the legal aid jar. This reminds me. Rolly; the first lawyer who told me not to worry, the duty man. Well it was said he was into the legal aid fund and more. My trial was his ticket out. He gave in; gassed himself in his garage with his car exhaust fumes. It was shortly after losing my brief. You can never tell what other people are about. Whatever he did or did not do he died an innocent man. The Mount is where the learned

157

friend is heading. Way down on the east coast. I should be first off the van at Garth. We stop at Home House prison for lunch, soup and a roll. Two hours in the van before I ask the question all children ask on a trip.

"Are we there yet? Where are we now?" I can't see out of the window. Only fields from my side-facing vista. That's when the girl officer tells me the lawyer's getting out first. I can't believe we are going past Garth on the east coast, crossing over the country and back up the west coast to Garth.

"Why are we going all the way down just to come back up again?" I ask.

"Back up to where?" the girl says.

"Well back to Garth for me?"

"You? You're not going to Garth. Evesham for you?"

"No; Garth. HMP Garth in Leyland, that's where they said I was headed for."

"They lied to you. Did you tell them you didn't want to go?"

"Yes; the S.O. told me he had sorted it. Garth he said." She's reading my file from the last year and a half.

"No you're down for Long Lartin here. Twelve years is that right?"

"Yes don't sound so hopeless will ya. I try to forget it's so long." She's standing at my door. Her slim shapely figure fills the long narrow window in the door. Twenty four years of womanly beauty. I can smell her warm sweet body. For the first time in a long time, since Malta, I feel like a man.

"How will you do in prison for so long? All the things you'll miss out on?"

"Like what?"

"I couldn't do it. What about sex? Twelve years without sex? I can't imagine that."

"There's more to life than sex but yes; it'll be the longest break I've ever had. If you like you could make it only four years of drought?" My time left if I am to get parole.

"It says here you are very dangerous."

"Don't believe all you read. What's your name?"

"Diana. And I don't."

"Don't what? Believe all you read? Or..." She cuts in.

"What about him. The Lawyer up front?"

"Unlike us Diana he isn't going all the way."

"It says here you chopped a guy up."

"It says Weetabix on buses but they don't sell them Diana. You can be my midnight express moment."

"In five minutes we'll be at The Mount. Do you want a drink of water?"

"Can I get out for a toilet break?"

"I'll ask when we get there. It's up to the prison officers Tony."

"I don't fancy the plastic bag to pee into."

"I can't let you have a plastic bag you might put it over your head."

"I don't think I would get my head in it Diana."

"I'll have to watch you use it; security." She smirks a cheeky smile.

"You don't say."

As we round the tree lined country lane leading to the drive I notice two boys cutting the grass with a ride-on mower. No fence. No wall. No way is this a jail. The van pulls up outside an old wooden building painted pale blue and cream.

Three prison officers stroll out to meet us. All grey faced, without that red, high-blood-pressure completion usually seen in any prison I've been in. Diana steps down from the van with a brown file and hands it to the first screw. He boards the van to inspect the new guy.

159

When the lawyer matches the photo on the file off he goes into the wooden building. No cuffs and no fuss. Diana asks for my toilet stop. After a long look at my file the answer is no. Too dangerous for a cat D prison to unlock me is the answer I get. With the help of Diana and a very heavy chain handcuffed to me and two screws I get to pee. The entire grass cutting has to stop for the operation and all inmates are put out of sight lest it might frighten them. Even I feel dangerous. In no time we're back on the van with an empty bladder. Robbing Diana of any show; for now that is. Somehow I think she was joking. Cross country to Evesham I work on the small hope given to me by the lovely Diana. Would it be six or eight years before by loins would move once more. She is looking sweeter by the mile. The final word from her is if we can get together without the door opening we are on.

Maximum security

It's seven in the evening as we pull up outside the prison gates. The radio from the driver crackles into life.

"Diana the prison is locked down for the night; we can't get in." The lockout means a night at the police station.

"How good is that? Good food with no rules to throw at me. Bring it on." Just as I say the words a mechanical din drowns out the radio voice of the driver. Slowly the white roller-door starts its way to the top. Revealing the dark airlock foot by foot. The same blue sign is fixed to the wall saying the same mission statement of all jails. I don't think anyone ever read it but for prisoners. Maybe it's in the wrong place. It should be hung above the key rack for the screws to read every day before they pick up their keys. It has words like humanity, respect, dignity that one's the best one. A prisoner has no dignity left after the first week in prison. Four times a day I'm searched, stripped twice daily, I use the toilet in the same cell as another person; have to sit in the cell while the other guy uses the same toilet. Even without another inmate in my cell the officers can spy on me any time. When they call me for a drug test I'm locked into a cell with no toilet until I have to go pee. I have to pee in full view of a screw. And it's not the lovely Diana. Dignity? The first thing to be taken before your name. Now I am a number in the prison system with a file of what I am. If it's not in the file it doesn't exist. The last thing to go is your mind. Sanity is a fine line that can be tipped to insanity by prison rules that make no sense.

In the floor of the airlock there are cameras to look under the van. An officer sits in a small window as if waiting for an order, in a drive-through burger bar. The intercom his only contact from behind the bullet-proof glass. Only when he's happy with the outside of the van is the door unlocked. The three aluminium steps are swung down so Diana can hand over my file. The light from a torch fills my face as the screw matches it with the image in his hand. With nothing said by him, or me the van door slams shut annunciating his exit. About ten minutes I've been in here while they make sure only one; me, enters their jail. The inner door of the airlock moves as the electric motors whine under the strain. We are in. One door closed. One door open. Twenty yards on is a large metal gate with razor-wire over the top; it stops the van once more. A screw waits to open it then close it when we drive past. A bend in the tarmac road hides the next gate until we reach it. The same procedure gets us through two more gates before a small yard with three buildings becomes our final destination. My door is unlocked by Diana. All my property is bagged and tagged waiting to be collected at the door when I leave. Only when I get to the steps do I see what's greeting me.

In an ark seven big screws stand shoulder to shoulder. I have to step down into the centre. Why so many? Why this reception? Picking up my bags, three in each hand, I take that long step down. The whole mass of screws move toward an open door in one of the buildings. I move with them. With nothing said we all enter the long thin corridor. In takes us up a slight incline to a wide blue door. All the time I'm a hub. The centre of this human ring as it moves on through the jail. I know jail. I know this is nothing I have seen before. I know the wing in front of me is not normal. Wide doors, wide wing, silence. Security above any I've seen. This is not good, why am I here? In the wing office I'm stripped off then given prison clothing that look like a star-trek uniform. My questions go unanswered. My property stays in the bags. My protests fall on deaf ears. My twelve years is a short sentence here so carries no weight. This is the lowest I can go. Why has God brought me to this when He knows I did not do what they said I did? Why am I now on a Close Secure Unit inside a maximum security prison? Living with prisoners who can't mix with each other. Let alone prisoners who are just inside for murder. The worst of the worst live on this wing of seventy six cells.

Out of eighty-five thousand prisoners in the UK these are the most secure. I am now one of them. But in the same breath, I am not. I am a lamb living among wolves. Half a pound of butter along with half a pint of milk in a cardboard carton is given to me. The cell door closes, the echo resounds, ringing in my head. My journey ends here. From way back when my world fell apart with the end of my first marriage, the loss of my children through divorce. My new life of crime, of drugs, Money, guns, women, doing it all my way. Even this, my trial I asked God to show me how to beat it. My way. I have taken God out of the box, or out of the bottle. Still I only ask for my way, my will. Now all I can hear is Jesus Christ saying. 'Your will father not mine.' The bible words fill my mind. The Lord's Prayer, 'Thy will be done.' I am the way said Jesus. Every knee will bend. Every tongue confess. All are sinners and have fallen short. The floor is hard on my knees as they hit it; but I don't feel anything. All I feel is the power of God covering me with His grace and mercy as I weep for forgiveness from His only begotten Son, Jesus Christ. Because of my sin he was nailed to the cross. Because of my way Jesus was taken in front of the law of the land and then unjustly sentenced. Now I am sentenced in place of another. Jesus gave his life, I did not. It was my will, my way that got me here.

163

"Lord Jesus Christ Forgive me, I am a sinner and I am sorry. I give my life back to you to do with it what you will. Come into my life now and show me your way Lord. Speak to my heart I am listening. Lord protect me in this place from anyone who would do me harm." I cry out.

I can feel the words in my heart saying. Where two or more are gathered there I am in the midst of you. I am alone, what does it mean? You are not alone I am with you and The Holy Spirit lives in you. This is only your darkest hour because I'm holding you tight in my closed hand. What I have given you will protect you. Don't worry for you are a child of the most high God. Peace fills my whole being. I can live here with God for as long as He wants me to. And I can live a Christian life. A shining light of hope in the darkness of prison for all to see. That's what I will be from now on. Even if I never see another prisoner I will eat, sleep and talk as a Christian.

The sound of footsteps are heading my way. The flap in my door opens and a woman's face fills the bottom half of the glass. Spectacles sit on the end of her long nose. The rest of her face I can't see. I think she must be on tip-toe.

"Are you OK?" She has a soft Birmingham accent.

"I'm just fine thanks. I could do with a cup of hot water and a tea-bag. Twelve hours on the van, I could do with a cup of tea." I ask her.

"I'm Wendy the nurse. Just seeing if you need any medication. I don't know if they'll open you for that. I can ask them, love." This must be my induction medical.

"Thank you. And I have no bedding so if they'll give me water with the bedding that would be great."

"You'll have to wait till there's six officers on the wing, love. They only open up on here when there's six

164

and an S.O." I've heard of this it's called S.O. and six unlock. I thought it was a myth. I wonder if it goes hand in hand with back wall. I've had a back wall unlock. They won't open the door till you are standing at the back of the cell and facing the wall. Who is so dangerous they will only open the door with seven big men while the prisoner is facing the wall ten foot away? Bob. Back in Durham on G wing is. I don't want to meet a person like that.

But that's me now.

The six officers come to my door bringing not water or bedding but a thought to my mind. It was six friends of Swindles' on that first day in Durham who concerned me then. Now it's another six. Without them saying I move to the back wall. Wondering if I shouldn't get under the bed. The safest place when you don't want to be tied up like an oven ready chicken.

"Your moving get your stuff together." I hear.

"Where to now? I'm OK here for now." I can't believe what I'm saying.

"Come on." He says. "Move yourself I haven't got all night." I move, trusting in my new found faith in God.

"Where we going?" Nothing is said till we get to the wing door. A tall blond female officer stands bursting out of her white blouse. My face is level with her breasts, it's hard to talk to her eyes when I'm confronted with such a beautiful sight. Her high-heels show off calf muscles fitting any ballerina turning on a music-box. She speaks to me but I don't hear one word. In the wing office, to the left, I can see my property. On top of one bag is my radio.

"I want my radio with me. I'm not going in any cell without it." I think I'm on a winner so I'm going for all I can. She's an S.O. with power over the whole wing.

"You can't have it till the morning." She says.

"Well I'm not going in there all night, on my own without it."

"Come with me." She says. "You're in fourteen on the twos." Off we go to the far end, rows of cells ring the landing. Now there's only me and the S.O. She opens the blue door, turning the white handle with one hand and the big brass key with the other. The wing is new. The cell in the cleanest I have ever seen. All the contents is new. Sitting on a small table is a TV set. On top of it is a remote control. Inside a clear plastic bag. All the furniture matches. The mattress is new with a pillow and bedding folded into a neat pile at the foot. I've paid money to stay in hotels not as good as this. A radiator gives a warm homely feel. There's two electric sockets behind the TV. No bars on the window that overlooks a large Yard. What can I say to the S.O?

"You have a colour TV in your cell. You don't need your radio tonight." I haven't seen a TV for two and a half years.

"Right." I stumble over my words. "Well I want it in the morning." Although why I would want an old radio that only works off batteries is even beyond me. If she says anything to that I don't hear it. Water, I need some water. Before I can ask for water the S.O. says.

"That jug." Pointing to the cupboard. "Is hot water. The tea pack is in the drawer. The toiletries are in that cupboard." I give in to the new life God's got for me. The S.O. must be an angel of The Lord. The TV programs are the same only older. Everyone is older but doing the same. Michael Parkinson is the first thing I see. This is the best night I've ever spent in any jail. God is good when you do His will, His way. I hope this is how it is going to be from now on. I can't wait to go to Church on my first Sunday as a new Christian. Two chapels next door to each other serve the prison. One for the Roman Catholics the other for the rest of the world. The guy at the first door asks me if I am a Roman Catholic. I don't know what I am now so I tell him.

"I'm a new Believer in Jesus Christ; he's my Lord and saviour."

"Next door," he says, "you're not a Roman Catholic." At the next door just a little way down a narrow corridor a voice makes my ears prick up, it's a voice from long ago, three hundred miles from my home town and this voice is from that area.

"Hi; Jim Lee, welcome." I can't pin-point the accent it's been so long.

"Are you new to HMP Long Lartin?"

"Where are you from? I know you're close to my home town, Whitehaven."

"Cleater Moor is my home town. What are you doing all the way down here?"

"You tell me I don't know."

"Come in and find a seat. I'll come and see you on the wing after the service, what's your name and what wing are you on?"

"Crowe CP3703, and I'm on P Wing."

"The new wing with in-cell toilets and water! Someone must like you."

He must be kidding about someone liking me. If he means God. Giving me a new cell with a toilet and running water in a maximum security prison three hundred miles from my home town is not what I call a good turn. If someone likes me, and that someone is God why am I not free? Why am I in prison for a crime I did not commit? Maybe he didn't like me then but now He does. Unlike HMP Durham where Sunday was a good time to get unlocked for an hour, here only the ones who want to be in Church fill the seats. There are no screws inside the Chapel and the peace of the place is intoxicating.

167

Jim comes in the afternoon for his induction visit. For an hour we sit in my new cell and talk, over a cup of tea. Two people chatting and drinking tea together, we could have been any two people, anywhere. The cell next door is the home of a drug dealer serving seven years, his hobby is crime; his expertise is the who's who in the criminal hall of fame. He points out the famous living all around us, some are that well known even I have heard of them. London hard men from the sixty's immortalised in films. When I don't know a bomber who the police took five years to catch he's amazed. Eddy is living in twenty four an old man with a six foot two frame and a pleasant manner. Only one man on the wing looks down on Eddy, not in a condemning way. Tiny is a huge man standing close to seven foot tall. He lives on the ones. The cell next to the snooker table. Tiny is not a well man has are a lot of others in here. Out of seventy five men only twenty are not lifers and ten are not Category A. prisoners. Out of the ten two are High Risk. That's one step up from Cat A It's like A+. Then there are the ones who are in for life. That is the never-getting-out people. We have four on here. Crusher, Mary, Streaky from the film Mac Vicar who is the holder of the title Britain's longest serving prisoner with forty five years done. He too is not a well man. The fourth member of this club is a guy who has done sixteen years and has just had his thirty-third birthday. I know about him because I was the one who he asked to explain his letter from the Home Office. One line 'Your prospects for parole are nil.' The question I ask him is what was your tariff? That's when I find out how he comes to have this letter. The time served is his tariff. That is, it's his tariff for the murder he did when he was sixteen, the problem he has is the murder he did in prison. For that he is never getting out. If you kill your cell mate you will get this letter. He did just that. I am not the right one to tell anybody of sound mind they will die in prison let alone an insane lifer. I send him to his personal officer with a pat on the shoulder. The benchmark of sanity has moved somewhat in my opinion. People who would seem mad outside don't appear to be that bad now. Categories are for the prison to hang on people not me. We are all inmates in this house of pain. No one asks what another did or how long he's in for, no "weeks-left-to-do" here.

My first job is to be in the workshops making wooden toys but before I can start work my friend Eddy, the bomber, informs me he is moving on to a new post in the education department. Eddy's work now is giving out the food on our wing. Unlocked all day and every day. With a fifteen pound a week wage. That'll do for me. A word to my all new personal officer who can't do enough for me and the deal is done, I start in one week. There are a few more on the wing who don't get locked in. Cleaning is a good job to have. Little cleaning and good money. Dave cleans the second floor; Danny is the bin man with yard cleaning duties. Rozan is a cleaner but I don t know of what. He has just started his nineteenth year in maximum security prisons so he can do just about what he wants. We have only one thing in common, both of us are in for attempted murder. Rozan is a P.L.O. hit-man who shot a Jewish diplomat in the neck. God was on the diplomat's side, he did not die. Rozan got thirty five years for his days work. Still after all this time he is a Cat A. prisoner. I asked him once how long he had been a Cat A.

"One year." He told me.

"Why after all this time did they make you a Cat A prisoner?" I asked him.

"For the last eighteen years I was on the book." He said. High risk. Some call it double cat A. There is no such thing. On the book, is a life of documentation, every minute of every day, and night, is written down in a blue book which has a photo in it of the prisoner it refers to. I seen one once in Durham when a mass murderer was brought to the dentist while I was waiting for my appointment. Did I say they have to have a dog escort when ever outside the buildings? That reminds me of Danny, the yard cleaner. My cell is on the yard side of the wing and every day I see a screw picking up rubbish from the tarmac yard. My enquiring mind leads me to ask Danny why? In his deep north London cockney he says.

"A. cat. I'm a cat A, can't go outside without a screw and a dog." I don't ask why they gave an outside job to a guy who can't go outside. A small bald headed guy empties the bins; a Turkish drug runner doing twenty five years for the pleasure 0f Her Majesty the Queen. For a reason I'm not sure of Rozan calls him Jew boy. Mr Tilly is not a Jew. The last of our cleaning gang is another Dave. Drugs are his down fall. His cell has wall charts of a nautical manner. Dave is doing eighteen for four tonne of pot, cannabis, or so they say. His boat was crossing the Bay of Biscay on its way back to the UK when it was boarded by the British navy. The S.B.S. boys landed on his deck from helicopter drop ropes in full combat gear, weapons drawn. When the boat was searched there was no drugs found. Dave was taken to the mother ship and the Special Boat Service, S.B.S, set off for the UK in Dave's boat. On the way, and some were not recorded on any chart, the boat sank!! Along with four tonne of drugs. They say. Not even enough time to take one photo of the drugs. However, on the trial day the customs wheeled in to the court a pallet. On it was four tonne of drugs. This is what it would have looked like, they told the jury. Now he is trying to find his boat and its empty hold.

Every Wednesday two men dressed in heavy cream coloured woollen jumpers hold a lifer meeting in the wing TV room. They work at HMP Wakefield full time and as a result of their success at Wakefield prison they have expanded the work to our prison. I sit in to get an insight into the mind of a lifer. First job is to introduce themselves to the sick. The word doctor is omitted from their opening gambit. First names only in an effort to win favour or may be trust. As in all walks of life no one wants to be on the bottom of the social ladder. Everyone in the room points to someone else who is a bigger offender than they are. No one, even in here, wants to be on the bottom of the heap. Personality disorders from childhood abuse is the main reason for the five minute of madness that led them to commit the life changing crime they now pay for. There are many ways to kill, some mirror the abuse of old. Some make up a whole new way when it came to taking a life. All are in a mental graveyard with these two jumper men being the way out. Sadly they don't know it. First concern is for their comfortable prison life. At the end of the meeting everyone is given a chance to have their say on how the therapy has gone. All speak out against the prison for not giving them what they want, when they want it. I raise above the good doctors expectations and speak of things in the positive. Using the philosophy of professor Dummer.

"I don t have any problems." I tell them.

"Why is that Tony." They ask pen and pad poised at the ready.

"Well," I start, "I expect nothing from the prison and I ask for nothing. I have contentment and they can't take that away unless I let them by wanting something from them. I do not behold to them. Whereas the rest of you are disappointed daily. If you expect nothing then get something, your life will be fantastic; even in here." My years of prison living has taught me to ask for nothing or spend months fighting for it against a corrupt regime. In the end you can't win. Like the comedian and the heckler in the working men's club, he has the mike. The only reason the jail gives me something is so they can take it off me if I don't play their game. Believe me it's a game played with loaded dice, whose rules are made up by the other side. Rules that are not so much chiselled in stone but written in pencil on the back of a fag packet. Rules that I am not permitted to see. The wisdom of a long term prisoner. I was asked once by some Governor or other.

"Do you know the rules son?" To which I answered. "No."

"Well when you break one we'll tell you," he said. The trouble is every time they tell you, they take seven days off your remission. A game, that's what it is. A game I can't win. So I don't play anymore. Have I won? Or lost? I know one thing; win or lose in the end it all goes back in the box. Just like life, rich or poor when this life is over like a board game it all goes back in the box. Prison is not forever. One day I'll get out. A new life in a new place. One day I'll die. A new life in a new place forever and that's a long time. I don't want that to be in another hell worse than this one. From now on I'm working toward spending eternity as a winner. Ricky use to say something what was strange back then.

"Now there was a man of the Pharisees, named Nicodemus, a ruler of the Jews; this man came to Him by night, and said to Him "Rabbi, we know that you have come from God as a teacher; for no one can do these signs that you do unless God is with him." Jesus answered and said to him, "Truly, truly, I say to you, unless one is born again, he cannot see the kingdom of

172

God. Nicodemus said to Him, "How can a man be born when he is old? He cannot enter a second time into his mother's womb and be born, can he? Jesus answered, "Truly, truly I say to you, unless one is born of water and the Spirit, he cannot enter into the kingdom of God. "That which is born of the flesh is flesh; and that which is born of Spirit is spirit.

I think I know what that means. It's from The Bible, John 3.

I am freer than any other man in this place.

Dear John

A letter from Dawn informs me she will not be visiting me or sending any more letters. This is what they call a Dear John. Did we not agree not to send this letter, just stop coming.

"Don't send cards at Christmas or birthdays I want a clean break." She wrote. What kind of break was not clean? Now I was cut off from the outside world. Just as Dummer told me to be in HMP Durham. My life is now me and my new found God. Maybe my madness is my God. I don't know how it works and nor do the Muslim inmates that surround me. We'll see. A visit out of the blue takes me by surprise. I haven't sent a visiting order out so I don't know who this is. At the gate to the visits room I glance round the low tables. No one I know is sitting at any of the three without inmates.

"What number." I ask the woman controlling the gate.

"Eight." She says, without lifting her head from the story book that is occupying more of her mind than I am. A grey haired, short woman waits on a seat in the corner. She sits on a beaded seat-cover designed to ease some lower back problem. Her bag spewing out documents in its fallen position under the table. Who is she? Not a visitor for me. There must be a mistake. I don't know her but she knows me.

"Anthony Crowe." She calls to me.

"No Tony, That's me who are you?" The seat at the corner of the table is where I sit down. The only brown one out of the four. Marking out the inmate from the visitors for the CCTV.

"I'm Mizz Hollings from Whitehaven probation office. I am your Probation officer for..." In I go.

"I don't know what they told you but I got Jail, not probation."

"You still have to have a Probation officer for when you get out."

"Get out? Are you serious? I just got in." I can't understand why she is talking about getting out. "I have a document from the jail saying my sentence expiry date is the tenth of November twenty eleven. Today is the; what?"

"That's not the point..."

"Point? What is the point?" before she can answer my rhetorical question, "fifth of December, nineteen ninety nine." I tell her. Out of a small brown handbag she produces a spectacle case containing half moon glasses. Resting them on her thin nose she opens the grey folder.

"You pleaded not guilty," Is the first comment, "do you still deny your guilt?"

"Why do you even ask that? Will you get me out if I say yes?" I have so much anger against the people who helped put me in here. In her I see them all.

"I have read the documents and it's clear you are guilty of this horrendous attack on..." I can't help it, I stop her again.

"Clear is it. To you? I didn't see you at my trial. Were you at the first one or the retrial? What have you read?"

"I've read the depositions."

"Really? Thirty odd pages of lies from police and drug addicts. Is that what you read? Did you read my police interview?" Knowing there isn't one.

"No I haven't got that."

"Have you read anything that I say about the case?"

"No but I would like to read your police interview. Where can I get it from?"

"You can't. There isn't one. I was never asked anything before I was in court and in the witness box."

"You must have been interviewed by the police."

"Yeah? Well you find it and read it."

"I'll do just that. Now, how do you plan to spend your time in prison?"

"Well first I'm going to try to stay alive. Then my aim is to not go mad. You may think I'm already mad, in that case madder. If I can get to the end alive and sane I hope not to be a drug addict."

"I meant rehabilitation courses. To address your Offending Behaviour."

"Nothing I don't have any to address."

"You are a drug dealer who rules by fear and violence."

"Who told you that? I'm in here for attempted murder not drugs."

"But you had twenty nine charges most for drugs."

"I was convicted of none of the drugs charges. What name is on that file?" I ask her.

"Anthony Crowe."

"Even that is a lie."

"I hear you ran all the drugs in the area by fear."

"Do you have statements from these fearful people in your bundle there?"

"Well no but that's what I heard."

"Well I heard about you. But I didn't believe it."

"I see you have two children. Do you have contact with them?"

"My children have nothing to do with this; or you."

"Why are you getting upset? It's been nine years since you split with your wife." I have never gotten over not having my children to hold or to love, but from afar.

"That is the last question you get. Good bye and don't come again. I'll refuse to see you if you do. When

176

I get back to my cell I'll be penning a letter of complaint to your boss." When I stand she mutters something about parole. The giving of something so they can take it from you game.

"I will do every day of this time I have been given unjustly. Then walk out of here a free man."

She asked why men do the things they do. I wrote this as a tribute to that good woman:

Poem Why do men do?

Why do men do what they do?

How is it that men do the things they do?

It's nothing unique or even new.

Men have forever done the things they do. They did it in the past and they do it still.

The words God used was man's free will.

Free to laugh, to cry, to love to sigh.

How is it that men do the things they do?

Do I know? Can I say? It happens every single day.

All do sin, all are sinners. In this life there are no winners.

With on your soul the barrier of sin there ai'nt no way God will let you in.

So why do men do the things they do? It's nothing unique or even new. Is it lust?

Envy or greed? Is it just a wanton need?

Are some men born good, others evil?

Or is that excuse just a bit feeble?

We are all cursed with mortal sin.

Since the beginning of mankind that's how it's bin.

Jesus came, died on the cross. What a man. What a loss.

On that cross he suffered; died.

At his feet his mother watched, cried.

He died for me, he died for you.

So why do men do the things they do?

Wasn't it Eve who chose with FREE WILL?

Wasn't her enticed, beguiled.

Her made Cain who was somewhat wild?

From Eve's womb came us all.

Both you and me the big and the small.

So why do men do the things they do?

If history repeats then it's because of you.

Anger

On the walk back to the gate that leads to that other world the anger is welling up. How dare she come here telling me how guilty I am. She has stolen my peace, my contentment. A fire has been lit inside me. All the people that told lie after lie to put me in here are sleeping in their own beds, eating their own food and kissing their children good night. The anger burning inside me will only be quenched by revenge. Yet my bible tells me to love my enemies and that revenge is God's alone. I have to forgive as I have been forgiven. How can I? The answer is always in the word of God so I look for it. My third Christmas in jail is my first as a Christian. So the police don't forget me I send them a greetings card. Kevin gets the only other card I send. Two cards sent with two different motives and emotions. What I don't understand is why I am in jail for a crime I didn't commit when there are more than enough that I did commit.

Nothing happens without God's say so. That's what Jim told me in the Chapel. Why would God want me in jail? Do I have a purpose here? Is there someone who I have to meet, someone who I am supposed to help? Over the last three years I have sat up through the night talking and listening to men who would kill themselves to become free of this place. I have protected people who could not protect themselves. Is it one of them? Is it the next person I will meet? What you did for the least you did for me, I read in my bible. Just keep on doing what you are doing is what I hear in my heart. The New Year is the millennium. Will the world stop? No one knows if the millennium bug will create havoc with all things electric. May be the gates of the prison will open and we'll all go free. Maybe just as the last two new years the prison will erupt into a cacophony of noise for five minutes on the stroke of midnight. Incarcerated men live to a unique calendar with New Year's coming on the anniversary of that first day. The first strip search, first bang of the door. The first time they cried in a strange bed. New Year for me brings another year of survival. On the second of January I'm a year older. This year a celebration with only two people, Danny and myself. Two of Danny's bins have been overlooked by the screws on their seasonal sweep of the jail. The hooch mooch is a game of hide and seek. Home brew is hidden in the jail and the screws try to find it. I attracted the attention of the screws when I thought I would use all the oranges left over from the kitchen to make marmalade. First job was to get sugar and lots of it. Then I cut them up and boiled them in a big pan until they gave up their pectin. Just as you would do to make hooch. Seems I still have a lot to learn. Danny's bins on the two's are this year's success. In full view of the wing office. That makes him king of the wing. For my birthday Danny cooks a curry, South American style. In our cons kitchen. With a banana and almond cake to follow that came from my own hand. The venue is Danny's pad, or peter as he calls it. It's a cockney term that comes from their word for safe. I don't get it but there you go. The most talked about thing is how you came to be in this place and we are no different. After Danny told me how he escaped from a prison van on the way to court fifteen years ago in London then went to live in Venezuela where he worked for the drug running Cali Cartel in Columbia. He told me he was kidnapped by the British customs. Brought back to the UK and given eighteen years total.

"Malta was where I was arrested, by Interpol," I tell him, "on a boat headed for Sicily."

"Did the Attorney General of Malta sign an extradition order?"

"No. There was no court case in Malta. I was put on a plane to Gatwick..."

"You was kidnapped kid."

"They had an international arrest warrant."

"You was kidnapped Tony. They have to have a court order to extradite you and did ya say you was on a ship?

"Yes, a cargo ship. The police boat came after the ship and took me back to Valletta. I skipped immigration. My mate got me on the boat without waiting for the clearances."

"You have a case for an appeal hearing. Bennett v R is the case you need. He was kidnapped from Zimbabwe by the British."

"What are you telling me Danny?"

"Get your guy on it mucker. Tell me your story."

"I'm sick of my story Danny. The police lied to their back teeth and set me up. First trial was a joke and the second was some other guy for some other crime. Sometimes I thought I was in the wrong court room."

"You've been had kid. Two trials? Was the first one hung?"

"Tell me 'bout it. Yes I got a nine three I think. One more and I'm home. Ten juries couldn't come to an agreement."

"What did you do in Malta for a year?"

"I had a great time scuba diving and living in the fast lane. The job I got was with a top diving school on Gozo. One time some mates came over from Liverpool for a holiday. It was a bit mad. You can take the man out of Liverpool but you can't take Liverpool out of the man. One week was as long as a month. Two hours after landing at Malta airport they were arrested for being drunk. They lost all their money so had to sell the drugs they had brought with them. They never lost the drugs. The first I knew of them was my boss asking me for five pounds. They hit him for the taxi fare from the ferry boat. I had to laugh. They told me how they had to sneak on the ferry without a ticket because they had no money. The ferry to Gozo is free. You only pay on the way back. They stole a free ride. When I first found, them sitting outside my local restaurant on the seafront, they were drinking jugs of the local beer. With no money."

"We've had three of these and not paid a penny." "They said. I told them You pay when you leave. That's when I found out they had lost all the money.

I had a car so when they got a bit rowdy we would go out of town. To somewhere I never normally went. Or over to Malta for the night clubs. After one week was up I took them to the airport. It was Thursday night. I parked the car and they went to find the desk number for checking in. All that greeted me was the girl on the Air Malta desk saying."

"You're too early sir."

"What's the problem."

"They are too early" She said.

"We'll wait." No way were they going into Valletta.

"No sir they are three days early." She come back with. They had a ten day return, not a week. Another three days? I was mad as a bear. I dropped them off on the way back at the night clubs. When we met up again money was no problem to them. I didn't ask."

"Sounds like you had fun to me. Once in Columbia I was taken hostage by a gang, they like taking Brits 'coz they have money to pay a ransom. The Cartel paid them three thousand dollars but told them I was one of theirs and to leave me alone. Two month later I was grabbed again on my way to the job. No money was paid that time. Two men came in the room where I was held and killed every one of them. I never had any more trouble after that."

"I sometimes wonder if I'm in the right place."

"How long have you bin an A. cat Tony?"

"I'm not. I'm only a B."

"The only Cat B. folk in here are the lifers on their first stage. You should be in a long term cat B. prison. Someone in the system doesn't like you Tony."

"Tell us about it Danny. I was told I was going to Garth in Leyland. I have mates in there."

"You've got them in here. Just keep away from the crazy and the queens of the wing."

"Mary was at me cell yesterday with a bottle of shampoo. He asked me if I had left it in the shower. He knew I had just come out."

"Don't you mean she?"

"Well even with the little red dress and the blue pool chalk eye make-up I still can't see him as a woman. Can you?"

"I think he looks OK. You haven't been in long enough."

"Don't forget his lover, Crusher. I don't think he would be too happy with Mary coming on to me."

"Do you know why they call him Crusher?"

"No but I know they are both never getting out."

"Natural lifers both of them and they are never separated. Mary was in Parkhurst on the Isle of White, working in the tailor's shop; some kid had a go and Mary put the big black shears through his neck. Already a lifer that got him his letter from the home office. No prospect of parole."

"What about Crusher? Why did he get the name?"

"When Mary got her second life sentence, and her letter; crusher put a kid's head under the steam press in the laundry, the big ones used for the bed sheets. The steam popped his head like a melon they say. Crazy folk kid."

"Sounds like true love."

"They'll do anything to stay together. They grassed some kid up for murder last year over on A. wing. Stood in court and grassed him."

"Was that the guy with the size fourteen shoes. The only one in the jail with size fourteen feet? He left his size fourteen imprinted on the guy's ribcage."

"There was that as well but you don't go pigeon on a fellow con."

"Honour among thieves? You really are from the old school Danny. How old are you?"

"Sixty; and we knew what it was to keep it in the family kid, none of this modern day first in lowest sentence."

"I was playing soft tennis with Eddy he's from your time zone. A nasty piece of work even on the court."

"Richardson? Eddy's all right. Better than them two queers from my side of the river. Why do you think they never went south kid?"

"Who you on about Dan?"

"The Twins Ron and Reggie."

"Are they still on the go?"

"Brown bread both of them, and the other brother Charley."

"Brown bread? You mean dead."

"That's what a said kid," rhyming slang unique to London, "do ya know the difference between the north and south of the river?" I shake my head and take a bite from an apple. One of the dozen or so in the dish next to the TV.

"In the north we have little blue plaques saying Charles Dickens lived here; south of the river they have yellow signs on the streets saying did you witness a murder here last week?"

"Very good but isn't my badminton partner Terry from the north? He belongs to the biggest criminal family in England."

"Europe kid; the biggest family in Europe. We was in Belmarsh together, down near the Dome."

"What's with the Canadian Dan.?"

"He's the Rolex killer kid, Killed some kid after taking his identity and moving to England from Canada. A swap if you like but the kid came back home and wanted his life back."

"Where does the watch come in?"

"He left a Rolex on the body when he dumped it in the sea. When the peeler found the body and checked the serial number it took them to the home of the Canadian, who by their reckoning should be dead. Amateur; he should 'ave wrapped the body, naked, in chicken wire to keep the arms and legs from floating off."

"Bit of a problem then?"

"And he was living with his daughter as his wife. Another crackpot kid just stay away?"

"We is the only sane ones in here and we live like kings."

"Like being in Hollywood kid. Pass me one of them apples over."

"Steak and leek pie for evening meal Dan, then a banana and custard tart topped off with fresh cream for afters. Can it be any better?"

"When I was in the joint over in the US I had lobster and wine once a week."

"You were in jail in the states? What for?"

"Gear kid same as here. It's me life kid. I was in wid some big guys; some of the family members. Me and the Teflon Don."

"To me this is Hollywood. I was in Durham for two years on remand. No heat in the cells and no electric. No cooking apart from toast made with a fire in the tin sink. No bedding from Argos and no first name terms with the screws."

"They're still screws kid don't forget it's us and them, and we are still in the us camp."

"Once I got an egg from the kitchen, a raw egg it was and that night I got me self a marvel milk powder tin, a knob of butter and a burning taper to cook it. Never have I had a better egg sandwich."

"Don't be calling the goons boss kid, guv is good enough for them, they a'nt no one's boss kid."

"Time for dinner Dan I'm off to the kitchen for the food; do you need anything from the boys in the kitchen."

"No I'm sweet kid, see you after lock-down. And remember; you a'nt seen me, right?" Dan always says that, then taps his finger on the side of his nose, whenever we finish talking.

Every meal time I go with the screw for the food trolleys. Colin comes with us, he has the job of wing laundry orderly one of the people you need on your side. At six foot and athletic build he comes in useful if things kick off. Being a Brother comes in handy as well. The first gate is opened when the small camera identifies the screw. I'm sure any white shirt would result in the gate's bolt clunking open. There are no keys in here to take from the screws. Security is of the highest order without it being in your face. On our way to the kitchen the gym class passes us headed back to the wing. One of their number is Ken; he walks with a sailor's gate, shifting his small frame from one foot to the other compensating for the motion of the sea. His silver hair perfectly groomed by the prison barber along with the jail pace removes any doubt about the length of his sentence. Behind him for the last fourteen years walks a screw holding the tell-tale little blue book of a high risk prisoner. Another from Danny's town down in the big smoke of London. We are outside the library when Ken beckons me to him with an upward nod.

"Hi Ken how's it going mate?" I ask him.

"OK kid, you going to the kitchen?"

"Yep what can I do for ya?"

"Guy on the fryer has got something for me would you pick it up for me kid and drop it off with Danny?"

"No problem Ken. Do you never get sick of him following you everywhere ya go." The screw is leaning on the window of the library and taking no notice of Ken or me.

"Who's that then kid?" he smiles.

"I guess not then, I know it won't be Ken, but I'm asking anyway; the guy in the kitchen! Nothing to do with drugs is it?"

"You know me kid, no, no drugs son."

"What was it again you got your thirty years for Ken?"

"Dealing in commodity's kid, they wanted it so I sold it. I never seen a drug-user kid till I come in here. Come to think of it, I never seen much of the cocaine neither."

"Well let's not keep our lapdogs waiting Ken; I'll see you after lock up."

"Maybe a game of tennis Wednesday morning, I'll reserve a court kid."

"Only if you go easy on me Ken. I'm only learning."

"Aren't we all kid, aren't we all." Is what he says disappearing out of sight round the bend in the narrow corridor.

At the kitchen a white coated con, dripping perspiration from his forehead, is standing next to the bay where P wing's food trolleys are parked. When Colin and the screw starts checking the content, lest the screw would have to come back for more. Or for the missing custard, a common mistake because it's always last to be put on the trolley. The con gives me a white envelope before slipping silently back into the steamy cacophony of the kitchen. Not one word is spoken and the note goes into my pocket. Being in prison for some people just means working away from home; Ken is still running the cocaine distribution for the south of England and who knows where else. An inconvenience that a man of his mature years could well do without. But he knows big crime carries big jail. One thing different from Durham is big criminals don't whinge. The people you need to have in your small group are the same whatever jail you're in. One from the kitchen, another from the stores department, Colin the wing laundry orderly is a must, and the all important fixer, this is the guy who can get things not permitted through normal channels. Someone in the gym is a good contact if the gym is your thing. But everyone works for a price and most jobs can give you a wage on the black market. My job on the food counter is no different. Meat-heads always need more food.

Rice wars

Back on the wing the shutters go up with Colin on the dessert, myself giving out the main course and the screw standing back; a silent authority. Over on the other side of the wing stands the wing S.O. Prison rules require an S.O. be in attendance at all meal times. Experience has taught them to have all hands on deck at this volatile time. All the meals have a number and the screw standing behind to my right reads them out for each con that passes. John, the longest serving prisoner in the system never brings a plate; one slice of white bread is on the palm of his big out stretched hand, waiting for the pie-of-the-day to be put on it. Never looking up he shuffles by. Forty five years done and never getting out till the day he dies. A life of jigsaw puzzles and the chapel, now that he's over the age of retirement is his life. One after another they come for their king's ration. One man one meal and seconds at the end if there's some left. Waiting until last is sometimes a good thing. No need to go back for more. But it's all about timing.

Smiler meanders his way to the hatch, dreadlocks swaying to and fro from his cat A. strut. A Yardie from south of the river doing twenty five for the assassination of a rival gang member. Knelt some kid down and shot him in the back of the head with a nine millimetre barrette for having the wrong post code. One of them yellow signs Dan was on about. He pushes the blue plastic plate under my nose nodding toward the curry. No trays in here.

"What's he on." I ask the screw who is more interested in scratching his butt than what Smiler's up to.

"Curry and rice." Without lifting his eyes from the clipboard doodling. I know the attitude of this hard man from over the river who in my opinion would do better if he got himself a belt so the jeans he wore stayed on his waist instead of round his buttocks. One spoon of rice and a ladle of chicken curry to comply with his religious doctrine is what I serve up.

"More." He says in his West Indian Patois dialect spoken extensively in the Islands of the Caribbean, where Smiler has never been. Born and bred in Brixton London. Turning to the screw I ask.

"Can he have more?" The shock on his face doesn't put me off. The decision is his and as much as he would love me to make the call I don't.

"Have we got extra?" Putting it back on me. He has the uniform on not me.

"It's up to you gov. There's more people to come yet. You have the list of who's to come." Then with total degradation of his duty he shrugs his shoulders. It's not my job to say who can't have more food. Taking hold of his plate with my left hand and the ladle with my right I put the whole of the content of the rice tray onto his plate. The plate is being pulled away from me but until all the rice is on it, or the floor, I will not relent.

"Now you have all the rice and there's none for anyone else." The wing falls silent and the S.O. rocks on his heels. You could cut the atmosphere with a knife. Smiler doesn't know what to do.

"And I'll tell them why. Next." I shout "We need more rice." I tell the screw. Now he'll have to go back to the kitchen. I'm not angry with Smiler; he only has regard for himself. The screw on the other hand has a job to do, like it or not. I can't imagine the Durham screw doing the same.

After dinner and unlock my job is cleaning the serving area for the next meal-time. My small outburst over the rice is forgotten. By me that is. The screws

190

have another view of the altercation. As I mop the floor my personal officer appears at the gate.

"All right Tony?" The Welshman asks me.

"Fine. Why wouldn't I be?"

"Well we was just thinking like, 'bout that bust up you had with Smiler like."

"No problem there. He won't bother me." I reassure him. "Thanks for your concern though."

"We aren't concerned for you."

"What do you mean by that?"

"Not me Tony. But the S.O. like, he's worried 'bout you having a go at Smiler like." Speechless at the view they have of me. Do they take no notice of me? Only my file is true to them.

"Me having ago at the assassin? That's a bit rich isn't it? Why do they think I'm the dangerous one?"

"You know people and have heavy friends in here. You're intelligent Tony."

"You can't put someone in a maximum security prison then hold it against them for knowing dangerous criminals. If I was that clever I'd be at home with my family."

In Durham I remember I was the one others would want to be associated with. One time Trevor, a young kid from my town, was in and out on a monthly basis. He was my eyes and ears on the outside. I asked him to find out things and let me know when he came back in. And he did. One day we were standing having a cigarette; it was association, when a short guy with a shaven head came over. He doesn't look old enough to be in a big man's jail. The conversation went something like this.

Trevor: Hi Carl what you in for pal?

Carl: Me-bird mate she's a cow.

Trevor: Where'd ya get the black eye?

191

Carl: Me-bird, the bitch hit me with one of her stilettos.

Trevor: Do ya know Tony Crowe? (I was standing next to him)

Carl: Yeah Mate he's the one who chopped up that kid.

Trevor: How do you know him then?

Carl: Business mate I did some business with him.

Me: Do you know me Carl?

Carl: No where ya from mate.

Me: Whitehaven.

Carl: So am I mate. You must have heard of me, Carl's me name.

Me: No don't know ya.

Carl: I do all the drugs in the town kid.

Me: Really? I wouldn't be telling someone who I don't know. KID.

Carl: What would you know 'bout it? Who are you anyhow?

Me: I'm the guy you say sells you all them drugs you say you sell. I'm Tony Crowe. And you are that little shit who runs errands for Ronny.

Carl: Sorry mate I was thinking of someone else.

I couldn't believe what I was witnessing before my very eyes. Trevor was laughing. He knew what was being said outside all right.

Back to here and now with my small crime and my twelve years.

"Your file says you are one of them dangerous criminals Tony. And you have another problem. The S.O. needs to talk to you." The Welshman says.

"What about?"

"Don't know, he'll tell you when you get there."

"When? Now?"

"When you've finished here like, would you come up to the office Tony?."

192

It's not a question, more of an order. Will this be another comment on my growing file. Another anti-bullying incident? The wing office is on the twos. Thick glass divides them from us. A sliding drawer is where they give out cooking tools taken from the shadow boards on the walls. Even knives are given out if you handover your ID card. Last week I saw someone take a knife from the drawer and push it into the neck of another guy as he walked past. I don't know if he had a problem with him or whether he just needed someone to stab. May be he wanted to go down the block. The safest place if you are on some one's hit list and can't front it. The segregation block is a hard place to get at an adversary. The intercom is how I call for the S.O. Pressing the button to open the channel I speak into the mic. He comes out from the side door to meet me.

"Come into the TV room Tony I need to speak to you about your clothes."

"My clothes? What can be wrong with my clothes?"

"It's not a big problem. Sit down. There's a Governor in the jail that is the spitting image of you."

"So how does that have anything to do with me?"

"If we let you wear outside clothes, and you had a suit say, the camera on the gates will think you are the Governor and open the door."

"Then why are you telling me. If I didn't know that I couldn't use it."

"We can't work on the idea you won't find out."

"What are you saying?"

"You can't wear your own clothes on the wing."

"Really? What's the name of this Governor then?"

"Can't tell ya that."

"Tell him to grow a beard."

"You could. Why don't you grow one, then you won't look like Governor..." His excitement nearly reveals the name of the Governor.

"I don't want to and it's not my problem. By the way, I don't have a suit."

The meeting is over. I get up and walk out. At the tea-time food-handout there is no sign of Smiler, which isn't strange; the rice was for his evening meal. My home made steak pie is ready for our Hollywood banquet just as soon as we are unlocked after our tea. Danny stays in his cell waiting for the pie. Every evening we are out from six till eight forty-five. A far cry from Durham now a million miles away. On weekends we get to walk in the prison field, that's the closest to the wall we ever get. Danny and I walk round in the clean air talking and dreaming of things to do when we get out. He has this plan of how I, with my knowledge of boats and scuba diving, could run drugs from South America. I know how the navy track shipping across the Atlantic Ocean. A firm have just come in for that very thing. One hundred kilos of coke on a catamaran. GPS was their spy on the boat. It lets you know where you are but it also tells anyone else where you are too. You have to do the trip without GPS or a motor, they can be picked up on submarine sonar. If you do all that the only other thing to avoid is the wake of phosphoresce that can be seen by satellites in space. I didn't say it was easy.

Lots of people on the exercise field have towels round their necks and some are padded out in the kidney region. My schooling is not complete but I know enough to watch for closed hands hiding a weapon and have eyes in the back of my head. Danny wants to walk the wrong way breaking from tradition. So that's what we do. Even in the snow we walk the field.

194

Sitting in Danny's cell eating our steak pie with the door open as a sign Danny's taking visitors. Who should put his head inside the door but my mate Smiler. Now when I said to the screw it was over I meant it. If this guy has a problem with me that's his problem not mine. One thing he does know is I serve up all his food.

"I is sorry man for dat ting bout da rice." He says.

"Not your fault mate. The screw copped out on me."

"I wasn't tinking man, don't want any bad ting man."

"I forgot it when you left the hatch Smiler."

"A knew man. Hey man 'av ya got an onion till pay day?"

"In that box behind the door take what you need from there and don't worry about giving it back we get them from a mate who works in the gardens. Give me an order and I'll get it for you. That box for one phone card."

"Yeah Man Will do. Well sorry 'gain bro."

Another customer for Danny and his fruit and veg black-market. The wing kitchen is not the place to be in the evening so Danny and I do our cooking when everyone is still at work, before bang-up. A perk of being a wing cleaner. A must for the Christmas dinner Danny made. Prison Christmas dinner is nothing like the one we have made. Screws wear red hats and think Jesus has no business hijacking it. Two days of fuzz is on my face from not shaving. Christmas is one time of the year I can do without. Staying in bed for three days is nothing for me roundabout now never mind shaving for work.

My mood is just right for the screw telling me to shave before the next meal time. When I get back to my cell I take hold of my razor, snap it in half and bin it. No more will I shave. No more will I live in the world of man's rules. I am a child of the most high God. I think this is the start of my madness. No more do I look like the Governor. In two weeks my beard is long enough to split down the centre and wax into two spikes. My moustache I train to turn up and curl. It reminds me of the eddies lifting off an aeroplane wing as it speeds through the smoke of battle. A new photograph for my file is taken and I get a new ID card to hang round my neck. Sanity is a fine line. Few come back once they cross over.

Routine is now set once more, every day exercise, but here I can go out and come in when I want, within the allotted hour. Weekends walking on the field. Evening meal is good food made fresh. Wednesday is canteen day when we get our shopping delivered to our door. Friday we change our bed sheets etc. When I can be bothered I sit in on the lifer meetings, with the two head doctors in the woolly jumpers; getting an insight into another world. The world on the other side of that line. Then there's the gym. I've started playing badminton four times a week. Terry, from the biggest family in Europe, as Danny calls him. This six foot plus tall guy with one eye is my new badminton opponent. Until, that is I put him in the hospital. We were playing when a mate came and asked if we would play doubles. There were no more courts available so we doubled up. My partner was Terry and he took the front of the court, I was to the rear. I don't know why but it happened, just as I hit the birdie as hard as I could he turned round. His good eye took the full force of the shuttlecock. Blinded he was taken to the jail hospital, no outside hospital here. They thought he had a detached retina. It was two days before Terry could see again. Thank God he was right as rain in a week. On Wednesday mornings I go to the weights room in the gym for a little workout. Nothing like some of the meat-heads who six times a week pump iron. Pedro is my meat-head mate in the gym. He lives on D. wing, one of the old cell blocks. There is no water in them and they have no keys for the doors. Here on P. wing we all have our own keys. Talk about the lunatics taking over the asylum. We also have toilets and wash hand basins in our cells. God is good to me. After lock-up the screws will unlock two cells at a time for the toilet. Fifteen minutes is the allotted time period. Even though we don't need out for toilet relief we still get the chance if we wish. My mate Pedro is sixteen stone of muscle chiselled out of black granite. From the waist up that is. His legs on the other hand look more like they are cut from liquorice. We are a good match because my legs are my strong point. When Pedro works my chest and arms so I can't wash my hair because I can't lift my arms. The next session I work his legs so hard he can't climb stairs for two days. All in the name of fun. But good for my new found passion of badminton. I leave the soft tennis for the old guys of the jail. Danny isn't one of them. For a week he has been under the weather. A trip to the jail doctor gives him the news. Shingles is the illness keeping him in his bed. For the pain they give him aspirin and for the virus they give him nothing. It can last for two weeks or two years they tell him. My visit to the doctor for a hepatitis jab is routine. I'm in a place where blood could be infected and where you could be spattered with it.

Becoming ill in prison is not a good idea. My mate Danny has me to help him with day-to-day comforts. The job he is paid for is done by one of the other kids. Nothing new about that. Ken is the aviary guy. He looks after the birds in the prison aviary where all the pet birds come from. True jail birds born in prison. To buy one you first have to buy a cage from the jail shop. No one puts the bird in it but you still have to have one. It's not unusual to be dive-bombed by a budgie on the loose, or to have a cockatiel buzz your head as it comes

197

in to land. They all know where they live and when they get outside through an open window or a screw takes no notice of the sign saying, 'bird loose in cell,' they come back when a mirror is flashed at them. My interest is poems and music. The legal writings over the last two years has given me a passion for putting my thoughts onto paper. What better way to relax than listening to classical music in the midst of madness. It reminds me of the book: Rita Haywood and the Shawshank Redemption where the main man locks himself in the Governor's office and plays a record over the PA system of some woman singing in Italian. Drugs take some out of here. Music and my writing takes me to places that only exist inside my head. One thing they can't take away from me is my mind; and my head is all mine. Fighting my case has taken up all my time and now I have the joy of writing poems. The words sometimes come out of the pen from somewhere I have never been to.When I read them back it's as if they were penned by someone else.

TV soon loses its appeal. I can't put my trust into something they could take from me. As a new Christian I read The Bible as a novel but it makes little if any sense to me. Stories from long ago. What is the relevance to today and to me in here? One thing I do get is I did some crime. We all did it's called sin. But Jesus paid the price for it. He did our jail. He was beaten and killed and much more for what I did. Who do you know who would take your just deserves? Who do you know who would let their only son take the punishment for you? The love of Jesus is overwhelming to anyone who understands what he did for them. I am no different. If he can love me why would I find it difficult to love him? I don't, he is with me in this prison cell. I read about all the good men in the Bible who were put into prison. The murderers like

Moses. The disobedient like Jonah. The apple of God's eye David, Daniel, and Joseph. It says Adam and Eve walked in the garden talking with God, I wonder what they talked about. Psalms are the poetry book of the Bible. Ecclesiastes is about life without God; over and over it says what is the point? When asked if I had found God I said no He wasn't lost I was, He found me. Deep in a pit and lifted me out. All I had to do was take a hold of His outstretched hand. That's just what I did.

Now that Dawn is not visiting my aged mother takes up the position. With help from the prison Chaplain Jim she comes to see me once a month. Two buses and three trains with a taxi ride out to the prison whenever Jim can't pick her up from the station. The visit is for two hours in the morning and again in the afternoon. For these four hours she is on the go for twelve hours. I need to get closer to my home town although it's been that long now since I was in my own town I don't think of it as such. Out of the blue one of my four brothers comes to see me. He has a young son who thinks his uncle is a hero and is somebody to look up to. David, asks me to put the boy straight. So he has brought him to see how it really is. How a hero lives in a caged environment with men who will kill for as little as a cigarette. Just like the film Angels with Dirty Faces I am Jimmy Cagney. If I could take him into the jail and let him live a day in my life the myth of the gangster life would melt away like ice cream on a sunny summer day.

Words are all I have to turn the boy away from my reputation. Away from a life of prison. Something I wish I could have done for my beloved son Dominic. His mother sent me a letter just after I got my Dear John. Your son, she started, but I couldn't help thinking when she went behind my back and asked the court to give the children to her there was no mention of my son. Your son is in a jail for children. The rest of the letter tells me it's all my fault my fourteen year old son is in jail and his life is a mess. If I could do the jail for him I would. I can't, just as I couldn't be a real father to him.

I can keep David, or Jaffa as he is called by his mates, off that merry-go-round I saw so many on in Durham. After being searched just to get in, young David had something he never had before in his sixteen years of life. Insight into another world. Famous, or should I say infamous criminals sit dotted round the large hall. Criminals who Jaffa knows about from glorified crimes in newspapers and books. After pointing out four or five by name to him, followed by their jail term, I ask him what they all have in common. They will all die in here or some other place just like it, I tell him. Life is about living. Everybody will die, that's not an achievement. I read this once so I tell it to him.

Reputation.

Reputation is what you are supposed to be.
Character is what you are.
Reputation is a photograph.
Character is your face.
Reputation is what you have when you come to a new place.
Character is what you have when you go away.
Reputation is learned in an hour.
Character does not come to light for years.
Reputation is made in a moment.
Character is built in a lifetime.
Reputation grows like a mushroom.
Character grows like an oak.
Reputation is made from a single newspaper report.
Character is built from a life of toil.
Reputation makes you rich or poor.
Character makes you happy or miserable.
Reputation is what men say about you on your tombstone.
Character is what the angels say about you around the throne of God.

"Your Dad has more character than I will ever have. If you want to have a good character; emulate your father. Don't think anyone of these in here have something you want. They all have nothing in this life and less in the next."

Young David then tells me he has been thinking about joining the army.

"If you're looking for character I think you'll find it there." I tell him. Men who live alone in prison cells are no stranger to the person they are. Most don't want to recognise their character only their reputation. That reputation is only for other people and does themselves no good whatsoever. I hope it won't take me a lifetime to show I have character and not reputation. I want to have a reputation for having a good Christian character from now on. Reputation got me in here but character will get me out, I know it. My first step is to put in an application for a move up north. Visits are a good reason so that's what I use. There are only five prisons for maximum security prisoners in the county; this one is for the Midlands. I need to get to the northern one in Newcastle.

"Pack your kit Tony you're moving." Is what the screw says at eight O'clock unlock on this Friday morning. July two thousand.

"Why? Where am I moving to?" I ask him.

"Ship out mate. You're on your way. Your request for a move has come through."

"Only took eight months. That's great. Frankland?" I ask him

"Not supposed to say but you're OK; Garth in Leyland."

"You are joking right?"

"No but don't let on you know till you get on the van."

"I know nothing, right?" I tap my finger on the side of my nose. Time to pack with one hour before I leave on my first positive move. Free from maximum security. Free in The Spirit of Jesus Christ. Free indeed. My three years here has ended in only eight months. As the prison gate screeches closed behind the van the world turns back into one of colour. I thank God for this impossible move.

A new jail and a new life in Jesus is my next story let me tell you all about it.

Praise be to God.

Deliverance

In with the old

Yellow broom with vivid green stems line the narrow way. White hawthorn bushes breaking up the garland of colour every few feet. An old oak tree reaching out for the sky. Soaring out of my limited sight. I strain my neck to see the top. Its boughs stretch out; leaves whisper in the breeze to each other. The summer fragrance? A mere trick of my imagination. The prison van rounds a bend in the meandering lane. The dirty-white wall of concrete and steel goes on forever into the distance. HMP Wymott, a category C. prison is behind that wall. Not to be my domicile. I have come from a maximum security prison and a Category B. is to be my new home. HMP Garth is beyond the staff car park. Beyond the neat well-kept flowerbeds that gives any visitor a good first impression of the house of doom. In the centre of the sixty foot high wall is the security airlock. That two door void where the van is scrutinised for anything that does not belong inside. The beautiful colours in the hedgerow and the wide open fields I passed on the journey from HMP Long Lartin are now behind me. Once more my world is black and white.

The reception is the same as any other. The screw behind the high desk, without looking up, asks for my name. And number of course. Given to me so long ago now. Scratching it onto my file. My photo I.D is the first problem, his eyes lift from the paperwork. Looking at me over the small reading glasses perched on the end of his bonnie nose; he says.

"You have a beard."

"Very observant of you. Is that a problem?"

"You don't have one on here," he taps his pen on my file, "did you get permission to grow it?"

"Well it turned out I was a ringer for the governor in Long Lartin, he didn't have a beard, so I grew one to stop me escaping by dressing in a suit, that I don't have, and looking like a governor, that I don't know."

"Stand on the black foot-prints and smile for the camera." He continues his scribing duties.

"I have my I.D badge if you want it." I hold it up showing him I have a beard on it.

"Just stand on the marks." A small stuffed bird is hanging at a jaunty angle. Held aloft by black gaffer tape wrapped round one foot; precariously perched on the web cam that takes my image for the new file. Not new but new for here. Now just under 4 inches thick.

My beard is impressive; parted down the middle and trained into two spikes it points slightly upwards. My moustache completes the set. I use Dax grease to curl it round in a giant swirl. The envy of any Bondi beach surfer riding the big waves if it were one. I think I'm just a bit insane now. The screw thinks I'm all the way round the bend. Just one more for his zoo of insanity. Out of the six bags of property I lose one full bag. The one pair of shorts and the Van Morrison music tape I lost when I left Long Lartin pales into insignificance. The list of "you can't have" includes my tin opener, my cigarette lighter, my typewriter, half my clothes, bath robe, slippers, any food in glass jars. More than half my music tapes. Only ten tapes or CDs allowed. I have to try to get something back.

"I need my typewriter for legal work." I start my inevitable doomed-to-fail attempt.

"Not allowed in this prison."

"Do you know anything about prison rules?"

"You can't have it." He thinks he is the rules.

"I think you'll find I can."

"You're not in a holiday camp here son. We are not the same as Long Lartin."

"Same blue doors, same uniform, what's different here then? Do I get to go home at the weekends?"

"You can't have it."

"One day. If I was a betting man I would put me hat on it. One day it will be before I have it in my cell." I tell him.

"I've heard it all before son. Do your request/complaint form all you like you're not getting it."

"I don't do R/C forms now I go straight to the court. Judicial Review is the new R/C form. Just as a matter of interest what's your name?"

"Get in there and strip off. You are going to love it here..." I stop him right there.

"I'm not your son and me and you are going to get on just fine. Once I get my typewriter back. God bless you."

A wing is for new recruits. The iron steps leading up to the third landing have a worn-out hollow on the treads where over time the feet of hundreds of men have eroded the steel away. The decorative design only apparent on the less used sides. The hand rail smooth from hands. I can't help being amazed every time when I think the paint and the metal has been worn away by nothing more than the hands of prisoners as they slide their way up and down.

For one week I will have to stay here for my induction period. Number 12 is open and the screw standing next to the door still has his key in the lock. Dragging what's left of my property behind me in I go. One bed is a welcome sight. Single cell. The door bangs shut behind me. Is it worth unpacking for one week? I don't like it here already and I've only just arrived. Why are all jails not the same? They're all run by the same rules; by the same Home Office. Why do I have to revert back to opening tins of food with the bed and a plastic knife? Why no lighter? Why am I even in prison? Why can I not have my typewriter? Even in Durham I could have it for legal work. I am being robbed of my joy; my peace has been taken off me by the reception screw. I just want to stay in this cell till I can go home. I want nothing from them and I don't want to know about their rules that don't make any sense in a grown-up world. I still have my God. Only because of this; If God is for us, who can be against us? He who did not spare even his own Son, but gave him up on behalf of us all is it possible that, having given us his Son, he would not give us everything else too?

But still I don't feel very Christian and that's what I tell the painted lady. The overpowering aroma fills my cell. A colourful woman with bright red fingernails who opens my door; asking if I'm a Roman Catholic, Church of England or other.

"What's another?" I ask her.

"Muslim, Buddhist, Pagan and if so which type, Sikh, Hindu, Jew if so what type, Scientology, Jedi warrior, and more; need I go on?"

"I'm a Christian and I just want to do me jail so if you don't mind; close the door on your way out please." Her wide frame fills the doorway. Light from the outside flows over her head and through her thinning unnatural red hair. Glinting earrings sway with the slight wobble of her head as she speaks. If it were Christmas I would swear she was the tree.

"I'll put you down as a C of E then." She enters a tick in the box on her form.

"See you in church. What did you say your name was?" I ask her.

"Pauline I'm the Assistant Chaplain."

"C of E, Roman Catholic, what are you then?"

"Other. Anglican. Like C of E."

"I give in. I'm just a follower of Jesus but I don't feel Christian just now. Still in the Old Testament I haven't got to the love bit yet so can you give me some room to myself for now?"

"Is there something you would like?"

"Only one thing; to go home." The door closes without another word said. That distinctive clunk followed by the clatter of keys coming out of the lock. High heels tapping out on the wooden floor dissipate bringing silence to my new world.

I don't think this is a good move but I'm here now and what can I do about it? My new cell is now an old dirty one. No cooking food, no friends apart from Rickey wherever he is in this mad house of pain. I have enough food for a day or two and nothing to do all day, apart from the all important induction. Visit the Gym, the library, see the governor, work allocation screw, to see what mind numbing job he can give me. The old daily routine of Durham is back. Only opened for food and no TV. My radio is back in use for music and late night talk shows. I can pick up Radio Liverpool and if I put it in the window on a clear night I can pick up a weak signal from Radio Cumbria. My so far off once home county.

When they open the door I close it. For three days I stay in bed throughout the day. My food brought from Long Lartin is better than the food here so I eat it in the evening after the screws are all gone. Four days into my induction period somebody opens the door-flap, the Judas hole. It's not time for the door to open so I lift my head from the rolled up towel I'm using for a pillow.

"Who's that? Get away from me door." I'm like a curiosity at Blackpool's wax works. The mad man from the big prison.

"It's me mate; Rickey. Do ya need ought Tony?"

"How do ya live in this jail? It's bad mate; I want to go back."

"You want a shave mate. You look like a nonce. They're all saying there's a sex-case on the wing mate. That beard will have to go. Did ya hear 'bout me appeal? I got four years knocked off. I'm doing twelve like you and I'm getting my first parole."

"Who says I'm a nonce? Tell them to come and tell me that then."

"I didn't know you were here till I seen your name on the gym induction list."

"What wing you on Rickey? Put me a word in to get on your wing."

"I will but that beard has to go mate."

"Here take this burn mate I don't need it." I flatten the packet with my foot and kick it through the small gap under the door.

"There's an oz of tobacco here Tony do you not want it?"

"I don't smoke."

"You can use it to..." I stop him mid sentence.

"No you take it I don't need it."

"When did you stop smoking? Do you not want to keep it just in case you need it?"

"I have no lighter they took it off me along with everything else I had to make life bearable behind my cell door."

"Do ya want some matches? Garth is a no-lighter prison."

"I don't smoke. It's too difficult to play their games."

"What happened to the fighter I knew in Durham?"

"He died in Long Lartin. Remember the man from the Pharisees who asked Jesus."

"Nicodemus; John 3?"

"That's him. I know what it's about; but I don't understand it. Do you?"

"You've lost me Tony I've got to go, shave that beard off and I'll see about getting you onto my wing. If they ask you what wing you want tell them D wing mate. I run the wing so get on D wing and you're made."

"Rickey its crap here. You only know Durham and that was bad but I've come from cooking your own food and clean cells with showers for one at a time and gym every day. I've lost half me stuff in reception. What's the work like here?"

"I've got to go Tony get onto D wing and you'll be all right."

I can't help thinking of what I've come from. Is this what I wanted? I have to move on to get to a category D prison. Will it get better or will it be like this whenever I gain something will I lose something? I still have the anger of being put in prison by lies. How can I be a Christian if I have no forgiveness and the pain of anger inside me? One day at a time. That first day in Durham after I was sentenced I was given the document telling me how long I would serve. It was given in days all four and a half thousand of them. Days are what I have to do. One day at a time sweet Jesus. A song from my youth. First job is to get back my typewriter. Take my mind off prison and the anger that I live with every minute of every day.

Here I am and here I will stay. Time to lose the beard and conform to this prison. The orange razor, standard prison issue, makes your face bleed as soon as you pick it up. The trick is to rub the blade on your thigh while wearing prison jeans. A tip given to me by an old lifer. I think the razors are the ones that fail quality control. Not deemed fit for the public. A bit like the food. Good enough for us, who live like kings with our cable TV and Play Station games to occupy the quietness of a trouble free life. Let them that say that swap places for a night or two.

Every night the proms broadcast the day's music from The Royal Albert Hall. I melt into the bed with my eyes closed and my mind floating far away from this jail cell. Handle's water music takes me to deep blue waters. The abundant fishy rainbow of colour that still fills my mind's eye. The blue hole of Gozo, Malta. My drug for that day out that all prisoners need from time to time. The low methodical thud of too much bass from a radio far off only reminds me of my beating heart and the life I have; wherever I may be.

The move to D wing comes on my week's anniversary. A wheeled trolley carries my depleted property bags to the new home. The same as any other cell that has suffered from overuse. The ravages of time have not been good to it. Nothing in it is clean or in good order. The TV has no control buttons and I don't see a remote control. Wires hang from the hole in the front where once long ago the buttons were. My first task is to meet the wing S.O. Not so he can welcome me to his happy band of men but to give him the old TV set.

"I would like you to take this TV and put it in the bin where it belongs." I put the broken box of wires on his desk and turn to leave the office.

"You'll have to put up with that one. We don't have another."

"I didn't ask for another. But if I leave that box of wires in me pad I may reach that level of boredom were one day I switch it on."

"You won't have a telly if you don't have that one. What will you do?"

"Without; is what I'll do. That," pointing at the black box, "is too dangerous to have in me cell. So I don't want it."

"What if I can get the buttons fixed?"

"You do that. But don't put yourself out for me. What you can do is tell the nice man in reception to give me my typewriter back and I won't have to write to prison HQ with a complaint."

"We don't permit them here."

"That's what he said. You do. You just don't know it yet."

"Why do you need it?"

"Legal work; I have to type paperwork for the courts and by law not prison rules, I can have it

"I'll ask the governor about it for you but..." I stop him.

"Very good of you. Now where do I get cleaning materials for that cave I have to call home."

"See the wing cleaner in number one."

The door to cell one is open but its occupant is absent. From down the narrow corridor muffled voices and that thump of too much bass drifts toward me. Two guys sit on the bed of cell number 7, one a gym-head with his huge bulk bursting out of the world gym vest hanging around his bullish neck. The other with less meat on his bones than that of one leg of his pal. Both the product of drugs I think. One steroids, the other smack, the new drug of prison because of its quick exit from the body. It was cannabis that took men out from the pain of prison; now the prison test for drugs every fourteen days, cannabis stays in the system for up to a month so heroin is the answer, it's gone in seventy two hours. That's the insanity of jail.

"Okay mate is one of you a cleaner?" I ask.

"I, mate what can a do for ya?" The small guy from lounging propped up on one elbow, sits up.

211

"I'm in number twelve and I need some cleaning stuff. Was the last occupant a pig?"

"He was a mank mate. You ever been in Strangeways jail? Those Manchester lads don't do much cleaning. Ha'way mate I'll give ya a mop and some hot water." The Newcastle twang takes me back to my early days of Durham jail. The first thing Gary wants to know is do I have any drugs. When I tell him I don't do drugs he asks how I get a head change. My music and my bible give me the respite from jail. But I tell him my head is okay where it is. Next the question never asked in Long Lartin; 'How long are you doing?' It's not a problem here. When Gary asks me how long I'm doing I tell him twelve years. Then he tells me he's on his fifteenth year in prison. I can't believe what he tells me when he says he's a lifer. His puny build, under five foot odd tall and standing at about fifty kilograms. Well I can't imagine how he could kill another person. He's nothing like any killer I've met. And I've seen lots up close.

With all the cell furniture out on the landing, one iron bed complete with old mattress. One small table, with wobbly leg, one locker come cupboard devoid of drawer front and one tubular-steel chair with its cracked wooden seat that nips your bum every time you move. I set about the filth. When I've mopped the worn-out muddy brown linoleum floor and washed the walls, toilet and wash-hand basin the S.O. rounds the corner carrying a new TV set.

"I told the governor about your telly and you're right it's dangerous to have it in your cell."

"Thank you. Put it on the table. But mind it doesn't fall off the leg's a bit dodgy."

"I think number four has a good table." He opens up the door to number four and I swap my table for the new one. No sign of a chair; cracked or otherwise.

212

"I need a locker, what about this one?" The one in 4 is better than mine.

"Yeah go on hurry up and get it." Like we're gonna get caught stealing! "Put yours in there then bang the door."

"Did the governor say anything 'bout me typewriter?"

"He's looking into it for you."

"What's his name?"

"Who? The governor? Brown he's the wing Governor. You'll see him tomorrow when he comes for his morning meeting."

"Can't wait. If only to thank him for the telly. Where's the remote?"

"Don't push it." I don't think I have a new TV for my delectation. How can they take away what you don't have? No sign of Rickey. All the cells are locked down and empty; the occupants are working in the prison workshops. Gary and his mate Pedro are the only two on the wing. Sitting on the bed playing cards midst the cloud of smoke. Their life sentence and home town of Newcastle give them a common bond.

Screws swarm onto the wing clattering and banging gates and cell doors as they unlock the wing for the imminent return of the inmates. The cacophony of chattering men grows louder as the wing fills up; reaching a crescendo then dying down just as fast when the doors bang shut. The last bang ends the raucous routine. 'All away' the screw shouts out. One by one the cells produce a muffled clue as to the TV channel favoured by its occupant. Sitting on the cracked chair; waiting for the door to open for lunch. The realisation of the mundane routine of life in jail is here all over again.

'Open up the twos'. The call comes. Again the noise builds as doors are opened. Closer and closer the noise

213

gets until my door swings open. Long Lartin was unlocked with the peace and quiet of a library. When the doors were unlocked the screw would just take it past the point of the lock-keep. At first I could easy miss my door being unlocked. Here the door opens to its fullest, with a bang, stretching the steel hinges on every occasion. Every unlock the screw moves on seven cells so the same cell isn't opened up first every time. Who says things in here aren't fair?

The line of men moves quickly past the food hatch, each with his plate. A small victory and a move up the ladder of privileges given to those who play the game of prison. Gone are the steal trays. I can't help thinking their demise is more for the screws benefit. They don't have to open up after meals to have the trays put outside the cells.

Although the room where the food is served is big enough to seat the whole wing. There are no tables and no seats. Just a pool table and a snooker table that couldn't be described as pristine examples of the green baize. The food is taken back to the cells to be eaten in your private toilet. The door's locked. Every cell holds a soul who calls it home. I need to make this cell my home and move on in my journey down the security corridor of prison. When, like me, you start at the top of the security ladder the only way is down.

The first job I'm given is just what I thought it would be. Mind numbing. One bolt, a number of different size washers topped off with a nut. That's what I do as a job. This is not for me. In days of old it was eight stitches to the inch. Sawing mailbags was the nut and bolt job of the time. I need to progress to something more befitting my skills. Rickey worked in the same shop when he first came here from Durham but now he has a job in the silk-screen printing shop. My faith points me toward the chapel cleaning job. A job that is a trusted position given only to a prisoner who is seen to be of no threat to the system. That's not me so I'll have to work on that. Maybe my file will be lost in some bizarre mishap. Who knows?

On Sunday mornings the call for chapel fills the air. A hoard of men stand at the wing gate; impressive. All these going to church? The last call goes out. Two or three of us standing at the wing gate go right to the chapel, the rest run to the left, heading to the gym. Even five yards, the short distance between wing and chapel is too much for us to go unaccompanied.

"Morning." The Chaplain greets everybody as we enter. He's just how I imagined he would be. Graham is from the old school of religious doctrine. Adorned with the modern garb of the priesthood, long white bed sheet hung over a black under garment. Dog collar of white plastic. His badge of office. Ex-army whose life has been one of rules and routine. There's no sign of Pauline, the painted lady. Ten men are scattered midst fifty or so seats. Ten men from the whole jail. A poor turnout, not impressive, but maybe the cream of the crop. The clean environment of the chapel, with the smell of furniture polish, is a pleasant sensory rest from the sweaty stench of the wing. The orderly is a lifer on his way down the security ladder. Soon to move on to a category C prison. After the service, tea and biscuits are served with a time of fellowship. No screws are here. We could be anywhere. I like the peace and I need the job for my walk with God to grow. I don't understand where I'm going or where I will end up. I do know this is where I am supposed to be. Still I don't fully understand what God is all about. Is it just a way out of hell when I die? What about here and now? What about the anger I have toward the ones who lied to put me in prison? How does it all fit together?

One thing I do know. I won't find the answers here. Even to say I'm in prison for a crime I didn't commit sends them all running for cover. No one in prison is innocent. Even on remand waiting for the court to declare your guilt you're assumed guilty. Why would you drug test an innocent man? That's just what they do. I only answer the question when I'm asked. Still they don't like it when I say I'm not guilty. I know what's to come. Gary the lifer is not guilty and every year he sits in front of a panel who determine his degree of regret and rehabilitation. The prison has a term for it. I.D.O.M. (in denial of murder). I have a day when I will have to be let out. Gary, or any other lifer, has to conform to get out. How can you say you are guilty when you're not? Truth is you can't, Gary is two years over his tariff. If he said he did it and he is sorry he could go home. He won't. I won't.

There is some hope. One of our happy band of guilty men went to The Strand, High Court, to appeal his conviction. Twenty-six years he's been in prison and still he's in a cat B jail. Not only does he get acquitted, it turns out there was no murder in the first place. I.D.O.M. was in big black letters on the front of his file.

Jed's a lifer who has served 14 years for the murder of his wife. Another murder that wasn't a murder. She left a note before she took her own life. A note that the crown say was written by Jed. I can't imagine the pain he's in. Not only has he lost his wife, who he loved. Still loves. He couldn't attend her funeral. Couldn't say good bye. Couldn't grieve. Being a Roman Catholic he takes confession every Saturday before mass. He won't work and has been in the same cell for 12 years. A very troubled man who the prison doesn't understand. The sister of his wife identified the hand writing in the note as her dead sister's. The expert said it wasn't hers. Guilty.

Peter's a lifer. He's guilty of patricide. To say he is a bit special wouldn't be out of place. Having the mental age of a small child but the strength of a four-times-a-week gym head I'm sure he can be a handful. He killed his father when he was a young boy. I don't know how old he was but he was a Y.O. (Young Offender) so he was under 21. He watched as his father repeatedly raped his sister. I don't know what her age was at the time but she comes every visit to see him now. She looks about two or three years younger than Peter. Anyway, one time he stopped his father's debauchery with his hands round his throat till he was dead. His mental state will keep him here forever. Mental prisoners are common place. This is a contradiction in law. If you are mental, or not of sound mind we'll call it, you are legally incompetent. You can't be put on trial. So before the trial the CPS prove your sanity and then when you are found guilty they try to prove your insanity. That's insane! One other guy is in for throwing eggs at cars from a motorway bridge, he is mad. If no one in prison is mental why is the medical hatch giving out more anti-psychotic drugs than any other? Sanity is a fine balance. A thing not to be messed with. One Flew Over The Cuckoo's Nest comes to mind.

I hold on to mine daily. I hope what I see in myself is what is really there, you can't see what others see in you. All have a story. All have problems. All are loved by God whether they like it or not. Innocence is a diluter of sanity. If it was a painting it would have to be 'Scream' by Edvard Munch. The torment inside can't be explained in words. It's a mental state. Manic depressive was one definition of the roller-coaster ride of emotional highs and lows; euphoria the zenith.

217

Depression rushing towards you, free falling into a dark pit of loneliness. Now the new definition is bipolar.

My mate Rickey asked me in Durham if I did it. I told him I didn't. Today walking in the small yard for our allotted hour, he tells me someone was in Garth and knew who committed the crime I'm doing twelve years for, so now he knows it wasn't me.

"Do you believe him Rickey?" I asked him.

"Aye, he told me how it went and that you weren't there."

"So you didn't believe me who you know. But you do believe some guy who you don't know from Adam?"

"I still think you must have had something to do with it Tony."

"I got found guilty didn't I? So I must be Guilty, right? Your mate Porter said I owned the baseball bat found in the house."

"Porter was lying I know that but I can't believe you knew nothing about it."

"Rickey, I know everything about it. It's what put me in here. I know where the machete is that cut him up."

"You know Swindles went into the pub and fronted Tanner. He told him he knew it was him and not you."

"And you still don't believe me? Tanner asked someone in Workington to hide a machete the same day."

"No, I do know. I know you weren't there when he got cut up like."

"Don't even go there. I just want to get to the end of all this."

"What about when you get out Tony?"

"You don't want to know Rickey. I scare myself when I think of the people who stood and lied in court."

"Let it go man."

"Not till everyone has answered my question."

"What's that then?"

"Why? Why did they do it? Then they will pay the price all liars must pay."

"You're mad Tony. Just let it go mate. Do the courses and get out. I've done all of them, I'm going to Haverigg, cat C open."

"I send letters and cards to the coppers on the anniversary and at Christmas. Counting down the time till I get out. It keeps me going. I have nothing to live for but revenge. They won't let me out on parole Rickey."

"It's not good Tony."

I know he's right; I can't help it. The last thing in my head before I fall asleep is anger and even before I open my eyes the anger floods in. When I say the Lord 's Prayer I miss out the forgiveness part. The bible tells me to forgive. But how can anyone forgive this? Let them ask me for forgiveness and I'll give it. I know that won't happen. I know the time and the day every one of them will go to stand in front of God and be judged. I'm going to send them there. I will send them all in a way befitting their lying tongue. Shooting is too good for them. I just have to survive long enough after I start my campaign of war to end it with all those on my list dealt with. I'll make Rambo seem empathetic.

The prison asks me all the time how I feel about the victim. He's the only one I don't have any anger about. He's a simple-minded drug-damaged guy who knows no better than to lie and cheat. His medical record is his defence. He's best described as, Oy veh, that putz has got to be mashugana, (crazy). My mother would for some reason I've never understand use Yiddish words like these. No, I want the ones who knew what they were doing and did it anyway. Porter did what he did for his friend. 'What greater love is there than that a man lay down his life for a friend?' That's what it says in my bible and that's what he did when he lied in court. In the same way the police dog-handler did for his friend and brethren. The others did what they did for themselves. All will be asked the same question; why did you do what you did?

Holding on to sanity

Governor Brown gives me permission to pick up my typewriter from reception. The same reluctant screw hands it over.

"Crowe CP3703. Sign there He slides my property list over the counter and tosses me an old battered orange Biro for my mark to prove the property has been taken by me. Wouldn't do for a prisoner to touch his pen.

"Sign this one while you're here as well."

"What's this then, you know I'm in here as a result of signing without looking first."

"And I thought you were in for chopping a guy up in his bed."

"So they say and for no apparent reason. It was a full moon though."

"It's to handout on your next visit all the property you can't have."

"Like me typewriter?" Silence. I reach for the door with victory under my left arm in the form of my Olivetti.

"Just a sec son. Did you get permission to shave off your beard?"

"Do me a favour mate." He can't stand to see my victory.

"I need a new photo for your file."

"Just throw the one with the beard away and use the other one. It's not difficult."

"New photo. Stand on the marks and face the camera."

"Okay seeing as how you are so good as to give me my typewriter. Why not? Have you got a comb?"

"Just look at the camera." Image once more robbed.

Victory brightening up my day. Back to my cell to transfer all my scribbles into documents. With two fingers I spend all my in-cell time tapping out the words that swamp my mind.

I need to start the process of appeal. I hope it's not a life-long task like poor Rob who walked from The Strand free. Kidnap is my new argument. I know now more about my return from Malta. The police bought my aeroplane ticket. There was no extradition. I was taken over a country border when they took me off the ship back to Malta, which is not on in the legal world. You cannot take someone from a place of safety over a border for the purpose of extradition. I have Crown v Bennett, the case Danny gave me in Long Lartin. I have a document from the police in Whitehaven warning the Malta police about a claim of habeas corpus if they don't get me to sign some other document that I have yet to find. Habeas corpus is the right of every one to ask to be brought in front of a judge to test the legality of his/her custody. Without a court appearance in Malta my incarceration is poisoned from the very beginning. My 12 years sentence is the fruit of that poisoned tree. According to the law, my legal custody only started when I arrived at Gatwick airport. Question is how did I come to be there?

Argos is the shop where I can order ribbon for my writing machine, a duvet and pillowcase to match. Where I can get my plate to make me a somebody on the wing. Even a new radio with a CD player and mini disc, to beat the volumetric control problem. With a spending limit of ten pounds plus any wages I may get from my nut-and-bolt job it will take some time for any big item. What I don't spend in the prison shop is carried over to the next week. First on my list is a new Hi-Fi to get the best out of the classical music that's become my way of spending some time in another place. It will take me 26 weeks or a hundred and eighty two days in jail time to save the money, then another week to wait for the prison to give it to me.

Time is something I have lots of. In a month I can move jobs. So I do just that. A cell move is first though. The south facing spur overlooks the grassy no-man's land between the jail and the prison wall. The only side of the wing where channel 5 can be picked up on the TV. Bright coloured ducks waddle around the grounds. So that's where I move to. Next door is Andy, another young kid. Twenty-one years old. Already been locked up for seven years. Stuck, as most kids who have been robbed of their childhood. Stuck in an emotional wilderness. Never progressing into adulthood. The definition of his damaged state is compulsive obsessive disorder. OCD. The screws think it's funny to move his things around his cell on their daily check for signs of escape attempts. It drives him mad to see foot marks on his highly polished floor. Moving his property from its proper place can only be mental torment. However that's not what sends him over the threshold of hopelessness.

He was locked up as a child for murder. The other victim in the altercation was in a coma for seven years. The seven years Andy has served in jail. Now the guy has died and the police have just told Andy he's being charged with another murder. Devastating news in his well ordered world. The now all too familiar commotion at three in the morning is the resuscitation efforts of screws next door. Andy has hanged himself after taking some sort of pills. He's so bad the ambulance takes him to Preston Hospital. What mileage is there in charging someone with a seven year old crime when he's on a life sentence? His father, who mentally abused him from the time he could understand what abuse was, is called to his son's bedside. True to form he cares more about the young nurses than his

223

dying son. He's the murderer. He killed his son a long time ago. In a week Andy comes home. Not to rob the world of its revenge. He still has ninety-nine years to serve.

The prison has a workshop building wheelchairs and other vehicles that can be propelled by hand. The chairs, for want of a better word, are sent to India for children with walking problems. If a child has a special need a vehicle would be made to overcome that need. When I was a school boy our metalwork teacher entered us into a competition where we, the class, had to design and build a manually propelled vehicle. All the schools in the county took part and the judging took place at a Maryport school. Our effort was based on a wheelchair. That's why this workshop interests me now. Our classroom's world-beater wasn't as good looking as the grammar school hot rod. It wasn't as slick. It would be fair to say our design was more wheelchair looking. The entries all had to be tested for various attributes: weight, stability, angle at what point it would tip over and last of all a time trial on a test track. Driven by the five man team, of which I was one. We were a rag tail rough bunch kept in line by 'Sir', a hardcore, no-nonsense guy who over the years had drawn blood on all my older brothers. Discipline was allowed in schools back then.

The honour of our school was called into question. It was always going to be. The five of us couldn't have made up a full school uniform between us. This was a good thing as it happened. Skipper, my then good mate, stood his ground in the face of danger when a posse of locals ambushed him outside the dining hall. Not having a uniform that identified our school meant the teacher that saw him fighting his way out of there couldn't grass him up. The problem was we were the only kids there bereft through poverty of a uniform. I had to help him out that's when Sir beckoned us with his chipolata index finger. We were both dealt with in Sir's unique way. Our wheelchair, named Ironsides came in the top five. Above the hi-tech pillar-box red grammar school street racer. Looks count for nothing if it can't do the job.

I move into my new job making mobility devices for the immobile of India, turning out one-off projects to be shipped to kids in need. At Christmas the guy who took them shows us all a video of the kids in India receiving them. What a joy to see how our innovation overcame the problems of the most immobile of children. We never knew if our solution to the child's problem would work till they tried it out. Too late to change it then. Like most good things the funding is cut and so is my job. Back to the nut and bolts.

There's another workshop that makes wooden rocking horses run by Jenny. They look more like strange pit-bulls or Chinese mythical dogs to me. When my children were young and life was normal, one Christmas I made a rocking horse. The kids loved it and rode it for years. I have photos, sent in by my daughter. I can show Jenny.

That'll put an end to my nut and bolt job. Paying fifteen pounds a week, a five pound increase. Without another day wasted Jenny puts my move to the labour board. In a day I'm on more than double the money I was earning in the nut and bolt job. All good for my shopping list at Argos.

Every day the prison goes into movement's mode where the inmates are moved en masse to the places that will fill their time between meals. Some go to the workshops; others go to the education department. Some like Jed go nowhere. The eyes of some men are empty showing nothing of the soul that once lived inside the body. Marbles for eyes they have; that led me to write a poem.

Marbles for eyes

Marbles for eyes all black and glazed.
No life in those eyes of haze.
Just empty windows of the soul,
Black; dead pupils so small.
Men walk by but do not see.
They look through their windows of glazed black at me.
Empty shells without a soul inside any more
Walking like rats in the closed corridor.
All going the same way.
First one way then the other back to the wing.
I don't know why I bother.
On every corner there's a screw.
Cameras in the roof to watch over you,
They must think there's something wrong I can do.
They don't see the eyes of marble and glass.
They don't see the empty vessels pass.
To them it's a normal sight
To see soulless men who have lost the fight.
I can't understand how men so young, full of life
can lose their souls.
I can't understand how men can kill their souls
Ending up with windows like dark black holes.
Will I one day have those eyes?
Will I one day have no soul?
Will I one day have no hope?
Just like these men will I need drugs to cope?
If I never get out of jail and my face ends up like theirs
Lined; pale. I will never sell my soul to a drug.
All that will do is make me a mug.
I will never have eyes of marbled glass.
I will never bring myself down to that class.
I hope!

The block is always full and they don't work or go to education. No TV and no evening unlock. Drugs are all they have to pass the time. Visits to the Doctor when their haemorrhoids burst from too much drugs traffic. You have to hide them somewhere, right? The one hour a day walking round the small exercise yard is a legal right but even that can be used to discipline a non-conforming con. The lonesome figure walking round and round is a sad sight. On the weekends, like in Long Lartin, the sports field is opened up. But not for them. The summer sun is soaked up by the grey bodies stripped down to the waist. Drugs are thrown over the wall to be collected by some lacy con. The screws take the drug sniffer dog out to find any parcels before we're let out. The trick, and there always is one, is to put the drugs inside a dead bird. When the dog goes for the dead bird the screw pulls it away thinking it's just the bird interesting the dog.

Football is a big distraction, wing against wing with a screw acting out his childhood fantasy of playing in the big league. Once there was a rugby match, I don't know who it was that thought it would be a good idea. The ball was only an obstruction that got in the way of the fight. There was never a re-match. On Sundays the prison football team play in a league. They only ever play home fixtures. Teams come into the prison and try out their skills. What they fail to understand is the prison team is made up of gym-heads who live in the gym and eat any food within reach. They don't go out on the drink and there are no women to sap their stamina. Fitness is all they know. The beep test that pro football players take is a competition in here. Ten beeps and you're premier league fit. This lot go to twelve and beyond the limit of the machine. The jail winger can run the hundred metres in less than ten seconds and bench press one hundred and eighty kg. Even if you catch him you're not stopping him without a gun. It's a blow to the team when a good player's given parole or moved on.

Steve's his name. A guy who's on his way down the categorisation regime ladder. Due for a move next week. Today however is Steve's birthday and his mates on the out think it's a great idea to have a plane from Blackpool fly over the field towing a banner with his name on it, wishing him a happy birthday. Buzzing the jail whilst smoke trails write messages in the sky. It's an exciting distraction. Cheering hordes stop playing their games and everyone looks to the skies. Everyone that is except Steve. With that much influence his cat C. is removed and he stays right here. The prison's security department is easily spooked. I had the company of a guy who was lifted out of a prison yard by helicopter. His mates hijacked one and busted him out. He's still in Long Lartin. And will be forever.

The yard can be a dangerous place. Not only for prisoners who are in debt to one of the jail dons, but for the screws that are over-zealous. In their understanding of the role of turn-key they often think it's their job to oppress and judge those in their charge. Forgetting the courts has already judged them. One such screw pushed just a bit too far. It was a warm evening out on the wing yard with the last rays of the sun warming up the eastern wall. A full complement filled the small suntrap overlooked by the chapel office window. The dog-screw sat on a wooden seat in one corner, overseeing the allotted hour. Cons sucked fresh air in breaking the draught. Warming their bodies in the dying evening heat. The larger than normal number of men out on that evening was a clue for the ones in the know.

Emerging from the door, to the left of the screw sitting on his chair, came a figure dressed in prison clothes, his head and face covered with the blue sleeve cut off a prison sweatshirt. Holes cut out for the eyes; one higher than the other resembling John Merrick in the move Elephant Man. In his hand, hanging down, just behind his right thigh, in a vain attempt to conceal it, was a mop bucket. In the mop bucket was a cocktail of human waste collected over the last few days for this very act of retribution. The contents of the bucket hit the head of the screw from behind. In seconds the warm breeze wafted the pungent aroma into every nostril. The whole yard gave a huge cheer. The effluent attacking assassin, having delivered his load with the aim of a marksman, left the bucket on the head of the screw before legging it back inside. By this time the riot alarm had gone up. The CCTV gave away the deed. Help was on its way.

When the shout goes up its all hands, or in this case, screws to the wing. The feculent, wheedling fugitive was half way up the first flight of stairs, still sporting the head gear of a guilty man, when the wing S.O. rounded the corner. Bang to rights. Still emitting the smell of his weapon of choice. As in life the soldier is in the firing line while the generals look on from a safe distance. The screw got a new name. Mr Pooh. The assailant got the block and a ship out. Now on the twenty-one day lay down; roundabout of trouble.

Badminton is my game. Football on the field is not for me. The gym has four full size courts and three times a week I play. My opponent is a seasoned player who takes great delight in my inexperience. I aim for one point; if I get two I call it a win. Week after week I play, trying for that two point victory. Fitness and gym workouts get me in shape. Every morning at eight o'clock I start an hour of fitness work in the gym. To those who stand the test of time comes victory. I win my first game after only four months, putting an end to my opponent's enthusiasm. He never plays me again. The next guy to take me on beats me in the first game twenty-one to two. And that's how it goes until I am too good for most cons. The gym screws play me when they need to sharpen up their game. My determination is my undoing. It's more and more difficult to find an opponent. Often I play two on one. Seven times a week I play badminton now. If I can't find a partner I hit the shuttle against the wall for an hour. Whatever I do I want to be the best at it. I buy the best racket, the best shoes, even socks made for badminton. I'm addicted to the game. Or am I just addicted to doing something other than thinking? Thinking is my enemy. My thoughts attack my sanity.

Judicial review

Out of all the cons on D wing not many are conducive to my lifestyle. I don't take drugs and I don't make, or drink the jail alcohol, hooch. I keep myself to myself and don't get into the loan business, where the rates are two back for every one given. Eddy, an ex goalkeeper, who played football in his youth for Manchester United, alongside George Best and other greats of the day, has become a good friend. He, like me, has nothing to do with the day-to-day problems of the wing. Unlike me he is guilty. Seven years for hitting some guy with an iron bar. Only right I hear you say! Eddy is one of the nicest guys you could meet. A gentle giant. So I know there is more to his story than meets the eye. So I ask him.

"Why did you hit a guy with an iron bar Eddy?"

"Some guy, right, comes to me house Tony and hits me youngest with this bar. Split his face open man. So I went out and battered him."

"With his own iron bar Eddy?"

"It was yeah. My young 'un was in t' hospital. Nine stitches Tony in his face. Down here." He runs his finger from his eye down to his cheek bone.

"So why did you get jail Eddy?"

"Don't know. He got let off."

"Have you any other violence?"

"Just some stuff a long time ago when I used to fight after t' game."

"I think you've been badly done to kid."

"I'm always telling me kids to stay out of trouble but ya know what kids are like."

"I do. I used to be one. How many you got Eddy?"

"Fourteen."

"What? To one woman?"

"No. Three women but I look after them now, the young 'uns. The old 'uns get on with their own lives."

"So do ya have a woman now?"

"No I won't put up wi' them not looking after me kids, right? She used to take them down t' pub and spend all t' shopping money on drink so I put her out."

"How come you don't have any visits from the kids?"

"I couldn't do with it Tony it would do me head in't have them come here."

"But you're doing a long time Eddy." His head drops down with the weight of pain he's carrying.

"When I get to a cat D I'll see them." The overweight, unfit and vegetating bulk of a man who was once a professional football player fills the seat. I'll have to work on him. See if I can't get him up to at least one beep on the beep test. Right now he's not fit enough to switch on the beep test machine. But first I have to find out why he drinks bottles of antacid liquid like its honey.

"Why do you have so much trouble with acid Eddy?"

"For fifteen years I've been killed with it Tony. I've 'ad the camera down; they want t' operate but I'm not having it, right?"

"You have helicobacter pylori Eddy and you need a blood test then two weeks of antibiotics. In two weeks you can be finished with all this acid. Do you trust me Eddy?"

"Why haven't doctors said I have... whatever you said it was?"

"Do ya trust me?"

"Yes. But I've had all t' tests and it's an ulcer in me..." My bad habit of butting in again stops him.

"The ulcer is not the problem, the problem's giving you the ulcer Eddy."

"I'll put in an application in t' morning Tony. What do I tell the doc, heli pill what?"

"I'll write it down for ya and don't let him fob you off with some old bull, Eddy; you have to stick to your guns if he won't give you the test."

"I will Tony."

"Don't come away without giving blood. If I'm wrong you keep drinking the white stuff, if I'm right you are free from acid forever. Is it worth giving it a go?"

"I'll do it tomorrow Tony. Write down that thing I have t' ask him." Eddy hands me a scrap of paper torn from the stage newspaper of a week ago, and a pen he's using to fill in the crossword puzzle and pick out his horses, the ones he would bet on if he was out in the world. He just has to find a copy of the next day's paper to see if he got any winners. That's his time filler.

I know how much pain he's in. Not from the acid but because of the separation from his children. I do know why he can't see them from inside here. It's not the shame of being a criminal or the environment of a prison visiting room. It's the loss. The loss of his children over and over again. Every time they go back to their world and he goes to his he loses them all over again. The one thing I could not do when my wife told me to move out was take my children on weekends to McDonald's for milkshake and burgers. The one day, not one day, a few hours of playing Dad then giving them back to their mother was soul destroying. I just couldn't do it. It was killing me in more ways than one. I lived in a one-room upper roof space in an old Victorian house in Carlisle. No windows and a shower down on the floor below. I think if there had been a window I would have jumped out of it.

My day was much the same from Monday to Friday. I worked till five, went home to my room and wallowed in self-pity with a bottle of vodka. Soon the bottle was too small to have the desired effect so I changed the colour from red to blue. It resulted in accidentally setting fire to my room and burning my feet and hands trying to put it out. The children wouldn't benefit from weekends with me when I couldn't hold my emotions together long enough to give them the love I had for them. It was my inability to handle the loss on a week by week basis that stabilised my pain. I had to let them go and that nearly killed me. After the fire I moved on to drugs and moved back to my old town, Whitehaven. I loved my wife and I loved my children but couldn't have any of them. The time was one of grieving. The life I had was without meaning. The work I was doing was pointless and I ended up leaving.

I took up the job of driving a taxi in Whitehaven for a friend of mine, who later on asked me to be best man for him, an honour I accepted with pleasure. The taxi job was a big step on my way back from the brink. People and getting to know the back streets of my old town again was fun. I didn't know where anything was at first. Even the big shops I couldn't find. It had been twelve years since I drove my motorbike round the roads of that old town. The same as the twelve years I have to do now in prison. Women seemed to have an affinity to taxi drivers and I didn't mind the attention but I would never again put my heart in the hands of a woman. When they closed the front door of their house I never looked back. Until, that is; I met Dawn. It had been two years when I walked into the taxi office and seen this twenty year old girl with her sweet smile shining through dark wavy locks up at me from the comfy settee in the corner. Her hands hidden in the pockets of her brown sheepskin coat. Her hair cascading down her pulled-up fur collar. The musty smell of the office was drowned out by her perfume.

The controller's radio chatter couldn't win my attention. That was the start of our seven years together. It was six months after we met before I gave up my harbour-side apartment for the comforts of a family home with two young children. Still not my children. But loved never the less.

I know something of Eddy's pain. Is it right to cut them off? It can never be right. I carry the worn-out photo of two small children who I know. My children who I said good bye to long ago. When one was eight and the other six. Now they are grown up people. The last time I told my son I loved him was when he was six years old. Sobbing half-way up the stairs where he stood. Probably wondering what mummy and daddy were crying for. Two weeks before Christmas she asked me to leave, so I did. The last time I saw my wife was my son's seventh birthday. The scuba diving business was bankrupt. She had sold the family home and was living in a council house. No internal doors. No carpets. No happiness. I asked her if she was happy and she said no. I went to the house to see him on his birthday, she told me I should wait in the car and she would send him out. We sat outside in the car where he opened his present and I wished him a happy birthday. A joke. I have never seen my now ex-wife from that day to this. She divorced me in the winter of 1995 without my agreement. Before anyone becomes a father he should learn how to become a husband. Will those small children forgive me for not having the strength to be even a weekend dad? How can I think of forgiveness when my heart is full of hate for the ones who lied to get me in here? The bible says I must forgive. It says God so loved the world he gave his only begotten son, (His unique son, whose son isn't unique?) John 3-16.

When the probation officer asked about my children she thought it odd that I should still be upset about the subject. I find it odd that she didn't know how I felt. Still feel. Does it become okay after a given length of time? How long? If it does I'm not there yet. Now I have another son to mourn over and I have just found out from the local newspaper Dawn; that girl I met in that taxi office has married some guy. Another taxi driver. The wedding photo in the pages of a local rag is the way I find out the mother of my son has given him a new dad, Darren. When she said no contact I guess she meant it. My daughter visits me here, now a beautiful young woman. My son I would pass in the street. Unless he still looks like the small boy stuck to the wall of my cell with a blob of toothpaste. That small boy crying on the stairs. For so long I have hoped for their return to me. Locked up in children's homes because his mother who fought to keep him couldn't deal with his unique intelligence. Is he one of the kids who stopped growing up at the gates of some institution? Damaged, lost and alone.

Eddy's trip to the doc is a great success. He has the bug that lives in the gut. Two weeks and the acid has gone. Now I can help him in the gym. He thinks I am the all knowing one. We start by walking round the gym hall for five minutes. Having been a footballer he thinks he can do more. Slowly is the way to go. The first thing Eddy has done in years is walk round for five minutes. The next day he can feel the lactic acid-filled muscles making his legs heavy as he climbs the stairway from the food serving hatch on the ones. The first time in fifteen years his food has not given him pain ten minutes later. The acid in his legs has replaced the acid in his gut. It will be a long time before he's fit for badminton, but time is not our enemy in here.

My yearly calendar moves on. The day I will get out in that far off year passes. Christmas goes by with as little fuss as I can get away with. Again I send the cards. One to Kevin full of good wishes. One to the police letting them know it's one year closer to their day of judgement. My judgement.

My savings bring that day when I can listen to good music on a good sound system. The most important date comes. The day I have to tell the prison how sorry I am for the terrible wrong I have done. Same questions. Same answers. Same anger welling up when some pseudo-psychologist going under the title 'personal officer,' thinks he has all the facts. First question winds me up fit to burst.

"So, Tony, it says here you are a driving instructor. Where did you do that?" Even this small fact is wrong.

"Mainly under water. I worked in Malta. Before I was kidnapped by D.S Hatwood. Does it say that there?"

"Sorry you worked where?"

"Malta."

"So you were a driving instructor in Malta?"

"No. I was a diving Instructor. Forget the R. I took people under water and swam with them till they ran out of air then we got out. If everyone got out alive it was a good dive."

"So where does the driving come into it?"

"Well it doesn't is the only answer to that. I drove the pick-up to the dive site, does that count?"

"Someone's put driving down here. I'll make a note in your file."

"Just change it. It's wrong so just take your pen and change it. Go on cross it out and change it for the truth." Why does it wind me up so much?

"I've made a note. How do you feel about the victim of your crime?"

"What crime are we talking about?"

"The…" he turns the pages of my ever growing file, "attempted murder. What else are you in for? Oh the drugs. I can't see anything else here. Swindles is it?"

"No not drugs. The victim! Why do you use the singular form? Are we not all victims in this? Is my mother not one and my children who had to read what their father is said to be in a newspaper? Who knew as much truth as you do?"

"They are all victims of what you did, yes, but how do you feel toward Swindles?"

"I don't give him any thought at all. If he wins the lottery or dies in the gutter with a pin in his arm it's all the same to me. The poor mug only did what his small drug plundered brain could tell him. He was used by the police to weave their web of deceit. I pray for him."

"Are you sorry?"

"That's the one. That's the one that will keep me in here till I have done every day I've been given. No, I have a lot to be sorry for but that's not one of them so put me back in my cell and I'll see you next year. Don't ask the next question, I am not rehabilitated from the desire to kill. You can't fix what is not broken. I am not guilty of this crime. Write that in my file then someone may read it and let me out."

"Okay Tony, what course work do you want to do in the next year? Advanced Thinking Skills will help you. Will you let me put you down for it?" He, like all the others before him, can't deal with innocence so he doesn't listen.

"I do enough thinking in here I don't need to get a certificate in it."

"I have to put a plan in your file for the next year. Why don't you go on the course and show willing?"

"Why do I need the course?"

"You can go on an assessment first to see if you will benefit from it."

"How many are found not to need it?"

"A guy last week was turned down. It was thought it would make him a better criminal."

"I'll do it to get you off my back. You've just given me the way out."

"Is there anything you would like to ask me Tony?"

"Can I go home?"

"No. When is your parole date?" he looks again into the depths of my file, "Only two more years." He says with a hint of encouragement in his voice.

"Forget it; I know I'll never get parole if I don't admit guilt. And that will never happen. No I'm here, or somewhere just like it, till November 11th 2005." Back goes my file for another year only to be taken out by some new kid on the wing to ask the same thing all over again. I shouldn't be so bitter and twisted I know. Gary has done this for sixteen years now. He has I.D.O.M. on the front cover of his file; In Denial Of Murder. He can't ever get out. I still need to get to a Cat D prison so I have a better life. With four years under my belt I should be close to a Cat C. One step away.

After my assessment for the all important course deemed me unfit to attend I get a tick in a box that helps me on my way. For some reason that I don't understand I have to make a case for my down grade to Cat C. I fill in the form that asks me why I should be given the Cat C status. I answer the questions with. 'In the last five years I have not tried to kill anyone.' For the question. Why do you think you should be given Cat C. I answer, 'self praise is no praise at all.' The answer to my request is a big fat 'NO'. No reason given just a 'no', try again next year. For one it's not a year on year situation. It's not an obligation to consider category status yearly but six-monthly. And a 'no' just won't do. Not for me anyhow. The outcome of my need for a real answer results in; 'too long left to serve'. A great answer and not legal. What other people say about you is who you are not what you say about yourself. I was once waiting for my turn on the pool table down in the dining room that's not a dining room but a games room. The two guys playing at the time had a small dispute regarding a foul shot. Kingy who is a Jamaican mank born in Manchester Royal Infirmary and who's never been outside Manchester apart from when he's been in jail said.

"Ask Tony if it was a foul 'cos he won't lie." Kingy was there when I was asked to go tell a lad he was wanted at the window by somebody. The lad said, "Tell him I'm in the shower lad."

I went back to the guy at the window and told him what the lad had told me to say.

"He says to tell you he's in the shower," I said.

"Oh; is he in the shower?" He asked me.

"No that's just what he told me to tell you. He was in his cell when he told me to give you that message mate." I won't lie for myself so I wouldn't lie for him. That's what kingy seen and that's who he know me to be. We should live the person we want to be and then maybe others won't have to ask 'who we are.

The time has come to put my typewriter into overdrive. When Argos no longer sold ribbons for my model of typewriter I was allowed a new one thanks to governor Brown once more on my side. It's sent in by my mother. My new electric typewriter has a memory and with the push of one button it prints off my words in machine-gun fashion. I need something to occupy my mind. All my appeals have failed. My kidnapping has been swept away with the claims of voluntary repatriation. That's the police line. The courts say I was extradited, but they have no documentation from Malta. I can't get Maltese papers. Interpol seems to think I have no right to know anything about my case. No wonder, I have documentation warning them about the dangers of habeas corpus.

On the way to the B.A. flight, waiting on the runway in Malta, I was given back the boat ticket money. I was amazed at the time. 'Sign the receipt to say you have it and away you go', the Interpol copper said. With my hands sporting chub handcuffs and in the orange glowing light on the runway it seems I signed my freedom away.

There was no reason given for my refusal only hours earlier in signing anything to do with my arrest. Or the answer I gave to the question asked by Interpol, 'do you want to go to the UK?' 'No' was the answer then and 'no' was my stand all the way through. I was taken from a safe place to the UK without legal rule of law. Kidnapped punishable my life in prison. If you're not a copper that is. I did find out my ticket was paid for using the private credit card of the police officer who kidnapped me. B.A. wouldn't give me a copy of the document. One thing I did find out is that I can make an application to the court for a Judicial Review. I could and should have done it for the abuse of power when the Crown Prosecution Service blocked my application to marry. You don't know what you don't know. I learn quickly.

The first lesson given to me free of charge by the prison is; don't keep papers you don't want them to see in your own cell. The day letters arrive under my door from The Strand High Court in London the interest from security screws increases. They turn over my cell weekly to find out what I'm doing. Stripped to my birth suit and standing on a towel in the cell.

My legal mail is covered under prison rule 37a and can't be read. They still try. In two months I have my case ready for the high court. But the prison's dirty-tricks department still have one or two cards up their proverbial sleeve. When I present to them the letter from the court with the court attendance date, they inform me I will not be going anywhere without a request by the courts to 'produce the prisoner.' I inform them I am not the defendant, the number one governor is, then serve him with a summons demanding his attendance on the due date. My letter to the court changes the prison's stand on my attendance and I'm told I can go. However, I will have to pay the cost of the trip. I'm ready this time, being forewarned by a fellow discriminated comrade. And by my good and loyal lawyer Kevin, who still works for me for free from behind the scenes.

"Please give me the costing and I need it itemised." I tell them.

The total bill is three hundred and fifty-four pounds. Transport to and from London, food for the trip, bed and breakfast in prisons the length of Britain, and the screws' pay to escort me. I have to pay for my own incarceration. How can this be so? Well it isn't. It's a ploy to stop me taking them to court. One that fails in one day. When I send the bill to The Strand along with the case law that beats it, the prison drops the fee request. They don't like Philadelphia Lawyers. I still have Kevin Commons on my side who isn't a Philadelphia lawyer. He sends me documents needed for The Strand, filled in and ready to go after I put my mark on them. Advance Thinking Skills? What a joke, I do nothing but think. My case is that the prison is wrong when it says time left to serve is too long as the reason for refusing me category C status. A life sentence prisoner always has ninety-nine years left to serve. If the prison was correct, a lifer would never be eligible for cat C.

The February crisp morning air leaves glistening glass spiders' webs hovering over the well kept grass lawns surrounding the gate-house. The trees that had so much beauty on my way here in the springtime now hold a new beauty. Their winter branches wave me on my way; stags antlers swaying in the light breeze. No leaves to give shade to the hawthorn below; or to whisper to each other in the breeze. No sun to make the trees wilt. Beauty nevertheless when the only colour you've seen for so long is pale blue walls or grey faces on men without hope.

The van eats up the motorway mile by mile heading back south from where I had come. One night in the local jail at Birmingham, breakfast and onward. London bound to The Strand. One night will be spent in Pentonville prison, where it's considered upmarket if you have a toilet seat. In the morning I'll be in The Strand putting my case to the High Court Judges of the British legal system. How I wish it was to put my appeal to them. I think that's why I want to go with this case, just to stand where I should have stood in my fight for justice. Two others on the van are on appeals against their sentences. The Victorian prison looks just like Durham from the outside. A tree is resting lazily against the wall in the reception yard. Over the road a sad old façade is hidden behind a scaffolding fascia.

"When was the last time someone got off from here?" I ask the escort on the van.

"Got off? What do you mean?"

"Escaped."

"Don't worry son you aren't staying here. Says on your file you have to be housed overnight at Bellmarsh prison."

"This is the jail for The Strand isn't it?" I say.

"Normally it is, yes. Says Bellmarsh here so Bellmarsh it is. Have you upset some one? It's a local cat A. prison. You might meet Charley Bronson there. He's up tomorrow on his appeal."

"So there's me and Charles Bronson. Both at court in the morning?"

"Yep, that's about it son. Have a good night's sleep and we'll see ya at eight o' clock."

The reception screw in London's maximum security prison, Bellmarsh, is big and black with a hand that makes his pen look like a toothpick. House blocks and three to a cell is the deal here. One night isn't long but I do want to be in a single cell. What good are friends if you can't call on them when you need them?

"Stand on the line boy; name and number." It must be my boyish looks he's addressing.

"Crowe CP3703."

"From Garth hey? What ya doing down here then?"

"Court. The Strand."

"Appeal?" rhetorical question. "Sentence or conviction?"

"No neither. I'm not the one in the dock. I'm taking the Governor of Garth to court." Screws hate Governors so I'm on good ground for me single cell.

"What's that for then?"

"Prison rules. He doesn't know them and I do. Call it a free lesson in his climb to the Home Office."

"House block 3 cell number..." I stop him there; me butting in again.

"Would that be a single cell? See I could do with a night of working on the case and I don't need some kid asking if I did what I'm in for all night. My mate in Long Lartin told me this was an all-right jail."

"Who would that be then?"

"Danny Burns and me old mate from north of the river David..." He stops me this time.

"One eye and six foot tall?"

"Ya know him?"

245

"Okay I'll sort ya out and tell Davy, Jerry says 'hi' when ya see him next man."

"Will do Jerry good on ya mate. Where do I go now?"

"Jail to jail you needn't strip off. Get some food and I'll have ya taken to the house block as soon as the doc has seen ya son." From boy to son; that's a result.

That's what friends are for, I say. My single cell and one night with association couldn't be better. For prison life that is. Barry George is here waiting for trial. They, the police that is, say he is the one that planned and executed the killing of Jill Dando. I somehow can't see it myself. This guy couldn't plan a shopping trip to the corner store. How do they come up with such suspects in the first place? I'm tempted to say they just look for the first local nutter and lock him up. But where would that leave me? I will predict a guilty verdict for the mastermind of the assassination of Jill. Then years of fighting until the public have forgotten all about it. Like Rab, he too will walk down the steps of The Strand a free man with the police saying 'we are not looking for anyone else in connection with this case'. Meaning we think he did it and the system let him go. What do the police not get about the word detective? For once do some detecting. Rant over, I digress.

The short ride to the rear entrance of the court in the centre of London takes twenty minutes through the rush hour traffic. Armed police are standing on the main gate, their black uniforms giving them a military-like role. Assault rifles across their chests, their bulk made bigger by the bullet-proof vest strapped to them. Not a reception committee for me. I can see, on the other side of the iron gate, the distinct markings of a cat-A van. We have to wait while the prisoner in it is moved from the van to the court cells. I can just see through the body of men as they open the van door. The walk to the court door is three steps. I wonder if it's anyone I know? For a second I see the beard of the man dressed in prison clothes, very bright yellow and blue. Only one man who I know could fit that beard. Charles Bronson; given the category far greater than Cat A. He is the most dangerous man in the prison system. I can only imagine the prison service hasn't met the same people as I have. This guy has never hurt anyone ever. Apart from in the boxing ring.

He pissed off the prison system and he has taken the odd hostage here and there, giving him his life sentence. But like I say, never has he hurt anyone physically. He's a lifer now and never been on normal location for years. Solitary confinement is good for the body; he's a big man and a strong man, holding the world record for push-ups. Not so good for the head and when, like Charley, not his real name, you have to live up to the reputation, you can't help but go a bit mad. But hey! The guy is okay and a good fellow poet. I wish him all the best.

When he's safe inside the stone walls of the court it's my turn to run the gauntlet. No gun-toting police for me this time. Just one Group Four guy, overweight, over-keen and underpaid. He hands me over to the court officers. Relinquishing his responsibility until he has to take me back. In the cell I have the last chance to cross the 'T's and dot the 'I's. I'm ready for the fight.

Ten o'clock the door swings open, two guys, handcuffs at the ready, stand outside. The cuffs on we set off up the stone steps, one guy in front, the other behind; me in the centre of the escort. The narrow tunnel walls catch my shoulders. The way winds upward; onward. An old brown wooden door blocks our progress; we stop. The cuffs are removed before the door opens revealing the impressive Dickensian court room. My position high up in the dock gives a good view of the public gallery to my left. The wigs and gowns are in the front facing the three Law Lords sitting even higher than my box. This is stuck to the wall like a swallow's nest under the eve of an old house. One seat and one door. The first problem is I am not on trial. The jail is. The Judge in the middle of the trinity asks the first question and I'm impressed.

"Why is Mr Crowe in the dock?"

"He is a serving prisoner M'lud." The wig pipes up from the floor making half an effort to stand.

"That may well be. However, he is not the defendant in this case. Is that not right?" Mr Greenhow The barrister is lost for words.

"Well yes but..."

"I would ask you to bring Mr Crowe into his proper place so he can put his case to the court in the appropriate manner."

"That would mean moving him through the public area of the court M'lud."

"And? Mr Greenhow. Your point is?"

"It may cause distress to the public. Seeing a prisoner handcuffed in the corridors of the halls."

"This is a court of law and as such it is inevitable one would see prisoners coming and going from time to time. Is it not?"

"Quite M'lud. I take your point." Mr Greenhow gives half a bow and sits. Back through the door we wind our way through the labyrinth. Down we go until we are walking through the wide open, bustling halls of justice. Courtrooms line up on both sides, numbered; starting at one and going on to I don't know what. The court looks even bigger from my rightful place next to Mr Greenhow. It's not easy to stay focused but I have to start.

"My Case is one of abuse of power and I bring it against the governor of HMP Garth M'lud. On a review

248

of my security categorisation the governor gave the reason for not downgrading me to category C as, 'too long left to serve'. I submit this is not a lawful reason but only one factor in the decision, not looking at all the other information regarding my progress in the prison system. I submit that the points regarded in the categorisation of a prisoner are not how long he has left or a life sentence prisoner would never meet the criteria. He having ninety-nine years to serve whatever the stage of his sentence is at the given time. No, the point is this; is the prisoner a danger and should it be made as difficult as befitting for him to escape? I am not saying I should or indeed should not be categorized as C. I am saying the reason given is not a legal valid one.

My next point is this M'lud. It says in the prison manual a prisoner's categorisation should be reviewed whenever there is a change to his situation and at least every six months. Garth has a policy of yearly reviews and will not look at my request until that time has elapsed. This again is a breach of Home Office rules. Can I add, this is a ruling by this court and here is the ruling on it." I hold up the legal document for the usher to take to the Judges.

"It only remains for me to say I have had every obstruction put in my way in bringing this case here. It is only through the help of the court and friends that I am here today. The prison service has no regard for any rights I have and they are contemptuous at every turn. I hope by bringing this they will understand they cannot disregard the law. Or the rights of those it is meant to protect, prisoner or not. That M'lud is my petition."

"Mr Greenhow I don't like what I am hearing here, what do you have to say?"

"Well M'lud the matter of category is one for the governor and it is given credence on individual merit."

"What is the answer from the governor to this charge, Mr Greenhow?"

"He has not given me instruction on this. However the prison service categorisation of prisoners is a matter for the prison that is holding the prisoner and if the level of public protection is such then the categorisation must reflect that. Mr Crowe is serving a twelve year sentence for attempted murder. The Judge said in his pre-sentencing speech, 'this is the worst case I have sat on in my twenty five years as a high court judge...'"

"That may well be. However, the governor of HMP Garth is said to have no concern for what my fellow colleague had to say, just that the time left to serve was too long for this prisoner to be a category C prisoner. Am I not correct?"

"I would have to take instruction on that."

"Then I advise you to do just that."

"The governor is not in the court M'lud."

"Then we will set a date one week from now when you will bring him to this court to answer."

"I have other commitments would it please the court if we could set the date for three weeks?"

"Very well three weeks; I warn you, I do not like what I am hearing. Mr Crowe thank you and may I say well done in the way you put your argument, we will meet in three weeks from now and if you have any difficulty in doing so please inform this court."

"Thank you for your time and comments M'lud." No time is wasted. The cuffs are on, the case papers are stuffed back into my plane white carrier bag and we're off. Back the way we came dodging as we go the floating figures dressed in black flowing gowns. Legal bundles tucked under one arm, looking at their watches strapped to the other. It seems they're always in the wrong place. A reminder of Alice in Wonderland's white rabbit. Or is it my jail pace that makes the world faster than I remember it?

The whiteboard in the cell-area is the only reminder of Charley's whistle-stop visit. Cat A. prisoners don't stay outside prison longer than necessary. A cartoon drawing of the Judge with the caption 'Hope you have a nice Easter judge' is the work of the most dangerous man in the system. I wonder if he knows it's only February. I guess he never won his appeal. I have to wait for my escort to have lunch before I start the long trip home. Two jails and an overnight stay in Birmingham's Winston Green is a price worth paying. Will I win in three weeks time? How can I lose? It's a done deal as I see it. Then I can move to the jail closest to my old town. Closer for my mother to visit. My now only visitor, along with my youngest son. I've been in jail all his life, bar the one year I was living in Malta on the run.

It's always a fight when I want something. I have a great gift of upsetting governors. If I lose this case I will have no hope of ever getting downgraded to cat C. I know that much.

Bryan the Buddhist is a new recruit to our happy band of men here in Garth. He lives a life of peace and karma as long as no one upsets his yin or yang. His favoured line is, 'what will it all matter in two hundred years?' He believes that the fly I swat on the window could be my uncle Jerry. Jesus, he doesn't do. Heroin he does do. Sixteen years is what he's doing now for selling drugs on a wholesale scale. The boss of the team fled to Holland where he is serving a sentence for drugs and corruption. The police in Amsterdam bugged his phone for the Liverpool police and found out he had half the force of the city on his payroll. People who listen at keyholes come to mind. Bryan's problem is the big crime should have given him a big wad of cash under his bed. The court wants tens of thousands of pounds under the Proceeds of Drugs Confiscation Act. When I was in Long Lartin my mate Steve lost three aeroplanes, two houses, four cars and still had an order for two million pounds slapped on him; for payment after he had served his twenty five years. Big crime carries big sentences. Confiscation orders are the new problem in the fight to earn a dishonest living. I lost my BMW and, well, all I had really. Not just money, my life was taken and thrown into the bin. Now I have what I can fit into two blue boxes that the prison gives me when they carry out a blitz on volumetric control. What will it all matter in two hundred years? Maybe I should get the little fat guy to sit on my bed-head. In spite of Bryan's Buddha-build he plays a good game of badminton. Now and again he wants to voice his disbelief at the odd line call, even when I tell him I can't lie. Unlike, it would seem, a Buddhist. But on the whole we have a great battle in the gym.

My small band of friends is growing. Split in two halves; the pals from the chapel and the non-God ones. Bryan has a foot in both camps. He attends Wednesday evenings in the chapel. More for coffee and biscuits than for God. He sells out Buddha for a chocolate biscuit. I'm asked all the time why I go to the chapel, what's the scam? They want to know. Life is the scam I tell them but they don't get it and I don't know if I do but I keep on going. It says in the bible, when Jesus asks if they will leave him, 'where will I go?' that's what I feel. Without God what is there? How can a fly be my uncle Jerry? Without God life would be pointless. I don't understand the bible but I don't understand how a caterpillar can turn into a butterfly, be it Uncle Jerry or not. But it does. And the new butterfly is a new creation. Nothing of the old caterpillar is left in the butterfly. Did you know that? I didn't.

I look amongst the small number of people in my life for the reason I live here. I still believe I have a purpose or I would be outside these walls of grey. But I also know I'm a prisoner of revenge. I still have the anger living inside me and where there is strife there is the devil in the centre of things. Do I have God or the devil living in me? When I listen to Greig or the Blue Danube I have the peace of John's gospel filling my soul. Other times I have the rage of a man wronged by men not fit to live in God's great world. I know the day I will bring them to book for their false witnessing. It's biblical! God detests lies. The judge said the best made plans of mice and men. I have eight years to make my plan. They will not go awry.

Serenity is easier lost

The biggest day in the Christian calendar is here again; Easter. The death and better still the resurrection of Jesus Christ. Time for the chapel to swell at the doors as the C of E Christians fill the normally empty seats. Christmas and Easter Christians that is, not Church of England. Free cup of tea and a small drink of wine pulls them in from every wing. Still we can't all do Easter together; Roman Catholics have their day and the rest of the world have theirs. Saturday for Rome and Sunday for R.O.T.W. (rest of the world). 'One God', they say in the creed that both recite every Sunday; or Saturday. One cup for all believers. So why do we have two Easters? Like I say I don't get a lot of it but I do know God is the first and the last. Easter isn't in the bible. The bible says it's the time of Passover. The last supper was the feast of Passover. I can't find baby rabbits or anything to do with eggs in there either. What I see in my bible is the giving of himself for our sin. Jesus went freely to the cross and paid the price that we should have paid. Why? Simple answer is love. He says, 'no love is greater than that a man lay down his life for a friend.' Like I've said before, he's my friend and I know if I was the only one he would have given himself just for me. My bible came from an old cell I was in. A King James written in old English. Bound in black leather with gold lettering and gold leaf pages. The date inside the cover is 1920. There's an inscription on the same page and it reads: 'March 7th 1923. A gift to Wilfred Chappell from his Uncle & Aunt, Bill & Mary-Ann, wishing him many happy returns of the day. Thy word is a light unto my feet & a lamp unto my path. Psalm 119, 105'.

I'm intrigued. How did it get into that cell? Who is Wilfred Chappell? Did this bible help him get through some hard times? If only it could talk!

I've heard it said if your bible's falling apart your life isn't but if your bible's in good condition it's not being read so your life is falling apart instead. This old bible needs to be read until it's falling apart. By me.

On Wednesday evenings an outside church group comes into the chapel. They sing or play music with joy in their hearts and a smile on their faces. Chocolate biscuits and a cup of coffee are served up by the orderly. My job if I ever get the chance. No religious boundary for this time of Christian fellowship. Just all-out fun in the madness. A screw-free-zone that lasts for one hour. One of the visiting happy-clappy Christians asks me if I'm born again. Visions of David Ike telling the whole world he was Jesus Christ in an interview on TV leaps into my mind under the banner of; 'Born Again Christian'. I don't think twice before distancing myself from this loony religious minority group. No, I don't think so. I tell her. Truth is I don't think at all, John 3 says I am. In the words that Ricky told me in Durham I am born again. I'm now under the religious heading of 'other'.

These evenings are a diverse experience with all manner of ways to give us a picture of Jesus' love. This night it's the turn of Gregg. His performance of the whole gospel of Matthew from memory with a dramatic deliverance is stunning. The words become alive. The vision he creates transports me back in time to the hills and the dusty roads of the bible. Jesus in the garden. The emotional rendition of the crucifixion is heart wrenching. The joy of the resurrection. A roller coaster ride. The peace of transfiguration. There's not only drugs can take your head out of prison for a time. Who was this man Jesus? When I'm back in my cell the

255

book of Matthew gets my full attention. The dramatisation has brought it to life. It sparks Pauline into a creative mood and she organises a play for us to perform. Nothing from the bible. The subject is history and the great plague. Throwing in for good measure the signing of the Magna Carta in 1215 by the then King John. Irony; seeing as in it is the first time Habeas Corpus was brought into law. Strengthened in 1679, the act is a procedural device to force the courts to examine the lawfulness of a prisoner's detention. A right that I'm denied every day I'm held without the explanation as to how I ended up back in the UK to stand trial in the first place.

Peace is fragile, even more so in prison. My next door neighbour is Barney, a guy from the North East, Ashington. The gift of wisdom hasn't been granted to him. Saturday the horse racing fills the day. Eddy's pad is the venue. Barney, not a partaker of the turf action, appears at the door grunting in his distinct native twang something about a mirror. The cell's full of TV pundits all opinionated over the next race but Barney squeezes his frame in. He addresses me with.

"Where's ma mirror gone?"

"What would I know about your mirror?"

"Come on just give us it back like."

"Are you saying I have your mirror Barney?"

"You've took it from me pad. Just give us it back like Tony." The mirror is a square piece of plastic with silver foil stuck to the back. You get a better reflection from the tin sink, if you clean it that is. I can't believe he's saying I went into his cell and took something; even if it is a useless piece of plastic. That accusation could lead to a cell burned out. Usually with you in it. I'm at the height of anger inside. Calm as a mill pond on the outside.

"Yeah. Let's have it back."

"Are you saying I went into your pad and took it without you knowing? Stealing it from your cell?"

"I just want it back." Ignorance is no defence in my book.

"Don't say another word and get out of here. I'm extremely angry. I haven't taken your mirror and wouldn't go into your cell or anyone's without them being in it. Get out." I move him toward the door.

"But I just want you to give it back..." He stops speaking when my hand cuts off his air intake and crushes his vocal cords. His feet lift off the floor, his eyes bulge. The cell falls quiet. The only sound is coming from Barney's chocking death rattle. With both hands now round his fat neck I slide him up the wall.

"Tony man what ya doing mate? You're gonna kill him mate," says Eddy. Kicking the door open I dump him onto the landing and close the door behind him. Me on the inside and him on the outside.

"Did you hear what he said? If you rob cells in my world Eddy you're gone mate. And that's what he was saying. I warned him. Didn't I warn him? I told him to shut up, but no. He had to give it one more go. Well that was once too much Eddy."

"I thought you was gonna kill him. He went blue mate. What happened to love and peace mate, the bible and all that?"

"Old Testament Eddy I haven't got to the love and forgiveness bit yet. I'm a work in progress. I gave him all the warning I could he wouldn't listen. I'm fuming. I can't believe I let that shit wind me up. I really hate it when someone winds me up. I'm the loser."

"I've never seen ya like that Tony, thought you wasn't gonna let go of him."

"What would I want with his good-for-nothing mirror?" The wing gossips spread the news of the day and add their little bits just to make it unique to them.

Barney? Well he'll survive to wind up someone else in some other jail. There's no telling where his stupidity will take him.

Far off in the distant blue sky, framed by the cell window, a surreal parade of colour drifts by. Every minute a blast of fire shoots upward into the kaleidoscope canopy of colour. Soap bubbles sailing in the summer breeze. Hot air keeping them from crashing back to earth. Freedom from the law of gravity. Just the thing I need to regain my peace. The hot-air balloons float away dropping down over the horizon taking my anger with them. As quickly as they came into sight they disappear. The sound of the fiery blasts from the burner fading away.

Shafted once again

Round two of another fight to be given my category C status. The two day trip to London sees me moving from jail to jail down the length of England. Hours spent in the small box with its plastic seat and mucus-stained decorated walls. Countryside flashing by as the world's pace overwhelms my jail plod. The stroll of the exercise yard has slowed my world to a snail's meander. It's strange being in the real world but at the same time being only a spectator, looking in through the van window.

Reminds me of the story I heard from somewhere, I don't recall where from now. There were two dragonfly larvae, nymphs, living at the bottom of a river. One day the two friends made a pact. They noticed all their peers were compelled to climb to the surface up the stem of a plant. Once out of the water they became a blurred shape stuck to the top of the reed they had climbed. Then they disappeared and were never seen again. One larva said to the other, 'when you are driven to climb the stem into whatever is out there will you come back and tell me what it's like?' The friend answered, 'I will and if you go before me will you do the same for me?' 'I will', the little nymph said. Soon after that it was time. Slowly the first larva headed off to the surface. He climbed and climbed till he was breaking into the spring air. The little fellow watched from the river bed as his friend became that familiar blur stuck to the reed head. Then he was gone. The nymph was now a beautiful dragonfly. Time was short for the dragonfly. He had to find a mate. For in two or three days he would have fulfilled his purpose in life. However, he remembered his friend who was waiting on the river bed. He remembered their pact. When he had found his mate he went back to tell the little fellow what it was like at the top of the stem. He found the spot where he climbed out. His friend was there still waiting at the bottom. But when the dragonfly tried to get back to the river bed he couldn't. The world he knew before was now out of reach. He lived in a new world and he couldn't go back. His friend will one day make that climb then he too will know what lies beyond.

One day I'll be back in the real world. Unlike the dragonfly.

The story is about death. No one has ever come back to tell us. People often say that to me. One person did; I tell them but they don't want to listen. Knowledge is not always helpful. If; that is, you can't deal with truth.

Knowing right from wrong. Having knowledge of the law. With a judge who is sympathetic to your case is a good start. Truth is a stumbling block and I fell over it in my trial. This too is a second trial, however they can't do the same here. Can they?

When I ask for a pen to prepare my case the dirty tricks begin.

"No you might use it as a weapon."

"What would I do with a pen? Write my way out of jail?"

"We've been told by the prison not to give you a pen while you're in the court cells."

"How am I meant to prepare for court without a pen?"

"Have ya used a pen as a weapon in the past?"

"No. They said I chopped a guy up, but I don't think they thought it was done with a ball-point-pen."

"We've got some documentation for you that they said you could have once you were in the cells." The court officer hands me a bundle of papers. The heading on the front page is; The Affidavit of The Governor of Garth Prison.

"How long have I got till we go up to the court?"

"Ten minutes." He says.

"When did they give you these?" I wave the papers in front of his face.

"When the van dropped ya off?"

"Did you not think I might need them right away?"

"We were told to give you them before you went up."

"You were told not to give me a pen and to give me the case put forward against me ten minutes before I went into the court? Is that right?"

"Yes." He shrugs his shoulders.

"And you think that's fine do ya. Do ya not think it's not quite playing the game?"

"I'm just doing me job mate."

"That's what Herman Goering said. Ever thought of getting a new job where ya don't have to think as much. Shut the door I've got work to do."

The twenty pages don't answer the question I'm asking. Why can I not be a cat C with the time I have left to serve? One flick through and I'm on my way through the catacombs leading to the court-room. My sympathetic judge has been replaced by Judge Masterson. Mr Greenhow starts his address.

"I have the sworn affidavit of the governor of HMP Garth M'lud and I think this covers all the points put to the court."

"Mr Crowe do you have anything to add to your case?"

"I do indeed. I was given this affidavit in the court cells only ten minutes ago and I have been refused a pen. As a result of this deliberate ploy to hinder my preparation, I am not in a position to comment on the statement in question. I would therefore ask the court for time to read it. With the advantage of a pen so I can pick out the fact from the fiction."

"Quite. Why was this not given to Mr Crowe sooner?"

"I have no knowledge of the workings of the lower annuls of the court M'lud. We made it available to the court last week."

"How long do you need Mr Crowe?"

"Two hours M'lud should be adequate."

"Mr Greenhow?"

"I have commitments later today M'lud and I have to be in courtroom 4 after the lunchtime recess."

"Quite. Mr Crowe, it is not right that you have not had adequate time. The officer will take you back down and he will give you a pen whilst in the cell. Would half an hour be helpful to you to read the documents?"

"Well I would like more time. I don't see how the court has had the affidavit for a week when they are in London and I was only given it here in the cells. The affidavit came from Garth and so did I. Why was I not given it in Garth?"

"Mr Greenhow do you have the answer for Mr Crowe?"

"I have no instruction on the matter. I cannot comment M'lud." The walk back to the cell takes five minutes. Time taken off my thirty minute concession. The statement has nothing to do with my attack on the governor's illegal stance of too long left to serve or the annual review. It centres round how dangerous I still am. That would answer the no pen question. They are showing the judge how even a pen is still not a safe thing in my hands. The one nail through my heart is this statement.

'HMP Haverigg is a prison that houses inmates in a dormitory environment. Mr Crowe should be housed in a cellular environment where there is more prison staff supervision.'

What this says is that not only am I a danger to the public but to other prisoners. I know I have no chance. No judge will overrule the governor's ruling on a matter of security. The white board still retains Charley's cartoon depicting the three judges who turned down his appeal the last time I was here. Ten minutes or two hours it makes no difference. I'm not winning anything today. It only leaves me to watch yet again as the web of lies works to my detriment.

"When the time for your next review comes I hope you are more successful. I would like to say you have given your case in a well constructed manor." I'm standing, gathering up the papers scattered on the lectern in front of my station. I lift my eyes to the Judge and speak.

"There won't be a next time. You don't understand. I knew when I brought this case that I was shooting myself in the foot. I stand no chance of being given cat C status now. All I will get is victimised. But I don't think it will change a thing in my life. I'm already on the prison's black list of prisoners who know too much and embarrass inept governors. No M'lud I will get nothing. More than nothing."

"Mr Greenhow can you reassure Mr Crowe that he will not, in anyway, be victimised because of this case?"

"No M'lud I cannot give that assurance."

"Why not?" The judge removes his glasses.

"I have no such instruction to do so. However, I am sure he won't be."

"Well Mr Crowe this court is here should you feel a need. We will not look kindly on any abuse of power."

"Thank you for that. Abuse of power is why I brought this case."

They are better at this game than me. I can't compete with professional liars. Still, I filled six months bringing the case and it cost the prison fifteen thousand pounds. If they won't buy new TVs with the money they can stand the bill from The Strand. Back to Garth where no one thought I would win. Some thought I wouldn't even get into court. One of them was the governor.

It's not only inmates that upset the governor. There's something going on in the peaceful world of the chapel. It looks like the dithering of the chaplain will be his undoing. Word is a new team is coming. Not for the Saturday Christians but for the R.O.T.W. Christians. Maybe they will tell me about this born again thing! With little fuss the news is given.

"Retirement calls so I will be standing down as chaplain." The announcement is made on this Sunday, no different to any other Sunday. Apart from this news, which we were all expecting and waiting eagerly for.

"I would like to introduce a new member of our team who will be joining us from today. She will be working with you; I hope you make her feel at home." Rita Carroll A new face who has taken the place of the, Vanessa Cardui, or painted lady. Rita is more of a Blue Adonis. The pastel colours blend tastefully together melting into a gardenscape resemblant of, Garden in Bloom by Claude Monet. The blue Adonis butterfly edged in white lives on her blouse filling the front ready to fly away. She has a radiating glow. A freshness that invites the eye to drink up as much as it can in one sitting. A cleanness that you have to see to appreciate fully. Hard to imagine her being part of my world where freshness and cleanliness don't exist, except in dreams of white sandy beaches on island paradises. Pearls surrounded by blue waters. Maybe just one more who thinks she can gain God's favour by working with the sinners of this world. Looking for a place in the next. What do any of them know about what I am going through? How can they? Let them walk in my shoes for a mile and then tell me how they feel. Let them tell me to forgive and let go of the pain and anger I own. Or does it own me?

She starts with the 'pleased to be here' speech. She's the only one in the room who would say that. Next the testimony comes. Why she believes in Jesus Christ and what He has done for her. Prison has made her who she is. Not working in one, although she has worked for twenty years in the service of prisoners and their families. Prison is where she gave her life to Christ, under a hut sitting amongst the snakes and all manner of other crawling things, she cried out to Jesus Christ. John 3 came true for her. She was born again. Rita Nightingale, as it was then, gave her life to Christ and he took it. Now He's using it to reach other prisoners like her. Like me.

Who can say to her 'What do you know about my suffering?' Twenty years for a crime she did not commit. In a jail that makes this one look like a rest home for those inconvenienced by the law. Humbling the hardiest of prisoners. Ironic thing is they called her prison The Bangkok Hilton. This is more of a Hilton hotel than that could ever be. I've never seen the power of The Holy Spirit, (Ruach Ha'Kadesh in the original text), but I see it now. I can hear God himself laughing at my thoughts of, 'what does she know of my pain?' The white edge of the Blue Adonis matches the white glow framing the space she occupies on the stage. The Sh'khinah glory of God shines on her. Unlike Monet's painting, she has more beauty with less paint.

At the end of the service Rita takes time to speak to everyone as if they are the only one in the room. Her meekness is matched by her kindness. Still, she does wear a belt with keys hanging from it and an attack alarm should some crazed prisoner accost her. Garth is what you may call a comfy-slippers jail. Long-term prisoners and lifers are quiet and just want to move on in the system. However, you can't get away from the insanity in here. Violence still fills every dark corner. Now it's just normal to our daily life. A woman officer was taken hostage last Christmas by a lifer. He was a rapist and it got out on to the wing that he was a sleeper. A nonce hiding, sex offender, beast, there's lots of names for men who invade the personal space of others. Four days over the Christmas period he held her in a store room. The jail was on lock-down, twenty-four-hour bang-up all Christmas. When he threatened to rape her the prison's hit-squad blow a hole in the wall and the siege ended. So did Christmas. No great loss in here. No loss at all for him; a Sikh.

More of a loss was the parcel sent from my friend. When I was working in Malta as a scuba diving instructor I met many women who I enjoyed sharing life with for their two weeks holiday. There was one young woman who was diving with a rival school. She was German, as were most divers. Black hair hung down her back. She filled a small shorty wetsuit perfectly. Her strong physique from working out was evident. Small but well proportioned she was an out-of-season magnet for the instructors. I first saw her when I was new to Gozo. I was hiding out; which was more on my mind than the trophy collecting that the rest of the instructors were interested in. In fact I was working on a pig farm at the time because the diving season hadn't started and I was a stamp missing from my logbook to get the licence to dive as an instructor. Anyway, I was sitting in the window-seat of Moby's restaurant in Xlendi (shlendi) bay Gozo, as I did most nights. Martina was sitting outside with her friend. The two girls drank the local soft drink, kino. Herman the displaced Cuban was first to try his hand. Then David; Jeff, Olly, John being the last to make up the quorum. Every night was the same. Every night they went home alone. One evening Martina came inside the bar. She passed by and acknowledged me with her deep dark eyes, smiling right into my inner being.

"What brand of perfume have you got on?" I asked her.

"What?" She was taken by surprise by my question. Still smiling she said. "Why do you ask?" Her English was better than mine.

"It's very effective. It's a magnet for men. I sit here every evening and your table fills with young men hoping to win your favour."

"It's not my perfume that does it. We are the only two girls on the island who are not local." She laughed.

"Why does it make any difference whether you're local or not?"

"Local girls don't go out with diving instructors."

"And foreign girls do?" I ask her.

"Not this one." A small gold dolphin hung on a thin chain round her slender neck. Her eyes dark pools of polished ebony. She dived three times a year in the clear waters off Gozo. Her home is a small town close to the German city of Nuremberg. Land-locked with the nearest lake hundreds of miles away. Being a diver is not the easiest thing to be when there's no water close by. I never spoke to her again on that trip. It was high season when she turned up again, divers' wall-to-wall. I now had the missing stamp thanks to a potato and some ink. Forgery was in order. Along with the stamp came my diving license for the archipelago. And a job with Moby Dives.

Martina and I would sit at the promenade bars talking about the size of the universe and the meaning of life. She was a university student studying something about medical stuff that I can't even pronounce. Why she had no man in her life never came up in conversation, it was obvious to all the rest. Well she must be a lesbian! Why would she not sleep with the instructors? Why did she only come with girls? I didn't know then what I know now. She was, still is, a born again Christian. Three years it had been since she was in a relationship with a man. No she wasn't a lesbian. She told me once, 'they all think I'm a lesbian.' I don't care what you are I said. 'But I'm not.' 'Just promise me one thing, when I try to take you to bed don't let it happen. I love you too much; sex always takes something away from friendships, it never adds anything of value'. I put the responsibility on her knowing I wasn't up to the self-denial of a beautiful woman. And she is a beautiful, refined woman with class.

When she was home again she would send chocolate parcels. The purple cow. The best in the world she told me. We had a joke about my address. She wrote Tony, Diver, next door to Pissy, Gozo. Keeping my anonymity. I always got the chocolate. Pissy being a famous singer in Malta, he was well known by the post man. This Christmas she sent a parcel to Garth. It contained a small tree and all the other things Christmas was on the outside. Even a small nativity. Not permitted for in-cell use. How I could use it to offend security I don't know but I couldn't have it. Maybe I could cut down the nine inch tree and make a ladder. My mother took it when she came on a visit, as she did every month. She set it all up and I got to see it in a photo taken on Christmas morning. It was a joy and heart tugging to know Martina cared enough to send it.

Rita, another woman who takes my eye, does her daily rounds of the prison bringing light into even the darkest of places. The workshop where I spend my days is her stopping off place just before lunch. Talking to as many prisoners as time allows. Whenever the painted lady entered the room, rarely at that, you knew before you saw her. The strong womanly perfumed aroma filled the air and for the rest of the day you could taste it. Rita has the experience of incarceration. She knows the small things that outside would go by as insignificant are more intense for a man, or woman, when senses have been denied for so long. Men in prison don't need reminding of a loved one's favourite fragrance. My station is in a fenced off corner at the rear of the vast work-space. The blue tool boxes that fill the wall space remind me of the ones holding the knives in Long Lartin. Shadow boards show the shape of a missing instrument. At the end of the working period all tools must be in the box and the box locked. I find it crazy that I couldn't have my Christmas parcel but I can handle cutting tools and knives that could do more harm than a carved inch long wooden baby Jesus. What they fail to understand is I have at my disposal all I need to make a fake tool, put it in the box and use the real one as a weapon. Good job I'm not that way inclined. Rita is interested in the rocking horses I'm working on but in the work area I only have wooden components.

"You need to see one finished to get the full appreciation of what we do."

"When will you have one finished?" She asks.

"I have one now. Waiting for collection in the storeroom, would you like to see it?" She glances down at her watch.

"Okay I would love to. Where do we go?"

"That door in the corner." Pointing over to the small blue door on the other side of the workshop.

"How long have you been working in this shop?"

"Not long. About nine month now."

"Do you like it?"

"I don't mind. Better than some jobs I've done in here."

"You've made two applications for the chapel orderly job haven't you?" I hesitate, wondering how she knows that.

"I have; I would love to work in the chapel but I've upset the governor so I don't think so."

"He's a Christian."

"Who is? The number one Governor?"

"Yes it's John's church that comes in every first Wednesday of the month. For the evening meeting."

"Well it was the one before him who I had my conflict with. What do ya think of that?" A rocking horse standing on its rocking frame is sitting between the stack of pallets.

"You made that?" Her eyes fix on mine as she looks right into me. But with a softness. Not as an intruder; but an invited guest.

"I did, what do think?"

"Where do you get the hair for the mane? And the saddle; is it real leather? It's beautiful Tony."

"Thank you, we buy the hair and the saddle from an outside firm. Jenny gets them to order. I made one for my son last Christmas. The jail sells them for five hundred quid."

"It's really good, you have a gift." Jenny calls from the door.

"Would ya come back in now please?"

"I think we've upset security protocol by coming out of the workshop. I come in here all the time so it must be you." I tell her.

"Don't worry I've worked in prisons a long time now, I know how easy it is to upset security. The job in the chapel is coming up again, would you be interested."

"I have no chance of getting a red band job."

"Would you want the job if you could get past security?"

"I would love it. I've worked toward it for two years. Turned down three times now." She picks up on my dejection apparent in my whole demeanour.

"I'll look at your file and see why you're being blocked."

"Don't believe all you read they can't even get me name right."

"I don't read files usually. I take people as I find them."

Jenny locks the door behind us. She looks at Rita with a disapproving stare. No doubt she got a phone call from the administration department informing her that CCTV cameras have no sight of the storeroom area where we had disappeared into.

Rita has more faith than I have. I don't mean in a biblical sense. But in the prison system with its secrets and opinions that they don't let you know about. You can't object to something you don't know about. What you are in your file is who you are to all who read it. I wonder what Rita thinks of my alter ego. The man between the cardboard sleeve, or jacket as Danny called it that grows daily. Now it will have written in it, 'went into storeroom with chaplain.' But she won't see that. Even the prison staff can only see part of my file. Security files are closed to all but the top of the pyramid of power.

John the number one governor came round the wing once. It was when he first joined Garth. The S.O. showed him to my cell knowing it was a safe bet for a good impression. He was well spoken and asked if he could look inside my cell. I was standing at the door so I moved and he entered. The cell door was wide open. Stood there in the door way the thought came to me and the S.O. at the same time. Governor John hadn't shot the bolt. If I close the door he would be locked in. Taking the governor hostage is impressive in the twisted world of jail thinking. Just as I looked at the apparent mistake from someone so high up, the door lock that is, the S.O. reached over and fired the bolt. Removing any temptation I may have had.

My application for the chapel job fails again with no reason given even with Rita on my side. The post goes to a guy I've never seen in church. A lifer. That means he's a murderer. Hard to accept a lifer is a safer bet for the security department than I am.

At last a New Job

The new chaplain turns up for his first service, socks with sandals at the onset of winter. His wife is part of the team. Music and songs from her acoustic guitar, Peter, Paul and Mary seventies style. A stark contrast to Rita. Andrew has never walked in shoes, let-alone mine. His sermon is all about sin and sinners given in the third person, distancing himself from it. Apart from his story of when he would get angry at being locked in the bathroom by his mother for a misdemeanour He showed antipathy by 'putting' all the items from the bathroom cabinet on the floor. When he heard his mother coming he would put them all back.

He has lived rebellion indeed. My bible says all have sinned and fallen short. His maybe doesn't. I love it when a chaplain gives the absolution with the word 'them'. Forgive 'them' they say, forgive, 'you'. Where do they come into the sin thing? It should be an 'us' thing I think, we're all in the same mess. There is no big sin; the commandments are not in order of severity. In fact it says if you break one you've broken them all. I like people who know they are sinners. They have more to thank Jesus Christ for. He came to set the sinner free. The prisoner but not from prison, from sin. I am free in him. Still I struggle daily with the torment of unforgiving. I know I should forgive those who wronged me. Rita knows only too well how I feel; she was set-up in Bangkok by her boyfriend. She carried the same anger in her walk through prison life. 'Give it to God' she tells me. And I want to. I ask for help to deal with it but when I wake in the morning there it is again, stronger than yesterday.

My mother sends the local weekly newspaper so I don't lose touch with home. That's how I heard of Dawn's marriage to Darren Rawcastle, the guy she told me was a great help to her. Now it gives me more good news, my old pal who told the court he was a friend of many years is dead. The obituary page half way down says Gary Porter died of a drugs overdose. The true meaning of the acronym DOPE, Death Or Prison Eventually. In this case death. No other details given. Overjoyed and full of the sense of justice. God's justice; I tell the world around me one on my list of must sees when I get out is dead. The feeling I get is euphoric. Rita's not impressed with my news and thinks I should be more thoughtful. He wasn't thoughtful when he said the baseball bat was mine. A bat he was never shown by the corrupt police. He was asked by my Q.C if the police showed him the bat from the house and he blatantly said 'NO'. So I wrote a poem to get it out of my system. This is it.

The good die young or so they say

The good die young or so they say and every dog has his day.

For lies there's a price that in the end they all will pay.

One down, more to follow. I know I shouldn't in my glee wallow but Gary Porter said he knew me well! Do you think he did? Did he like as hell.

Porter stood in the box.

Swore on the book, with cunning of a fox but when asked what he knew you wouldn't believe what he was about to do. Know? Says he.

Are you talking to me?

Says he.

That's when the QC began to shout so the trial stopped.

They took Porter out. That did the trick. He was back in a tick.

With knowledge all in order and neat. Now after talking to the police.

He was quite able to weave his web of deceit.

For that lie and many more told by him not once but twice before his life was ended with a rush. The rush of smack running through his veins.

He was always simple he had no brains.

Who will speak up for him now? Who will defend his lying-tongue?

Who will he have to lean on?

On judgement day what can he say? He bore false witness and that; he knows full-well.

I hope he spends eternity in hell. Maybe then the truth they'll tell.

I find it funny that a preacher, whatever their denomination, can put people into heaven when they conduct the funeral service. I've never heard one tell the mourners 'well he or she will have to stand before God and tell Him why they didn't accept Jesus Christ as their saviour.

Truth is, only Christ can get you into God's kingdom.

I saw a film where missionaries went into the rain forest of Ecuador.

The son of one guy asked his dad if he will shoot the savages if they become threatening. No he said they aren't ready. He meant they weren't saved and if he killed them they would go to hell. Whereas if they killed him he would go to heaven.

He was ready to die. They weren't.

Powerful statement. More so because it's a true story.

The savages killed him and the son witnessed the salvation of the whole tribe years later.

All down to that one man.

I wonder if the ones on my list are ready!

Delivered

The new inmate in the chapel job is going to his cat C prison next week leaving the job open. Rita again asks if I still want the position.

"What's the point in even asking?"

"Do you still want it if I can get you in?"

"I do. But I think you're wasting your time."

"You don't know what can be done. I'll talk to the number one. The last guy was the pick of the Roman Catholics. He wasn't that good so I have the upper hand." Who does she mean, number one? Governor John? Knowing Rita it could be God himself.

"Well there's nothing in it... If I don't get it. Why not?"

"Is that a yes then?"

"I've nothing to lose, go for it. My security category review is tomorrow. That's the time I get told I'm not rehabilitated enough to be in a dormitory with killers and thugs.

"Can I sit in on your review tomorrow?"

"It's a bit boring. They ask if I'm dangerous, I say no. Then they say I am and it's all over for another year. But if you want to sit in I don't mind. The S.O. will call me up in the morning before work."

"At breakfast unlock?" she asks.

"No I go to the gym till nine o'clock. After that in the wing office."

"I'll have a word with the S.O. just to ask if I can sit in. There won't be a problem."

"See you in the morning then." I head off to the gym.

"Put in for the chapel job Tony." She calls after me.

"Tomorrow. I'll ask Jenny to do it in the morning after my categorisation hearing. Got to dash. Badminton time." More important right now is getting a court in the gym. First come first served. That old saying in prison. If you're not fast you're last. Buddhist Brian with his 1966 world cup shorts meets me on the court for the grand finale of best of fifty-three games. For a big man he's quick on his feet. When he's not he calls it out. I don't mind too much. I need to play and if he wants to win by whatever means it's no big deal. What will it all matter in two hundred years? As he would say.

When the cell door opens at the morning unlock the words that many dread comes my way.

"Crowe CP3703?" The official address is the first clue to trouble coming. He knows who I am but still he has to ask.

"What now? I'm seeing the S.O. after the gym." Racket in hand and dressed for battle I sense disappointment coming.

"Piss test son," the finesse of jail slang.

"I'm going the gym can't it wait?"

"No you're on me list. Come now and I'll do ya first an' drop ya off at the gym. Can ya give a sample now?"

"I pee on demand now gov." I tell him.

"It's just a dip-test so it won't take long." No paperwork just pee in a cup while the screw watches then a test paper dipped in to see the colour change.

"Dip it in the toilet there and you'll get one."

"Can't do that. Can ya not go again?"

"Whose pee do you think is in there? I don't see anyone else in here."

"It has to be on the camera mate." His eyes lower in his embarrassment.

"I always keep some back for you boys. Never know when you'll need it, come on let's get going." The test, as usual is clear and he takes me to the gym giving me a half-hour workout. Better than nothing. I should have known I would be on top of the list. They would love to have a failed drugs test to prove I wasn't ready for cat C status. Another certificate to add to my pile of passed test results. What does it profit a man to abstain from drugs, or anything for that matter, that he never partook of in the first place? No it's not difficult to do something you never did in the first place. But still it impresses the accusers.

The S.O. sits with my file open and he has his pen ready for the answers I give him.

"Is the chaplain not coming?" I ask him.

"Yes I phoned her, she's on her way. Did you ask her to sit in?"

"No she asked if she could. I don't know why. I'm putting in for the chapel job maybe that's why. The guy doing it now is going to Haverigg next week."

"Do ya think you'll get it? How long have ya done now?" He turns to the first page of my tome.

"Too long. Only four more years to serve." I tell him. Rita comes in. Stuffing a bunch of keys into the leather pouch fixed to her black belt. Not an accessory matching the predominantly pink floral dress flowing round her pretty pale blue shoes.

"Sorry I'm late please go on." She sits next to the S.O.

"The S.O. was asking if I stand a chance of getting the chapel job. What do you think?"

"I can't see why not."

"Maybe a better chance if I was a cat C prisoner in a cat B jail. Then I would have a chance." A sly quip lost over the head of the S.O. But not lost on Rita.

"What have ya done to address your offending behaviour Tony?" The S.O. starts the farce.

"My file tells you I've never been on a nicking in the four years I've been in prison. I've never failed a drugs test. I've not tried to kill anyone in the last four years. I don't know what more I can say."

279

"What about course work?" The stock prisoner answer is 'intercourse is the only course I need'. But with Rita here I resist the vulgarity.

"Advanced thinking skills said I was not suitable for the course."

"Anger management?"

"Are you kidding? I've lived in jail for over four years and never lost me rag and you ask if I need anger management?"

"You look angry to me Tony."

"I am. I'm pissed off and I don't see the point in all this pretence. You know and I know that if I don't admit to the chopping up of the dick-head so called victim I'm going nowhere and getting nothing. I understand you have a job to do. But it gets tedious after five years. Just do what you have to and lets all get on with life. You can put me in a hole in the ground and throw food in three times a day for the next six years then you have to let me out."

"What about parole? You can ask for parole in two years Tony."

"Are you kidding? I can't get cat C, never mind parole. I don't want parole and I don't want to hear about rehabilitation. I can't even get a job in the prison chapel."

"I'm wasting my time then?" He slams my jacket cover closed.

"Like I said you just do ya job and put me back in me hole in the ground for six more years." The SO launches my file into the air and says.

"We won't bother then. Let's just not bother." I start to stand up. Papers falling like confetti on church steps at a wedding. Covering the carpeted floor.

"Is that us then? Are we done?" I take his silence as a yes and make my exit before his head explodes. Hot on my heels is Rita. On the other side of the door, out of earshot of S.O. Al Durham, she asks.

"How can you say you don't want parole? You selfish man. What about your mother who comes to visit every month. What about your son and daughter?"

"Sons plural I've got two. I know. If you don't know, let me tell you. I have no chance of parole without saying I'm guilty. I'm not, so I will not say I am just to get parole. We're talking about something that will not happen. Why waste his time or mine?"

"You don't know that you won't get parole. But if you don't work toward it you'll never get anywhere."

"Go and talk with little Gary and then tell me I stand a chance of parole. He's four years over his tariff. Why? I'll tell ya why. IDOM that's why. What's on my file? In Denial of Attempted Murder? IDOAM. You've seen it; you tell me."

"I was serving a twenty year sentence with no early release on parole. I asked king Bhumibol of Thailand for a pardon and everyone told me the king will never give you a pardon. He had never pardoned a drugs offender. Or a foreigner for that matter. When the list came out on his birthday my name wasn't on it and they all said I told you so. I told them I would petition him again next year. A month after that he gave me the royal pardon. Don't let anyone tell you it can't be done. God is still in control."

"Why am I in prison? Tell me that. What does God want from me? He loves me so much He keeps me locked up in here."

"Forgiveness. Ask him. And get rid of that anger it'll kill you. Don't hold on to it, give it to God."

"He doesn't want it."

"You want it more than he does. Give it up and if you can't, then ask God to take it away."

"I ask Him every day for help with the anger; resentment fills my mind every day."

"Only when I gave up the anger did God get me out of that jail cell." I know she's right about the anger, it's my whole life. More time is spent thinking about the people who stood against me than those who stood with me. It's not good. Every day I ask for deliverance from the torment. I fail in my bid to be re-categorized once more. But I do get a shorter six month review date; that's a first. Maybe they want to bring me to the zenith of anger twice a year.

Tuesday mornings the labour board sits behind closed doors appointing jobs befitting ability. Not much call for robbers or thieves. Jenny is one of the board members, giving me a problem with my application for the chapel job. She has no one to take my place if I go. She's already asked me why I want to go. Even offering an increase in pay from fifteen pounds, a vast amount, to eighteen if I would stay. I need to be in the chapel job, it's where I feel I belong. The pay is six pounds but the peace is priceless. If she's offering more money I must be in with a chance. I can't wait till Jenny comes into the shop. At the end of the morning work-period she returns.

"Tomorrow you start in the Chapel. Stay in your cell till someone comes for you."

"I can't believe it; are you kidding?"

"No you're the new boy in the church from tomorrow."

"Thanks Jenny," I could kiss her.

"It was a close thing but Rita put a request in for you. I told security I've had no problems with you. And you've never been on report. That's amazing."

"Not bad for a crazy drug-dealing psychotic failed killer, is it?" That look I've seen before hangs on her face. She knows who I am. Not what they say I am.

"Get out of here and I'll see you after lunch." The whole world thinks I'm mad for giving up a good paying job for the post of church-lackey. I've had money outside prison without happiness. It's no longer first in my life. I'm not of this world. Along with the job more drug tests come and more working days. The Saturday mass is a morning's work and Wednesday evening is a loss of association. I attended every evening meeting anyway and Saturday is another day I get to be with Christians. Win win all the way. What's money in jail? I had all the money I needed outside. It did me no good. My first day on the job I ask the S.O. for my red band depicting my trusted position. The shadow-cupboard in his office has all the armbands hanging on nails. Each one has a photo encapsulated in clear plastic fixed to it; taken from the file of the trustee.

"You don't have a red band Crowe."

"Yes I do I'm the new Chapel Orderly." I can't help being gleeful.

"Yes but the job isn't a red band job."

"All Orderly jobs are red band."

"Not now they're not. The Chapel isn't a red band position."

"Since when?"

"Since you got it this morning. Security has removed the red band from the job. You have to wait till someone takes you to the chapel and you'll be brought back. No free movement for you Crowe."

"Is that right? So how do I get to work? Why can I not just go with work movements?"

"If there's no one to meet you there you'll be locked off the wing."

"So no red band for CP3703?"

"NO." Why did I think I was going to be treated just like anyone else? One thing is in my favour. All orderly jobs are now on a twelve pound a week pay day. A 100% pay rise from the expected six pounds. Thanks to Rita.

My new duties are cleaning, making tea and general dogsbody. The quiet and serenity of the chapel is outside my chaotic mind's conception. I can feel it filling me. It slowly rises from my feet. Blocked in my chest by the torment of anger held in my heart. The removal of the red band is an effort to rob me of the joy of getting this new position under God's roof. I will not be robbed of this small victory that took so long to come to pass. It's the first time in prison I can say my mind is empty. For the short time I've been free of all thoughts.

Ricky has a new job as gym orderly. Although he's a sixteen stone bulk of a man it comes from breeding not pumping iron in a sweaty gym. Brett the gym screw is his new mate. Ricky doesn't know about the 'them and us' situation of prison. His criminal companions in the cacophony of clanking, in the clutter-filled weights room consist of two cousins and one old man. All have a common interest. Drugs; Ricky with his big import from Ecuador. The old man a big player in Liverpool and the two cousins who ran a large operation in the North East. The Singh boys have the longest sentence with 18 years each. Then there's old man Archie with sixteen. Ricky comes in last with his twelve years. Having started with sixteen before winning an appeal against sentence in The Strand.

Archie is over sixty years old and laughs in the face of the beep test. No one in this prison, or any other I would say could stay with Archie. Morning noon and night he works out. When not in the gym Archie does cell workouts. Fanatic is the only word to describe Archie. Warming up with 500 sit-ups and half an hour on the exercise bike is nothing to him. A full workout for fit men is just a warm-up for Archie.

The Singh boys are not really gym-heads. Easy work is their inspiration. The gym screws look after their boys with little treats from the real world. A curry or a piece of leftover cake never goes in the bin. Vegetarian food is the protocol in the Sikh world and the Singh name is the other. All carry the same name. A sauna in the, out-of-bounds to prisoners, Swiss pine cabinet, is a treat enjoyed by the gym Walla's. More to take off you if you offend. All are red bands. All are still dealing drugs. All heading for a fall. We all do jail our own way. No way is wrong or right just do it, one day at a time. Or in the waiting room of the drug test room second by second as the clock on the wall ticks away your life.

Stories of officers are not a part of my life but the vulnerable are not all behind blue doors. A young woman, who has no business being a prison officer, can't go unmentioned. She is a lamb midst a pack of wolves. Already she's been corrupted by prisoners in Walton Prison, Liverpool. The answer to her problem is her new position here in Garth. A solution to her problem agreed on by the powers of the establishment. Out of the leaking lifeboat and into the shark-infested waters is what they have done for her. What they don't appreciate is the prison version of the world wide web of information. She is here one week when the Singh boys have her nailed. Her private life is a mess. Ripe for picking off. A lame fawn limping at the rear of the group. When the mufti squad spin her personal locker a large quantity of drugs are found. Her chaotic life just paled into insignificance. Jail is going to be more than her job. It will be her life. A life on the wrong side of the door.

The Singh boys are top of the list of suspects. They're the only ones on the list. All the attention befitting such activity is rained down on them. Unlike the lamb, the wolf is a worthy opponent for the hit squad. Nothing is found. No doubt a page or two is added to their jacket for some future event to be resurrected as a reason to deny their progress to freedom. David Reynolds paid a screw in Durham to bring in whatever was in the packet given to him. No questions asked. The money is the only thing you have to get right to have what you want in prison. With a wage of £25,000 a year and prison staff being the largest debtors in a keep-up-with-the-Joneses' lifestyle, it's a breeze for a criminal to meet the price of a man, or woman, who has a mortgage exceeding his/her income. Sometimes a teacher, always the same principle. Mr McCormack's economics of Dickensian Britain still works today. Earnings £25,000 expenditure £24,900 Joy. Earnings £25,000 expenditure £25,100 abject misery. The price for David is the words, CORRUPTS PRISON STAFF, written on his file (jacket). The misery is bounced back onto him. To follow him for the next ten years. Prison to prison on his twenty-eight-day lay-downs. A time deemed too short for alliances to be formed between con and corruptible couriers of contraband. A carousel journey going round and round; the Grand National as it's called, achieving nothing.

For a different reason Nicky is on the same ride. His face tells a story that needs no words. He has a permanent smile given to him in HMP Frankland. The scar on his cheek, running from the corner of his mouth to his left ear, tells anyone who knows the workings of prison justice that Nicky is a grass. A lower life form than a nonce to some people. Whatever he did to warrant the grin of a grass isn't important. People will make up the story that best fits the situation at the time. Most of the time the tale told will have no truth in it. However, that shouldn't get in the way of condemnation readily evident from his scar.

In 1966 England won the football world cup. Early on the morning of Friday, 21 October 1966, after several days of heavy rain, a subsidence of about 3–6 metres occurred on the upper flank of colliery waste tip No. 7. at 9:15 am. More than 150,000 cubic metres of water-saturated debris broke away and flowed downhill at high speed. It was sunny on the mountain but still foggy in the village, with visibility only about fifty metres. The tipping gang working on the mountain saw the landslide start but were unable to raise the alarm because their telephone cable had been repeatedly stolen – although the official inquiry into the disaster later established that the slip happened so fast that a telephone warning would not have saved any lives. The Aberfan disaster was a catastrophic collapse of a colliery spoil tip in the Welsh village of Aberfan, near Merthyr Tydfil, killing 116 children and 28 adults. It was caused by a build-up of water in the accumulated rock and shale, which suddenly started to slide downhill in the form of slurry. A day I'll never forget.

On the same day I was a small boy playing along with my older brother and some friends. All young boys playing boys' games. I was eight years old. It was a Friday afternoon. We had found a space ship lying in a lay-by that was to become a bus stop when the workers were finished. A capsule that in a child's imagination was the lunar moon landing module that three years later would put the first men on the moon. The yellow pilot's-pod called for a pilot; and I was it. Climbing into the mouth of the monster-in-disguise I took up my position. Lying on my back with my feet planted firmly on the side. My small hands gripping the metal paddles I was ready for blast off. Slowly the whole ship started to spin. Round and round it spun. Faster and faster it turned as my brother and friends rotated the hunk of steel. I gripped tighter and tighter. My fingers turned white as the blood flow was cut off. The small blue dot of sky swirled above me. Like the best fairground rides it slowed until it came to a rest. The space mission over, with a successful re-entry, I loosened my grip and started pulling myself out. My head was just starting to appear above the rim of the cement mixer cum spaceship when the locking pin that stops it tipping its contents out, usually concrete, worked loose. Instead of going, as it had, in a spinning action, it inverted.

The opening was heading downward, along with my protruding head, the back of which struck the heavy steel frame. My face or rather the bridge of my nose hit the rim. In a scissor action the mixer took off the top of my head and half my face. I spilled out onto the sandy washings-out beneath the blood stained machine. I was about two miles from home. At the bottom of a steep hill. My brother who was two years older said we should head for home. I had a better plan. The phone box ten yards away was my lifeline. Holding my scalp in one hand and bleeding profusely from the face, I dialled 999 and asked for an ambulance. The name of the road was on the house wall next to the phone box. Screel View. Then a woman that every Friday spoke on that phone with her husband, who worked away, opened the door to chase us kids, who she thought were messing about in the phone box. When I turned she was overwhelmed. I was taken into the house next to the phone box. Wet towels stemmed the blood flow then off to the hospital by ambulance. Blue lights and sirens all the way. My mother was out collecting food for Christmas hampers to be given to the old and poor.

When I speeded past her she said to her friend 'someone must be in a bad way'. She couldn't have known it was her youngest son. Two hours in theatre. One hundred and fifty stitches. And blind I survived. My sight came back in a week and the stitches came out after ten days. The scars left to this day tell a different story to those who don't know me. They see a man who must have lived a life of violence. Bearing the battle medals of war. Scars that identify a man who got into a fight he didn't win. I did win that fight. It was the fight of a small eight year old boy for his life. The damage to my brain was the confusion I have with words. I'm sure of it now. They look but they don't see. They don't see me. They see who they want to see. The jury saw the scarred face of a guilty man before they saw me.

The wounds we can't see are more damaging than the ones we can. Abuse is the hidden wounds of small boys locked away inside men. Compulsive cleaning. An ordered life. They are the scars of the soul. Deep wounds that fester and rot a man from the inside. Self-harm, depression, suicide are not just a cry for help, by this time they don't want help they want end. Tired and broken they crave death to heal the wounds deep inside their soul. In reality it's just the start of a bigger problem.

Prison is a small world. Even with its membership of over eighty five thousand. The information network is amazing. Not only about staff. When a guy comes in its only a week at the most before all is known about him. The inmates have a better network than any security department I've seen. It takes two hours for the identity of a rapist to be unveiled. Moving on to another jail where his lies will again be uncovered by truth. Then ther's the chance of encountering a fellow criminal who you may have offended against in the past. It's a common thing to throw partners-in-crime to the police when the going gets tough. Only in the top flight, and even then not all are true to a brother, in their honour among thieves old school philosophy.

Back in Long Lartin there was a guy who was the brains; I use the term loosely, in a kidnapping. The guy they decided to hold for ransom was only the boss of a criminal family in Newcastle. As if that wasn't enough of a mistake they tortured him. A hot iron was put on his chest, and no they weren't trying to iron out a crease in his £1,000 suit. Well all they got was jail and lots of it. Now I was told the story by the mastermind first hand. Who am I now hearing the story from? The brother of the guy who was kidnapped. It's a small world. The question I have to ask is how the police found out and what was the evidence given in court. Criminals don't involve the police; they certainly don't stand in the witness box. He starts his version with, "ah well!"

Gangsters, but when the going gets a bit hot they need the police to sort it out, I know what a true gangster would do, he would keep them out so he could pay them back. Maybe I'm thinking about myself. Why didn't Swindles come after me? When I had a small problem with the drug addicts in Whitehaven did I run to the police? When their boss told me he would do me in did I take cover in the law? No I dealt with it the way criminals do. When I showed them the ex- Hells Angel still had the ability to call on his past they changed their attitude. Sometimes you have to speak the language people understand. But if you go that way you have to be the meanest rooster in the yard.

In Durham, Alan was waiting for his trial. He was abducted by the local mob. A victim of the drug wars. The craft knife they used on him left its mark. All his body bore witness. Scars ran the length of his torso;

diagonal slash scars covered his back. His face was given that same permanent smile; scars ran from his mouth to his ears. He never went to the police even though he was fighting for life on a hospital bed. When he recovered physically he executed his retaliation. That's what he was in prison for this time. Then would you believe it? The guy who cut him up was brought in and put on the same wing. You couldn't make it up. Alan was skin and bone standing five foot six tall. The other guy was a giant of a man still no match for Alan when intent on revenge. They say when seeking revenge dig two graves. Tit for tat all done, a truce was met. Turned out Alan was the wrong guy and should never have been cut up in the first place. Even urban justice doesn't get it right every time.

There's a lot of ex SAS in prison, if you listen to the talk. The prison barber here is one. A lifer inside for killing the mother of some woman who he says hired him as an assassin. Not to kill the mother; he messed up. The woman told him he was the love of her life, you know how it goes. If he was to kill her husband they would have the insurance money and live on a Pacific Island eat fish and coconuts. I can picture the scene, the problem was she only wanted rid of her man and didn't want to replace him. Not with another man that is. Money is what she was interested in. All was planned and the day came for the murder. Simple plan as are the best plans, walk up the garden path knock on the front door and when he opens the door shoot him. Like I said a simple plan what can go wrong? Yep the door opened and when the guy saw a gun-toting killer wearing a ski mask, he closed the door. Out of sight behind the closed door the mother of the guy came to see what was going on. Are you getting the picture? SAS man shoots through the door and kills the mother. The wife is the first suspect and guess what; she blows him right in. It's funny when someone tells his story and you've heard it before from someone else. It's like a new tale with embellishments but if it fills the ego of the teller so what? Mr SAS's crime made one of them true crime documentaries and the story there was more embarrassing for him.

I often get asked who I know from Liverpool, London or Manchester. I always say no one. But sometimes I bump into a friend of a friend or some runner for one of the heads (big boys) from my past life. This time it's Peter from Liverpool. He ran with a mate of mine so knows me and all about my case. I try to keep my life outside to myself so I don't want him bigging me up to the £10 a bag drug dealers who want a leg up the drug-dealing ladder. He tells my story better than me with the main point being I wasn't there when the deed was done. I could have done with him in my trial. I keep him in phone cards and some smokes until he gets his black market income up and running. The news of the old firm is crazy times of war and territory grabbing. The easy money is robbing dealers from out of town, woolly-backs usually from over the Mersey. A dangerous game to play when you don't know who the drugs came from, heads don't take it lightly when one of their boys gets had over. Acid from a jiff lemon container squirted into the eyes is a high price to pay for a few quid. The revenge is for cheek not the money or drugs. A head can't let someone walk in and take liberties without retribution. There can be no limits if you want to be the top head. I never give a referral from jail. Who you see inside is not who they are outside and if my word gets them in it's my reputation that stands as the guarantee they won't turn grass.

A new badminton partner is on the wing today. I nearly met him once when I was shopping for "commodities" but he was dealing with some business, taking ownership of a car if I remember right. Some debt unpaid by a customer of his. You can't play the game without the capitol. I heard he was on his way from a friend of his who works in the rocking horse shop. Skeggy is a larger than life person who would never be lost in a crowed. Badminton is where we now have a common interest, and he's good. We play most days and my game moves to a new level. At the expense of my pride; not a high price. The screws know him of old and the local cons know him; or of him. He has a reputation that paints a picture of a ruthless no-nonsense, straight-talking guy who carries two things in the boot of his car, a spade and a shotgun. To be used in that order. I remember his mate telling me about a time when Skeggy threw a spade in the boot and the gun on the back seat of his BMW. 'Come on', he said, 'we have a job to do,' His mate thought someone was going to be topped, turned out Skeggy was just going to dig a hole for the gun. I don't know if it's true but I know Skeggy. He is an inspiration to me. I take notice of all his stories of revenge so I can use them in my future plans. Plans that keep me alive.

The chapel work is growing with the introduction of Christian based courses: Alpha, The Sycamore Tree, and my favourite, Skills for Living. Restorative justice is the new way. Rita is the reason for the increase in Christian methods of rehabilitation. Even the prisoners who don't come to church enjoy the groups. Earl, who is a brother from over the big pond, amuses the group with his faith in prayer.

"Before every bank job I pray that I won't get caught," he says

"And do you think God answers that Earl?" Rita asks him.

"Well ye mam. A didn't get caught for a long time. It says ask and ya git it mam yeah?" He says in that southern comfort drawl.

If he wasn't such a bulk of a man the room would be in uproar. Rita gives him a suggestion as to the will of God. Pointing out the fact that God is good. Maybe it's not his will for Earl to rob banks and ask God to be an accessory before the act. Maybe advanced thinking would be good for brother Earl. The rest of the gang attend, diligently taking down the important points. Important to them that is. Rita and I work well together as I become more hands on. By the third or fourth time the course is run I know it word for word. I know where it's leading to. The same questions come up so we can sound all knowing. My weapon of choice is the twelve apostles of Jesus. When Jesus was killed they ran like rats on a sinking ship. After the resurrection, of those we know about, all died because they would not deny Him. That's a turn around. Would they all give their lives for a conman? Maybe one would but not them all.

Thursday lunch time a beautiful sunny day, the cell door opens, time for work. Rita usually waits at the wing gate to walk me the fifteen feet to the chapel door. The screw at the gate is overwhelmed by the volume of bodies trying to pass him so he doesn't much care about me ducking under his arm holding the iron gate half open. The hoards of men are gym-heads pushing and jostling for position so as to secure the best equipment in the gym. Our wing is the closest to the gym but sometimes other wings are let out first and ours is held back so that it's not the same wing first every time. The screw knows I'm going to work in the opposite direction so he lets me escape the crush. Rita's not waiting so I head for the chapel.

The chapel door's closed but unlocked. I enter the foyer and make for the office. The first floor window facing the exercise yard fills the back wall. Light pours in illuminating the room highlighting the dust particles in an animated state of flux, slowly falling downward, followed by more and more in a never ending cascade in free fall. The desk sits in front of the window at the centre or the room. Rita raises her shoulders, and straightens up. Standing behind the desk. Window behind her. Light resounding all around her. It makes her appear translucent to my eyes. Angelic. From the doorway where I'm glued to the spot, a hand enters my chest. It reaches into my heart; takes hold of my anger closing its grip that tight I feel my heart stop. For what feels like ten minutes not a word is said. The reality is not even a second has passed before the fist full of hatred, anger, sorrow and pain is gone from me. The hole that should be left quickly fills with love. A spell is cast over my heart right here right now. I feel full from the soles of my feet to the top of my head. For the first time in years I'm full of something other than anger. I feel nothing towards the people who forever have been my reason for living.

At this moment. In this room. Brought together for the first time in my life is my past, my present and my future. My whole life is standing on this spot. All combined into one existence. The first time I came into the chapel I was empty. Now I'm full of joy, peace and love.

"It's all gone." I break the word fast.

"What's gone Tony?" Rita looks right into my watery eyes.

"The anger, the unforgiving, the pain. All of it, it's gone."

"That's great Tony you'll feel better for letting it go. It was doing you no good." She doesn't understand what just happened.

"I didn't let go. It was taken away just now when I walked into the room."

"Did you ask God to take it?"

"Every day except for today. I was feeling good today. Not as good as I feel right now."

"I can see it in you. You are fresher. Renewed in spirit. God will not leave you in a bad place Tony."

"In less than the twinkling of an eye it was taken from me and there's no emptiness. Do you understand Rita? I don't think I do."

"You're delivered from the hold anger had over you. I was only free when I let go and gave it over to God. Only then did I get out of Lard Yao prison."

"How can something so strong just go? I feel like I've been washed clean from the inside to the outside."

"It's the Pagan day today so keep that feeling for when the witch comes in. And pray thanksgiving to Jesus and The Holy Spirit who now lives in you."

"I do and I will keep on. Never have I felt anything like this in my life." The love is overflowing. Running out of me like a river. My future? Well that's in this room I now know, its Rita. I have a loving heart and she is in direct line of fire.

Rita doesn't know but I feel love for her that I never knew existed in life. The bible says if you say you know the father but don't have love for each other you don't know love. Or something like that. But how can I love a woman who lives in a world I can't even imagine? I know my love will be one way and that only in my dreams will we ever be in each other's arms. Soon she'll be in Ireland where she won't give a thought to HMP Garth or to me. When she comes back I'll be gone. My cat C will come and I'll be in Haverigg. My poems are an insight to who I think I am and for the last month I've put them together in a book. The cover I got Little Gary to print in the screen print shop. His new job. However he still holds the trusted post of custodian of the only bathe plug on the wing. The card for the cover came from Nicky the Triad lifer in education. And the glue for the spine from Jenny's wood shop. Eight copies for people who influence my prison walk and my walk with God. Kevin Commons gets the first one for the friendship he has given me for no reward. The sign of a true friend. Fraser gets the next for being a straight-forward preacher. The Salvation Army old boy gets one for his devotion without selfish gain to the prisoners. Rita gets one for the love I have for her, to let her know who I really am. But only when I've gone from here. I give her it on the day she finishes work for her holiday to Ireland.

Waiting for that day when I'm deemed safe to be let among men who I, in the past, might kill, according to my prison jacket; my category C. the needed requirement for my move to Haverigg prison. A post card under my door from Ireland. 'Thinking of you and having a good time... Rita.' No sign of my move and time passes. The holiday is over now Rita's back at work. Nothing about my book of poems, Words of a Demented Prisoner, maybe she tossed it aside. Kevin sends me three great books of poems. An early Christmas gift on the anniversary of my incarceration. That time of year when some just can't take any more torment. Along with the promise of a fishing trip to the salmon rivers of Scotland when I'm a free man.

My words are an interpretation of the things I hear and see from living inside the walls of this steel and concrete world. Sometimes words don't mean what you think they do. Nicky the triad lifer in education was asked to interpret a Chinese word or phrase that was tattooed on the forearm of a hard-core meat-head. He told him it didn't really make sense. The best Nicky could do was; "like broken washing machine The meat-head told Nicky it should say ' mean machine', to which Nicky said, "you can't translate that into Chinese I often wonder now when I see these tattoos what they really say, then I smile at the memory of little Nicky telling the guy he had broken washer on his arm.

The work I do as a listener: helping by caring without judging. Listening without giving advice. Showing love without actions. Keeps me occupied weekly. But some don't ask for help, they suffer in dark silence. The silence of their small prison cell. Made even smaller by mental torment.

After 12 years of living in the same cell without working, going to the gym, or taking part in any of the normal prison activities, Jed's time to move-on has come. He has no desire to leave his dark silent cell of safety. It's became his substitute womb. Like a foetus safe from the outside world he curls up; only to be attacked by his own mind. The governor is adamant, telling Jed 'if I have to body-belt you and carry you from your cell to the van personally I will do it. In the morning you will be on that van,' he tells Jed. The words of Jed's dire warning fall on deaf ears. 'Over my dead body.'

Jed was carried out of that cell that morning but not by the governor. Not in a body-belt and manacles. In a body-bag. Just another number for the black list of deaths in prison. I believe the prison killed an innocent man that day that never got to say good bye to the wife he loved and lost to the same fate that showed its face once more to him. Prison is a simmering pot of emotions that can boil over at the slightest change or sign of an injustice by the gaolers. Secrecy of the circumstances around Jed's death does nothing to calm the men. Inquest is the answer to any questions. His sister demands to know what happened. In one year, this year, Jed has lost his aunt, who was in fact his mother, his brother and now himself to death. How could they not see the pain? How could no one know?

He confessed to the brother from the Benedictine Order of Catholic monks every Saturday. The day Roman Catholics hold their mass. But no one saw what now is all too obvious. The monk's spiritual eyes didn't see. As if Jed needs penance. That's what his earthly spirit father gives him. Praise as an atonement. Where is that from? Some people don't ask for help with words. Their eyes scream out in pain but no one wants to see. Prisoners hold their own sanity, their own life in their clumsy hands. Staff are blinded by familiarity, hardened by years of turning keys in cell doors that hold people without faces. Without names. Numbers on a file. A file opened once a year for the ritual act demanded by higher powers sitting in an office somewhere in a bureaucratic swamped building in the heart of London, who have never seen a prisoner or the inside of a cell. Our life in their hands is even more precarious.

My love for Rita is hidden, even from Rita. I can't just come out and declare my burning love. I can't seem to show her my passion by my demeanour. Maybe my writings will reveal my heart without getting me removed to the furthest most prison in the kingdom. Poems with a personal undertone will melt her heart and turn her eyes toward me. The years of romantic starvation have built a wall around her. Ten long years have sailed on by, each one a winter storm as Rita keeps the depleted family home in order. A secret garden hidden from view. Seclusion.

Only by climbing to the cap stones. By straining eyes in an effort to see through the thick thorns can I see her beauty. A rose garden in all its splendour, every flower tended with loving care; bar one, for none to see. The gardener's pleasure is the only purpose. The rose wilting in the heart is sick. A Blake worm-eaten flower. 'O rose thou art sick. The invisible worm, that flies in the night in the howling storm; has found out thy bed of crimson joy: and his dark secret love does thy life destroy. The cause? Love lost; the cure love found, my love will invigorate, put flight to the black heart killing blight.' The wall has to come down. The thorns have to yield to my poetic-prose-pruning, revealing her fragrant heart, her dew moistened petals. Once again the warmth that love radiates must fill her womanly desires. One stone at a time my words loosen their hold. Cemented together with tears of hurt.

The words flow from my pen to Rita's innermost, posing briefly on the page. Small love notes I leave in her desk drawer, written by my hand. The origins of which can only come from my new infilling of joy in the spirit of love. I am in a prison no more; I am free. These walls are not my prison. They never have been. The anger I held in my belly was the prison I couldn't break free from. I am free to liberate this beautiful woman from her bondage. Too long she has been separated from her womanhood.

The chapel is now a faith room and the prison's new ruling is that all faiths can use it. The toilets have the urinals removed and in their place, foot baths are installed. So much for, 'have no other gods but me'. For me it's work and lots of it. When the Muslims use the chapel all Christian items must be removed or covered. When the pagans have their day once a month the witch comes in and she doesn't have any demands. The rest all have their own requirements. It's a bit like the abomination of desolation in the bible. To close the rift between religions the governor holds a multi faith day in the 'faith room'. Representatives from the main factions sit on the stage ready for questions. After a short description of their beliefs the floor is open to questions. The guy sitting next to the Muslim leader comes out with the statement born of ignorance fed by lies told to him by his Muslim teacher. 'The bible was stolen from the Koran'. I can't hold my words. With this rebuttal I attack. 'I think you'll find the bible is over five thousand years old and Islam is only one thousand four hundred years old. You need to ask him next to you to give you the facts about the organisation you've joined. The Imam looks sheepish and has nothing to say in defence of his uninformed student. I finish off with. 'The truth is the bible was stolen from the Jewish book, The Tanakh. But as Jesus is a Jew it wasn't stolen but given freely'. Silence fills the space and kills the moment. Andrew says 'well' about four times before he takes back his authority. In all the jails I've been in I've never met a Jew. Or a Rabbi for that matter. That in itself, I find amazing.

November is over and so is Ramadan, the Islamic month of fasting during daylight hours. The 'faith room' is the venue for the feast to end the fast. There are no seats and the floor is the table. Food in plastic containers is given out to the men, to be eaten with fingers. Curry fumes fill the air bringing to mind that back-street balti house I ate at once in Aston long ago. Sort of a curry café.

As the herd break their fast. Suffering from the dill oil and the yellow saffron stains, the carpet cries out to be rescued. It makes me wonder what the reason is they don't eat pigs. May be they have an affinity to their eating habits. Appeasement overrides common-sense but it's only one- sided. The Sikh community held their feast in the chapel. I was amazed when they asked for pots and pans and told me that the Muslim ones would not fulfil the requirements of their religion. The meal was an ordered affair with no mess and all cleared away by themselves at the end. The Christian feast to celebrate the birth of Jesus is here. Christmas.

Two days before Christmas day, the 23rd, a Saturday, It's just like any other Saturday. In the morning is the Roman Catholic Mass after which I'm free from work duties for the rest of the day. Lunch over and my cell door is unlocked. Eddy runs his horse racing Saturday club for those who wish to partake in a small wager on the outcome of seven televised races. I take the spectator's role only joining in on the friendly banter.

"Crowe." The S.O. shouting my name in the distance breaks through the chatter of men cheering on their particular nag.

"Here I am what do you want?" I walk down the wing corridor towards him.

"The chaplain asked if you would go and help in the chapel. You don't have to, if you don't want, it's not a work day."

"Who's the chaplain? What do they want?" I can't understand why they want me.

"Rita, she didn't say. Just asked if you would go in for a while. Do you want to go or not?" Intriguing. She never comes in on Saturdays how can I resist.

"Maybe she needs something moving, I'll go see, will you take me over?" I'm already heading toward the gate eager to know what she could want.

"You can go alone and I'll tell her you're on your way."

Turning his key he unlocks the gate sending me on my way. Rita's not at the door waiting for me. My hand reaches out for the door handle in an uncommon act testing the door to find it unlocked. We never open doors ourselves. Entering the vacant foyer, no sign of

Rita, I walk on. The same office she stood in when I was delivered from the anger is where she stands. Pastel blouse decorated with a floral design blends tastefully into a long-flowing, pleated dress. The top two buttons are unfastened giving slender length to her neck. A small necklace breaks up the nakedness of her soft skin. Blonde hair rests on her pulled back shoulders, spectacles frame them brown speckled eyes that pulled me in long ago. Perfection standing before me. I am back in the same spot I was then. That place where my past, present and future came together. Now is the time for my future to show itself. Rita opens the exchange with.

"What's going on?" Shivering within from the confusion. Emotions working. Removing stones from that wall around that abandoned garden faster than she can replace them. I say, "What do you mean?" I can see panic, trepidation as she waits for my answer to the question that makes no sense to me.

"Are you just messing with my head? Am I just to be a conquest to you? I was driving home and I had an uncontrollable urge to come here and see you."

"Wow, well what can I say. You're not a conquest Rita." Still not really understanding the moment. I have accepted the fact that all my efforts to win the heart of Rita have failed and have been consigned to the dream bin of what could have been. Who was I kidding to think this woman from another world could fall in love with such a good prospect as me? How many prisoners have tipped their hat in the hope of something more? Nervously she delivers her next statement.

"I love you. But where do we go from here?" Wow.

"I'm not messing with your head. I am serious about my feeling for you. Rita I've loved you for so long I can't remember not loving you."

"This cannot be." Her denial is the futile attempt to rebuild her wall of stone protecting that dying rose of William Blake's. I know she is now mine. We move across the room towards each other not knowing or caring who may see us. The embrace is one of two lovers who after being lost for aeons have found each other once more. As we hold each other close, for what must be hours, the moment of reality awakens the sleeping passions. A kiss that is sweeter is a thing of dreams for there can't be one in real life better than this one. We are in love and we both know it's going to be a new beginning. Words aren't needed to express what we feel right now. And none could replace this embrace.

"We go forward Rita; with God's blessing. But we must honour God with our love. We can't give into our desires. We can only kiss and hold each other."

'Only' is the wrong word. To do just that this morning was impossible in my mind. I still can't believe I'm holding this fantastic woman. Tears from a woman are never fully understood by a man, but I know that these tears are ones of joy. The wall is broken but the thorns still block my way to this sick rose watered daily with a different type of tears. Tears of a hurting heart. We are now in a position that has led many to their doom. Forbidden love because of the circumstances imposed by the prison on me, and by the need to earn a living on Rita. Love knows no bounds, striking at the heart of men and women regardless of the position they hold in life. For every man there is a woman waiting to be found. Only one person is right for another. As Eve was taken out of Adam so Rita was taken out of me. Now we are united once again; two parts of one being coming back together as one new creation, just as it was in the beginning. This day will never end in my mind. Lying in bed will bring this day to life over and over again. Dreams of a new life will dance at the foot of my bed. But for now the fire burning inside must be kept out of sight. Life as usual when others are present. Is it possible to hide a flaming torch set on a stand?

Christmas day service is a first for the Christians in Garth. For the first time there is one church service/mass. C of E (rest of the world Christians) and Roman Catholics will worship together. I have to set out the chapel for the historical event. The piano is in pride of place at the front. Ray, a lifer on license re-call is our pianist for the day. He's not a believer that I know of, but he's a graduate from a school of music out in the real world many years ago now. His bald dark head sways from side to side as he fondles the keys. The little Stevie Wonder of Garth prison. His small frame is hidden behind the wooden frame of the instrument.

On guitar, strumming away to her own rhythm is Judy, the wife of Andrew. Unlike Ray, Judy isn't a scholar of any music academy. She took up the challenge while ministering to the poor people of Africa. Not poor necessarily by having no money but poor for having to endure the random chords and key changes of Judy's impromptu musical recitals. The music group is complete with Sister Cecilia bashing on the tambourine. Graduate of The Holy Family convent, where they must teach austerity as an attribute. The coming together of the two religions stops at the altar. For the bread and wine there can be no neutral ground as Bob Dylan once said. Two tables are set up, one for Fraser, Methodist and good for all R.O.T.W. Christians the other table is for Father Steven a monk from the Benedictine Monastic Order. We all say the same creed. One God. One body. One cup. One blood shed for the forgiveness of all. One bread broken. Father

Steven holds the cup of wine (gold-plated goblet) high above his head until his old shaking arms threaten to spill the contents down his white flowing gown. A wizard without the hat comes to my mind. Returning the vessel safely to its resting place he genuflects, I hold my breath as he vanishes out of sight. Will he have the strength to pull his frail body back up? Slowly he rises from his knees. The small round wafer gets the same ritual treatment and one of the boys in the back gets the nod to ring a small bell denoting the moment the sacrament became Jesus. I've done it myself many times in the past and sometimes I would delay the ringing of the bell. I liked the idea it was me who determined when 'the mystery', as they call it, happened. If I could control Jesus' coming what did that make me?

Fraser's approach is no less reverent but without the offering up or the going down on one knee. The bread is just that, bread, crumbs and all, the wine is next to it, and the blessing covers them both. No bell. No white robe and fuss. The line of ROTW Christians for Fraser's sacrament is on the right, father Stephen's on the left. I can't help thinking about the time Jesus did the same for his believers in that upper room. Jesus even gave it to Judas. Here they're a bit more selective.

With all the worthy blessed by the wine and bread or blood and body of Christ for Stephen's boys. My time has come to slip out of the chapel to brew the tea. My bible says ONE NEW MAN. Where is this one new man that is nether Jew or Gentile? All believers are called children of Abraham! I only hope I never have to become religious and lose the friendship of Jesus. He said 'no love is greater than that a man lay down his life for a friend.' I want Jesus as a friend not as a religious icon.

Chocolate biscuits for Christmas with Jaffa cakes supplied by Rita. I can't resist copying the TV advert. The small cake held in my right hand I say 'full moon' then I take a bite and say 'half moon' as the chocolate crescent moon disappears into my mouth for the third time Andrew is bewildered and totally confused when I finish the reminiscent act with 'total eclipse'. I don't think he's ever seen the add so now he just thinks I'm crazy. All the with-it people laugh but more at Andrew's bewilderment than at the acting out of the TV add. Andrew once went to a self defence day held over the road at Wymott prison. When he came back I asked him if he had learned how to ward off an attacker. He sheepishly nodded not knowing I knew where he'd been. 'I'll attack you and you can see if it works', I said. His face was the same as it was now total confusion. So funny. You have to be here. And his pink shorts for his gym workouts are legendary. The gym screw asked Rita if he was a pillow biter.

Operation plan B

The New Year is a time for a new plan. I still have to try and get my security categorisation lowered. Jail advice is never a good thing to listen to, I remember Dummer in Durham. But when all else as failed you become susceptible to crazy plans. This crazy plan is to get out of prison. Not to escape but to go out with an escort and return without any incident. This will be written in my file and it'll go in my favour. All I need is a reason to be taken out. Time to visit the doctor. I say doctor but I think if he was a real doctor he would be working somewhere else. Still I don't want a real one who I can't influence. I know how difficult it is to even see him. When I had a verruca my request to be seen was ignored, until, that is, I filled out the application in an imaginative manner. The form asked 'what is your problem?' I wrote; 'I have a highly infectious viral infection of the epidermis'. Without the viral bit in my description it looks like scabies. The prison is terrified of an outbreak of the little scabies mite. Once in Durham, when I was on holiday in HMP Preston, there was a scabies wild fire epidemic. They had to close down all contact between wings and burn bedding from the infected wings. It took weeks to clean it out of the prison; and cost money. The financial damage to the budget was their biggest concern. Here the same fear of an epidemic was enough to get an appointment the same day. When I seen the doc he asked.

"What seems to be the problem?"

"I have a verruca on the ball of my right foot."

"How do you know it's a verruca?" he asked.

"It looks like one, and it feels like one. In my experience that usually means it is one. If it walks like a duck and quacks it's a duck."

"Take off your shoe and I'll take a look," scribbling on my file as he shows no other interest in my answer. After a scrape with a blade and a poke-about he says, "I can give you some cream for it. There are two creams: one you can keep in-cell and apply it three times a day, the other one you can't keep in your cell, you would need to come here and the nurse will treat you with it. What would you prefer?"

"Well, the one for in-cell use. What's the difference in the creams as far as the treatment goes?" I ask.

"The one for cell use doesn't work and the other one does."

"Oh. Well of course I want the one that doesn't work! What would be the point of taking something that doesn't work?"

"You can have it in your cell." I suspect this is his attempt at satire. I take my hat off to him. Then he says, "If you do nothing they usually go away by themselves; just cover it with a plaster."

So I take the cream that will do no good and stick a plaster on it. And in a week it went.

Some years ago now I was told by another quack I should have a scan to investigate my man bits. With this perfect out-of-the-doc's-remit of competent ability my plan is simple. The doc suggests a visit to Preston hospital for the scan. The date of my outing is kept from me for security reasons but I know it'll be within the month.

The routine is easily found out from a guy who went last week. Jim had a swollen big toe that baffled the doc. After the trip out Jim was returned to prison minus his toe. All I want to lose from my trip out is my security risk. Before breakfast unlock the S.O. opens the door to tell me it's the day of my appointment at Preston hospital. No contact with any other prisoners from now until I return means breakfast in reception.

Two block screws are to be my escort with two chub handcuffs as my restraints. One set is for my wrists the other is for me to be joined to the big guy who has a neck bigger than my thigh. After locking the cuffs he hands the key to his companion who is no lesser of a brutish bulk.

Waiting at the door a normal car is my transport. After the air-lock security check the door opens, light flooding into the darkness takes away any sight of the well kept flowerbeds outside the gate. The air seems cleaner, brighter, and fresher than on the other side of the grey wall. Even in winter when the trees and fields are sleeping till spring, the brown with patches of green looks like a vivid drug induced world to me. The short trip to Preston is over before I adjust to the speed of life in the world. One thing good about being in handcuffs is there is no waiting around. The screw with the handcuff key books us in at the desk. Quickly we're taken into a side room where the others can't see us, or may be so I can't be rescued by accomplices. The two screws talk to each other like I'm not there.

"How many overnights have you had this month?" asks the key holder.

"I'm doing OK this will be my fourth one. Did you get to do the guy who had his toe off?"

"I did yeah, he's back in. They had to take his foot off. It got an infection."

"Who's with him?" The question isn't concern for Jim. He just wants to know who's getting the overtime payment.

"Arthur from C wing, he's on his own. They reckon the guy can't run with one leg." He laughs at Jim's predicament. "He's having it off from the thigh now. I don't think it looks that good for him." What do they mean by overnight?

"I think you'll find I'm only having a scan. I'm not in for the night," I pipe up.

"Is that what they said? They told us it was an all nighter son." The nurse will confirm my version, the door opens. Nurses have that pleasant peaceful appearance; this one is all the way a looker. In her hand is what must be my medical file.

"Tony?" She looks right into my face ignoring the handcuffs along with the screws, not seeing a convict only seeing me. "Tony Crowe? I have some forms for you to sign. Do you know what we are going to be doing for you Tony?"

"I was just telling these. I'm having a scan." She smiles one of them smiles that says 'well yes sort of'.

"Well you are. Often the scan doesn't show clearly what we need to see." I can't help but stop her right there.

"What do you mean; need to see? I hope there's nothing to see."

"To make sure we may need to look inside. The operation is simple and you'll only have two small holes where the camera goes in. Around your belly button." An operation to reduce my security level now seems a bit drastic.

"I don't think an operation is what I come in for. Just a scan was the deal." She hands me a form and her pen.

"You have to sign this form; we'll only need to look inside if the scan isn't clear. You need to sign just in case, to save time later. Someone will come and explain things to you. The doctor will see you." The form signed I hand it back. What am I doing here having an operation now when there's nothing wrong? Jim was here for a sore toe and now his leg is for the chop.

The scan reveals nothing, well it wouldn't there's nothing to reveal. A room just off to the left of the main ward is mine for the night. From prison wing to hospital ward. Handcuffed to the bed, guarded by one screw as they take it in turn to slip outside for a coffee and smoke. The doctor comes to explain what will be the procedure.

"The scan was not conclusive so we need to have a wee look see what's in there, OK?" A rhetorical OK. "When did you last eat?" I know that means a general anaesthetic, it just gets worse.

"Well I had breakfast that must have been..." The screws pipes up, "7.30am but he's had nothing since then." He wants his night's overtime and is not about to let a breakfast rob him.

"Breakfast, yes nothing since then doctor. But why do I have to be put out for it?" I ask.

"That's fine we'll take you to theatre at 5.00pm. We need to remove the handcuffs and the prison won't sanction that unless you're anaesthetised I'm afraid."

"I see. Doctor can I ask you something?" I don't like the idea of an operation for no reason other than to affect my security level. So I see this as a chance to have a vasectomy. "Would it be possible to give me the snip while you are messing around in there?" It just gets crazier.

"We could do that if you like. Are you sure that's what you want? If we do it from the inside you can't have it reversed later. We cut the tube higher up."

"Well it seems a waste to go in and not do anything; at least I won't feel that it's all been for nothing." He looks through my file nodding his head.

"OK I can't see why not if you're sure. You'll need to sign a consent form. Nurse could you bring Mr Crowe the form."

"Yes doctor," the young woman says then heads off to the nurses' station. The screw never lifts his head from the newspaper. Concentrating on the crossword clue that's giving his mind a mental workout. Inspector

312

Morse's first name. When that's the only one he has left I'll tell him the answer. Endeavour Morse.

On the hour every hour the nurse takes my vitals and logs them on the chart hanging on the foot of the bed. Every hour the screw stretches his legs with the walk to the car park for his coffee and cigarette, swapping duties. The only time I can go to the toilet is when they change over. Only when the two are both with me I go to pee. The toilet chain is pulled out of the brown leather bag used to hide it from public view. The battered bag must have been in use for longer that I've lived. Ten foot of chain with a handcuff on each end, one for me, one for the screw. Reminds me of Cool Hand Luke when he had to shake the bush as he took a leak so the screw knew he hadn't ran off. Again the key is given to the other guy. If this is to work for what I planned it to work for I have to show no sign of trouble. I need a good report on my prison file from these two goons. Putting up with this is part of the price I suppose.

The hospital porter and a nurse come to take me down. Chained to the bed, screw on each side I'm pushed to the lift. From lift to door to corridor my bed is steered expertly by the porter, arriving in the operating theatre's outer room. I can see the table where I'll go under the knife with its light hovering over it. A space ship hovering.

"If you could take off the handcuffs now officer we can prepare him for theatre," says the nurse.

"When he's under. We can only take them off when he's out."

"Well I need to put this shunt in his hand, can you cuff his other hand to the bed please." The key man steps forward, clamps the new handcuff round my free wrist before removing the other one for the nurse to perform her task. Into the shunt she injects the drug that

313

removes all consciousness leaving no concept of time passing. The sharp pain when I try to lift my hand and turn over in a half-a-sleep stupor returns my consciousness. The handcuff digs into my wrist like a knife as it rattles metal to metal along the side rail of the bed. My eyes only see shapes, shadows. My mouth a desert as dry as Gandhi's flip flop. The first voice is one I know. Rita is at my bed side. Though I can't see her I know it. In my drugged half lucid state I reach out for my love, oblivious to the circumstances of my predicament. Attempting to take hold of her in an embrace shared only by two people in love. Rita, knowing what my intention is keeps just out of range. Beyond the reach of my restraining chain, whilst trying to bring me into the world of reality. That world that existed before I went to sleep. Slowly my senses return to me. The screw next to the bed. The chain holding me to the rail. Rita the light of the room. Love mixed with compassion on her face. Just the prison chaplain doing her rounds is the impression we have to portray.

"I was visiting Jim and I thought I would come and see how you were getting on. How are you, you've just come from the recovery room? The officers will be staying with you so if you need something let them know." She's letting me know that I am still it prison and that there's screws in the room so I don't say or do anything that they will see as more that just chaplain and prisoner. My cognitive senses return quickly, understanding the situation I suppress my desire to embrace Rita.

"So how's Jim doing then?" I ask her.

"He's not so good. They have to take the whole leg. It's got an infection and if they leave it he'll die from the poison to his system."

"But he only had a swollen toe didn't he? Where did the infection come from?" I can't help thinking if he got it in here I could get it too.

"I don't know but you know what it's like in prison, it's not the best place to have an open wound. He's not so good Tony. They don't know if he'll survive the operation." Her eyes are telling me there's not much hope for Jim. Well no more overtime for the screws from Jim's misery. I'll bet the screws are gutted. Because of the anaesthetic I have to stay in overnight. The first night I've slept in a bed that wasn't in a cell for years, five years. The next morning I'm given the all clear to go home. Double-cuffed with my two escorting goons in tow the trip back is just what I planned, uneventful. Not only have I had a trip out without incident, but a night out without incident. That's got to be worth a cat C. for sure.

Two days after my return to Garth the doctor wants to take a look at the wounds and asks if I'm OK. Knowing what Jim went through I don't trust the medical staff of the prison.

"I'm fine, if anything looks like it's not I'll let you know." I keep him at bay.

"You have to come back in ten days with a sample to see if the operation was a success." He reads from my file. He doesn't understand why I had an operation. Not that he remembers why I went to Preston. He can't believe I would be allowed out for the snip. And by the way they found nothing wrong with my manly bits. But I knew that before I went. The small holes where the scope went inside my lower abdomen are looking a bit red by the sixth day. I know my body and I know I heal in seven to ten days. I know this redness along with the heat coming from the wound is not good. Antibiotics and not small ones are needed. The trip to the doctor is always a mental pain because most prisoners just want a drug of some sorts and he knows it. Every prisoner is treated as if he's trying to con the doc. But not in the way I just did.

"What's the problem?" he asks me. He never makes eye contact. The file on his desk is his distraction.

"I need antibiotics for my operation wounds, they have become infected."

"Why do you think they're infected?" he asks me.

"I don't think they are. I know they are so if you could just give me the pills that would be just great doctor."

"Well it could just be a reaction to the stitches. The redness is just part of the healing process I think."

"I'm not being funny doctor but I don't want your opinion. I want the antibiotics. See if you are right, and you may well be, then there will be no problem with me taking the pills. Now if on the other hand I'm right, and I don't take the pills I die. It's really a no-brainer for me."

"I'll give you the antibiotics for your peace of mind. But I don't think you need them." He writes the chit for a ten day course of tablets; 500 milligrams each.

"Thank you and may I say 500 ml tablets are some peace of mind placebo. Who was it that told Jim he didn't need to worry?"

"Jim who?" He has no idea.

"Jim who? Jim who just died in Preston hospital of what started out as a swollen toe. Diagnosed here in Garth Prison."

"I don't know him. You can get the pills at the hatch, if it gets worse come back and see me." Still looking down at my file he finishes off, closing the blue cover and tossing it onto the job-done pile.

"Thank you doctor I'll do that. But with these," I wave the docket he's given me, "I think it'll be fine now." It takes another seven days before all is well and the price of my efforts to reduce my categorisation is finished for now.

Seeing a dentist is even more of a task. He only comes to the prison once every two weeks. When I had toothache they gave me two aspirins. When I went to the gym I asked the screw, Brett, for the pliers from the shadow box in the office and with them I pulled out my right upper first molar. One week of pain is all I could take. It's not easy to pull out your own tooth but when the pain is so bad desperation kicks in.

Stolen love

Rita and I find a blind spot where we can kiss and embrace without the cameras seeing us. There aren't many places in prison out of sight of security. Losing the red band turns out to be a blessing. Once a week I have to change the towels that are used in the chapel. The storeroom is on the other side of the jail. Out of my range of freedom to roam without the red band. So Rita has to escort me, unlocking doors that hinder our progress. The stairway leading down to the storeroom is our spot. Halfway down, out of sight of both doors top and bottom; we take time to have our romantic interlude. The towels seem to need changing more and more frequently and our trip is now twice weekly. Fire is leaping back and forward when we are together. It's not long before the boys on the wing see that fire and ask questions like 'have you two got something going on?' My mother whilst on a visit sees the fire and warns us. She has never been told of the love we have for each other. 'It's obvious', she tells us.

Every day we're together our love grows stronger, but that wall protecting that flower still has a strong hold on Rita. Problems seem to come from within that long-standing safe place but with every concern I speak just the right words to calm the waters. Ten years alone is a long time and when you are the one who has run the whole life of a family and house, letting someone into your world must be hard. It's the first time I've got to know someone first. I've usually had sex first and then why do you need to get to know them? We are really getting to know each other and any concerns are dealt with. Rita is here working for the first time as a full-time employee of the prison service. For years she's worked between prisons all over the North West. A day here and a day there. No entitlements such as holiday pay or pension. If she had a day of she didn't get paid. This kind of life is always destined to collapse. And it did. Driving on the motorway Rita didn't know what day it was or what prison she was heading for. She stopped the car as soon as she could and heard God say. 'Okay super woman what are you going to do now?' Then a song came on the radio. Rita said to God 'please don't leave me here'. That was two years ago. It's time now. God is fulfilling that request. But she has to step out in trust. The travelling is over along with the being alone.

Rita has time off work coming up and I don't want to be out of touch for so long. The security of jail says she can't give any address or phone number. After finding her post code and dropping it into her handbag she gives in and tells me her phone number. Now I have the number I just have to circumnavigate the jail phone system. I can only phone approved numbers. I can't add Rita's number to my list for obvious reasons. And I can't add it to someone else's, a trick to hide who you're ringing.

A mate of mine from years ago was a Telecom engineer and I remember him telling me about call transfer. When I had my SCUBA diving shop we would divert the calls out of hours to our house. You phone the shop and it would ring in our house. I wonder if it would work now. On the next visit with my mother I hatch my plan. I explain my twenty-first century scheme to my nineteenth century mother leaving her with the instruction 'tell Mandy to do the divert; she will know what to do'. Mandy being my sister who lives with my mother. For you who are now lost let me tell you just how it works. My mother is one of my approved numbers so if I phone her all is good in the world of jail security. When I hang up Mandy knows to put the divert plan into action so when I ring right back I get Rita's home phone but the records of the jail show I phoned my mother twice.

Every day we talk on the phone Rita goes to visit with my mother in Whitehaven and we speak on my mother's phone. Rita bless her has not lived in my world of intrigue so she slips up now and then with things like 'I'll see you this afternoon' or my mother in the background calls out her name. But hey the prison holds eight hundred people why would security listen to the tapes of my calls? For the next four month love blossoms into talk of marriage and our life together outside prison. Without hesitation we both know we are to be husband and wife. On one of our Wednesday evening meetings I'm introduced to Rita's best friend. Monique has a sharp eye for a scam. She's worked with prisoners for years; her wisdom gained over time is priceless. She's not influenced by love. With one look into my eyes and a shake of my hand she has the measure of me. Her report to Rita is that she'll get away with nothing now. Compassion and passion is what Monique sees. Someone who can take the roll of the man of the house and the spiritual leader. Which I find strange when Rita has more spirit in her pinkie ring finger than I have in my whole body. The good report is a confirmation. One she really knew anyway. Monique gives me the new title of' Hunky Chunk. Better than some things I've been called.

Now I have a reason for parole and the wheels are set in motion. But will it be too late for me to persuade them that I'm safe to be let out? Reports time once more means answering the same questions I've answered for the last five years. This time I need to convince the parole board to let me out. The first report started back in December before Rita fell in love. Before I had a purpose in life other than revenge. My brother in Shetland has put himself forward as a place to live and has a job for me to go to. The parole board won't let me go to Whitehaven and if I have a job they can see I'm willing to earn a living by legal means. The prosecuting QC at my first trial asked me if I had ever worked in my life. For the jury to see I was a drug dealer and nothing else. This is what I told him.

'When I left school I started work in a print works where I spent twelve years. Then I was married and moved to Wigton. I worked in a cellophane factory for ten years. I started a scuba diving company with a club and shop. I worked as a forklift truck service engineer. Then a taxi driver. I started and ran a marine salvage company and at one time I sold door to door home security systems. So the answer to your question is yes I've worked.' He never asked me in the second trial.

Where does moving to Shetland leave us? I don't know is the answer to that. We both know we wouldn't stay in the UK when we marry. There's nothing here for me now. Only Rita who will live where ever we choose to. I still haven't got my cat C. Dream on. The probation guy from the jail has to interview me for their report. A nice guy with a quiet spoken voice and a frail build. The notepad on his lap records his thoughts as we talk for what must be over an hour. Then he says.

"Well I think that's enough Tony. I'll submit my report and I hope you are accepted for early release." He nervously taps his pen on the notepad resting on his crossed knee. Wanting to say something but not sure whether to or not.

"Can I ask you, do you think I have any chance of parole?"

"I don't know but my report will recommend it Tony." He's agitated. Fidgeting worries me so much I ask him.

"Is there something I should know, something you would like to tell me? I know it's a long shot so don't

321

bullshit me. If you know I've no chance then just tell me."

"Violent crime is always difficult to call Tony but it's not that. I've been a probation officer for fifteen years, most of that time spent in prisons. In all that time I've never before said what I'm going to say to you," now I haven't the slightest notion as to what's coming next.

"Okay just tell me and we'll get on with jail, only two more years and I'm out of here on time served." Then I hear words that twist my insides that tight I can't speak.

"I believe you are not guilty of this crime. I have interviewed hundreds if not thousands of people and I know you are innocent of this attempted murder. Are you okay? I've never told anyone that before. I really believe it Tony. Unfortunately for you it doesn't help and if I put that in my report they'll just disregard the whole report." Silence floods the room. I'm speechless with anger welling up inside me at the thought of the system telling me 'we know you didn't do it but it makes no difference to your incarceration'. If you've never been there you can't understand why it enrages me to be told by someone in the system I shouldn't be in prison.

This poor man doesn't know what he just did. He thinks he's helping me by believing in my innocence. Instead he has just shone a spotlight on the injustice of this farce that holds me wrongfully behind bars.

"You don't know how that makes me feel, but I can see you mean well and I thank you for telling me. Sometimes it's good to hear it from someone who is outside it all."

"You don't look pleased with what I said Tony."

"Sorry but you can't understand what it means to me to hear you say that till you've sat here." He's confused. "Your comment is painful to hear for me."

Even I don't fully understand why it's so painful to hear someone say with all honesty they believe I'm not guilty. Rita knows it but that's not the same as some guy who has nothing to do with me other than to write his report. Just doing his job. A task that he's undertaken thousands of times before and only this time is he moved by my situation to make this bold statement. His recommendation will help balance the scales of injustice. Some of the other reports may well be against my early release. November 10th is still a long way off and if I can get to Haverigg prison before then the scale will tip a little more in my favour.

When you're in love what can the world do to rob you of the joy? What can man do to me that would take away the delight of falling asleep with thoughts of my new love? Waking in that same seamless thought? Love letters and tokens of our affection flow to and fro between two youthful, hopelessly smitten children in love. A red rose made from bread is my valentine gift. To a fragrant rose I give a rose made from bread. Whatever I can use to turn into a token of my love in this limited world. The pen is my cupid's arrow striking that dying rose right at the centre of that walled garden. With music I speak words that tell Rita the passion burning in my heart. I arrange a mini disk player for her to listen to the tunes that span decades. From Dylan to Edvard Grieg. From tangled up in blue to the mood changing serenity of Morning Mood from Peer Gynt. Shakespeare's Duke Orsino in Twelfth Night married music and love like this.

If music be the food of love, play on;
Give me excess of it, that, surfeiting,
The appetite may sicken, and so die.

That strain again! It had a dying fall:

O, it came o'er my ear like the sweet sound,

That breathes upon a bank of violets.

I've got a woman way over town and she's good to me. Sam Cooke with his great collection of love-filled lyrics. The father of black music lost on the youth of this moment. A bother asked me who was singing the tune drifting from my cell. Cupid; that classic Cooke track from the50s it was. When I told him it was Sam Cooke his response was, 'who's he then?' She's my brown-eyed girl. Big Barry White may have said it all with 'you're my first my last my everything'. I Belong To You is the best love song ever written. The Duprees sung it in 1962, The Band and Dylan performed a memorable version in the film Natural Born Killers. The trance invoking repetitive boom boom of modern music isn't any food that I've ever tasted. That food is best left for those who have never tasted fine wine off the lips of a passionate woman.

Our taste in the same music is just another piece of the puzzle that fits perfectly into its rightful place. Our faith in God without the bondage of religion is another. We are not perfect people - who is? - But we are perfect for each other. I know why I had to be here. Why I needed to stand on that spot. That was where I was always headed. If we had met anywhere else we wouldn't have fallen in love. Life is a journey with twists and turns along the way. We take the dirt track sometimes not knowing just over the next hill there's a wide open road waiting to welcome us. I've walked through my valley and now I can see the green pastures.

This twist Rita was divinely shown. One day like any other day in the life of prisoner CP3703 holds big changes. Rita comes to collect me for work.

"I want you to give me all our letters and cards. Anything that we have together; I have all our letters in a big brown envelope. Reaching into my property box I ask her.

"Why. What's going on?"

"I don't know but this morning driving to work I felt the Holy Spirit stronger than ever before and he said 'go and get all your love letters out of his cell'. I've emptied my desk drawer of all yours. Something's going on I just feel it in my spirit Tony."

"Well here that's them all in there, what about me mate teddy?" I hold up the small gold furry teddy Rita had left in my cell one day.

"I think you should keep that. We all need someone to talk to." Her smile lights up the small cell.

"So what now?" I ask.

"I don't quite know. Work as usual. Come on if you're ready."

"I'm always ready to spend time with you my love."

Work in the company of the woman of my dreams. The excitement of our stolen love. The secret kiss. The out of sight touch of hands. Lunch time bang up is a time of reflection. A time to dream. To wonder what this morning was about. Is there something about to happen in our world? The peace and quiet is broken by the clatter of steel gates and keys turning in locks. The screw passes me by. A boot on the door brings him back.

"You haven't unlocked me."

"No work for you Crowe."

"What do you mean, no work I'm unlocked even if there is no work, I'm an orderly. Open the flap so I can speak face to face."

"I've just been told to leave you locked His voice wanes as he moves away from my door.

"Gary I shout over the corridor.

"Hey what's gan on like Tony?"

"I don't know Gary. I think I'm getting Shanghaied mate. Hang around the wing office and see if you can hear what's going on."

"Wey aye man. I'll be back soon Tony. Do you know ya self like?"

"Rita I think."

"I knew you two had a thing going on."

"Where do ya think I got that tin of corn beef for you?" I asked Gary what food he would like if he could have anything. Corn beef was his answer so Rita brought a tin in. Before little Gary gets back six screws and an S.O. stand on the other side of my locked door. Looks like we're going to have a bit of rough and tumble.

"Crowe put all your stuff in these bags." Six clear plastic sacks with the prison logo printed in prison blue on them come under the door.

"Why? What's going on?"

"Just pack, Crowe, you're going down the block son." There isn't a screw on the wing who doesn't call me by my first name. Without seeing the mufti squad outside I know they are the meat heads who eat testosterone for breakfast. Victims of the school bully trying to prove to themselves they are real men now.

"Open the flap so I can see you." Through the crack in the door I can see them; an S.O. and a business (my collective noun for screws) of goons who I don't recognise. The good news is they aren't kitted up for war. No helmets, shields or batons. The shampoo can stay in the bottle for now.

"Just pack. We'll be back in ten minutes." With that last word on the situation they head off. The wing is empty, even the cleaners aren't there. Is it the calm before the storm?

"Tony man what's gan on mate. They're gonna block ya pal."

"I know Gary. Looks like I've got that move I've been after. But to where I have no idea."

"You'll be okay man do ya want me to tell Rita?"

"No I think she'll know by now Gary."

"Drop us a note to tell us where you are mate."

"Will do. Now I have all this gear to bag up. I hate moving even when I know what's going on. Are you banged up?" I ask Gary.

"Aye man the whole jail's on lock down mate. They must think you's gonna kick off like, ha ha," he laughs.

To lock the wing down is one thing but the whole jail it's a piss take. Bags packed and sitting on the bed waiting for the return of my escort I can reflect on this morning's revelation given to Rita. But I still don't know what it is they know or think they know so I'm keeping ignorant until they tell me what they have.

"Back wall Crowe and put your prop away from the door." Extraction by the numbers even though I've never been nicked in five years. Even though this is my parole year. Why would I now do anything to have a black mark put on my file? I comply with all his commands. The key drops the tumblers in the lock and the door opens. My hands behind my back I anticipate the restraining steel bands that are now just a normal part of life.

"Turn round Crowe." The S.O. and two others are inside the door. The S.O. says. "You're going down the block for a while; the governor wants to talk to you. You'll be back on the wing soon after. Are you going to walk down without trouble?"

"Really! Well I would be a bit of a lunatic to say no now wouldn't I? What does he want and why not talk here?"

"You'll be told everything in the seg," I reach out for my bags. "You can leave them. I'll have them taken down for you later." After security has rifled through it all I think to myself. Prisoners are always extracted at lunch time when most inmates are sleeping or as in this case when work duties keep the inmates out of the loop. When I step onto the landing the ones who are banged up shout and bang their doors showing their disdain. A shout of 'where you going mate?' is answered by the S.O.

"He'll be back later on." I correct the statement.

"I'm out of here. I' won't be back on here mate I'll see you on the roundabout." That ever-turning rotation of prisoners trawling the blocks of HMP

Just as we get to the wing gate who should walk out of the wing office but me old mate Skeggy. Panic issues akin to the fox in the hen house. Skeggy being Skeggy ignores the obvious. And asks.

"Where you off to Tony?" turning to the S.O. he says."It took fewer men to arrest Ted Bundy. I can't believe he's done anything to put him in chalky."

"Can you go to your cell please. He'll be back soon."

"No more badminton for us mate I'm off out of here. See you around," I tell him.

The Segregation unit of a prison is not a happy ship of contentment. It's full of angry, at best, crazy at worst prisoners. Rebels like Dummer who think cooperating with the system is a sell out. Hurting people who are wandering in a wilderness of desperation. Fierce men on the outside but broken little boys on the inside. If left there their sanity is lost. The seg, block or chalky; whatever we call it the purpose can only be to break a man's spirit. The way to deal with it is not to become a part of it. Reception is the hub of movements.

"Take off your clothes and put on these." The block S.O. drops jail rags on the bench next to me. There's no point in saying anything, so I don't.

"What you been up to then?" The smirk on his face makes it a question he thinks he already has the answer to.

"When will I get my property back?"

"When we get it down here you'll get it son."

"I'm not your son and you aren't the daddy. So just put me in the cell and get the governor here so I can find out what I'm doing here." Everyone put in the block must be seen by a governor within 24 hours.

"All in good time. Don't tell me you don't know what you're here for."

"If you don't tell me then how would I know what rule I've broken?" I've not broken any is the truth. But Rita may have done.

"You know why you're down here so come on don't pretend you don't know."

"I only know what I've been told so why don't you enlighten me. You seem to be a man who knows all things." Waiting for his retort when a screw saves him.

"Sign there Crowe." He turns a sheet of paper and throws a pen on top of it. Not his pen. The one that only cons have ever touched.

"What's that then?" I don't even look down at it and sure as God made little green apples am not going to sign it.

"It's just to say you know why you're in the segregation unit."

"Well you tell me and then I'll sign it. Does that make sense to even you?"

"You are here to be interviewed by a governor."

"Well how 'bout you tell him I don't want the job. Interview over."

"Are you going to sign or not? It makes no difference to me pal."

"I think you know I'm not. Let's get on with it and get out of my face, PAL. When we go drinking together, you can call me pal. Until then stick to Crowe or 3703."

At that I head off to cell number two. A cell is a cell and what the wing is called be it house block or dorm it's still just a cell. Soon the guys want to know who's joined the selective band of down and outs. Shouts from windows soon identify the new transgressor as myself. I need to know where I'm heading to. My jailers aren't forthcoming to my request for information. If I refuse food they can't move me. One, I'm not fit to travel and two; no prison will take a hunger striker. When the door opens to serve food from a wheeled trolley I ask the screw.

"Where am I going from here?" He still has his key in the lock and his arm is lying across the open door.

"I don't know, are you not just here till the governor sees you?"

"No I'm for a ship-out But I want to know where to. If you can't tell me you can stick that food."

"Are you refusing food. 'cos if you are you have to take it into your cell and..." I stop him.

"I have been on hunger strike twice so don't lecture me on your stupid protocol of starvation. Shut the door and don't open it again till you know where I'm being shipped to."

No more screws show up till morning breakfast. The same reception greets that screw. I feel a bit like an Old Testament Christian again, if you can be such a thing. Blood and guts kind of a believer right now is what I am. I'm ready when the door opens at lunch time to keep up my solid stance.

"Come on Crowe reception The S.O. says.

"I want to know where I'm going. Don't treat me like a mug, just tell me and we'll get on a lot better."

"You're going to Preston so come on and let's all be grown up hey?" As much as I hate Preston it's not Wakefield or Dartmoor.

"Okay that's all I ask. Why the big mess about?"

Reception holds another surprise. Prison is not all the same although the same rules apply. A list of what I can take with me could be written on the back of a fag packet. No Hi Fi. No typewriter. No clothes. No bedding. Out of six sacks I'm left with one half full. That all sorted the chub handcuffs clamp my wrists together. Handcuffed to the shaven headed sixteen stone goon with another set of blue bracelets. The van is waiting at the door twenty yards away. One screw leads the way opening the door and holding it till we pass through it. Stepping into the noon sun light on this June spring day. Rita is walking towards us. I smile as I glance down at the hand cuffs. Sadness in her eyes breaks my heart and my smile melts away. When will I see her again when will I hold her in my arms. The soft skin of her neck. When will I see my love again? What will be the cost of our love? When Adam ate the fruit he didn't do it unknowingly. If his woman were to die then so was he. He didn't want Eve to die alone. Romeo and Juliet weren't the first to die for each other. I can't help her now she has to do this for our love to become stronger.

The stinking waiting room at Preston is just as I remember it.

"Crowe CP3703." That's my call to the desk.

"That'll be me then." Standing on the line at the required distance from the desk.

"Do you have any objection to sharing a cell?" Never been asked that before.

"Yes."

"Why?"

"Well I like to eat and use the toilet without an audience. So single cell for me will do just fine," I tell him.

"We don't have single cells here."

"Well why did you ask me?"

"Why have you been sent here?" He's reading the file that will now say 'Corrupts prison staff' but it may not say how I got that warning marker put onto my file.

"You do have single cells. The block. They're all single."

"Says here..." He stops.

"Yes what does it say...? What about my single? I came from the block so prison rules say I go into the block; right?"

"They told us you came off location. Have you come from Garth block?" He looks in disbelief at his buddy.

"They lied. Did you swap one for one? And you got me. Well I feel better knowing they even lie to you lot. That's funny."

"You're going on the reception wing overnight and tomorrow you're going in a double cell. Get some food over there and wait to see the Doctor. Murry!" He shouts for the next guy waiting in the filthy waiting room as he waves me on my way.

Food and Doctor done the overnight wing is an effort to quell the first night suicides. Screws with a good bedside manner and a nice cup of tea. Oh and the all important reception pack.

"Smoker or non smoker Crowe?" You can have a fiver in smoking gear or in phone card and sweets. Now my phone could be compromised but these cards are good for any number until they can set up your account. Could get a smoking pack and swap with this kid who's come in with me. To confuse the spies.

"None smoking gov for me," I say "Can I use the phone now my people don't know I've been shanghaied. I've a visit coming up and I'm not there."

"Yes you can use it in ten minutes just let me sort the rest out first."

"Is there any chance of a single cell gov I really need time alone to sort me head out."

"We don't have singles, and we like two in a cell for the first night."

"My first night was five years ago and I'm doing twelve years. You know what I mean? Come on I'll keep me head down and I'm a listener so if you need me I'll help you out."

"We have room for you to be on your own but if we get more in you'll have to double up."

"Great I appreciate it gov. I don't want to face the world right now."

Number two of the twenty cells is my new resting place for now. The phone call to Mandy fills me in on Rita's situation. She is suspended pending an investigation into an inappropriate relationship with a prisoner. The phone is now a problem. The spotlight will shine on all aspects of Rita and me including the tapes of our phone calls. I was once given good advice; when you have nothing to say in your defence, let them hang you. Don't open your mouth and tie the knot in the rope for them.

****

Rita:

Without seeing you or holding you I'm keeping this diary of my thoughts for that day when we can once again be together my love Tuesday 1st July 03

It's been 19 days since I saw your sweet face. Pain, pain, as your medal says...'the courage to know the difference'. Nothing we can do, but put our trust in God & hold on to our special love that knows no time or distance. I love you every minute of every day, our love only gets stronger by our separation.

My heart aches for you; of what you're having to endure there, you're right I do know your days there & it causes me much pain my darling, but you will know because our hearts are one. When will you read these words? Only God knows, but you will read them & with me in your arms my precious one. No regrets indeed my darling, no matter what we have to face I don't regret one minute of our precious time together, God given indeed. What a shock that Thursday lunchtime. I was in a daze driving home & just went on automatic, it was that night that it hit me & I cried, I cried, not for me my love but you. Where were you!! Such despair to not know what had happened to you. Should it have been such a shock that morning?

Driving to work the clearest voice of God I've ever heard 'get all the cards out of the cell', so strong. God is with us in this my love. Never doubt however painful; & it is. He is with us. Trust, at least I have your words & music. You have nothing. But you do my darling because my heart is in you & we must draw strength from each other. To get your card & letter was unbelievable joy but also tremendous heartache. I know, as you do, they will use it against me. They don't need any proof. I am not free my darling, big brother is also with me. Listening to my phone as well no doubt. All we had built upon to do everything right & honouring God, still stands before him, but after talking with my boss at H.Q. I was devastated to hear it will only be my word against all their malicious thoughts of what we had been up to on a daily basis. It seems the experience of the prison service of Chaplaincy is quite shocking to me. Six chaplains in the last 4 years have been sacked for having sexual

relations with inmates; staff both men with men &
women with women!

How then will they believe in my integrity when they
no doubt have heard us on the phone pouring out our
love to each other? Their measure is not ours my
darling & they will think what they will, indeed
rumours around the prison & beyond, what I haven't
been up to. Including trafficking is not worth hearing
about & although that brings discomfort. We know &
God knows & that my dear is what really matters,
whether they choose to believe the truth is out of my
hands. What is important is that we know & God
knows. The future? Us together my sweetheart for the
rest of our lives. For without that there is no future that
I desire. Together forever, I love you with all of my
being xxx.

****

The screw leaves me alone for a week in that
overnight cell before he calls me to the office to inform
me I'll be moved after lunch. A. wing has a cell with
my name on it and someone else's. Top landing where
the pigeons roost, cell number fifteen. The window
looks over the old sand stone wall, blackened from the
traffic fumes of the inner city bus route. The wing, like
Durham, is a relic from the Victorian era. Wrought-iron
walkways hanging off the wall under the blue doors
with their white handles lining up like teeth grinning
back at me. Suicide netting stretching across the void.
Still without all my property I take up residence in cell
fifteen top floor. What I call the threes but they call the
fours.

"The first floor is the ones right?" I ask the guy
serving food.

"No that's the twos mate." But there are only three
floors, or landings.

"I'm on the threes in fifteen mate so whatever the guy before me ordered that's mine." When you first get a cell on a new wing the meal for that cell is what you get till you can fill in your own menu for the coming week.

"No three fifteen has gone mate we're feeding the fours now. You must be in four fifteen."

"But there are only three landings. How can I be on the fours?"

"The block's the ones mate."

"The block? But this is A. wing and that's the seg. Two different wings."

"I, mad isn't' it mate but believe me you're on t' fours mate, are ya in with deaf kid?"

"Yes William." He's standing beside me next in line.

"Chicken pie mate. Chips or mash we' that?"

"Chips pal. This place burns my head out."

"It's one way an' know mate you have to go back the other way."

My cell mate William has been in here for a week. He has two cases ongoing in two different court districts. When he's in Preston court he stays here and when he's up at Manchester he stays there. Preston jail is a local. Not that it's close to home. No it's a jail where people wait to go to court. Like Durham. I'm back with remand prisoners. I don't even ask William what he's in for. For one I'm not interested and two William is profoundly deaf. He has two hearing aids but the batteries are dead and the jail just doesn't understand what he wants. Still he doesn't ask questions and he doesn't mind the radio on late at night when the radio Mersey talk show plays requests for prisoners in between chat.

****

Rita: Spiritual Diary 1st July

336

Prayer need; peace for financial provision for my children - fear - not enough money to provide with a different job - what can I do?

Answer. My child, the scene of isolation experienced in treading my way is a stage which I see as necessary for you (I do feel isolated from my work, all that I've known for many years. My focus.) There is a temptation to feel too much is being given up. To feel, even that you have been mistaken about the rewards of the spiritual life. Did T & I make the right decision? People will think what they think anyway, rumours!

You have my promise that the stage of feeling isolated, perhaps discouraged, is a very positive one in your growth. You will find that nothing (harmless in itself) which seemed to be coming between us & which you have surrendered, will ever be subject to regret. What I give to you is of infinitely more worth than earth's riches.

In what the world may see as isolation (suspension, fear, shame.) you will find companionship at the deepest level, a sense of being lifted through uncharted areas of difficulty. Affirm very strongly when tempted to feel discouraged that I belong to you!... Aware of being provided for in the fullest possible sense.

I will go with you and prosper all that you do (Exodus 33: 14) I am with you.

Rita: From word for today 1/7/03.

There were many lepers. The only one cleansed was Na'aman .Luke 4: 27.

It's easy to believe God for something you've already seen him do before. Na'aman's circumstances were unique nobody he knew had been healed. Are you being tested today? A unique situation, your Job? You don't know of anyone who's beaten your particular problem, (all Bob W. words of 6 others in 4 years!) Stop focusing on the circumstances & start focusing on

God. He doesn't need anything to begin with in order to solve your problem. Remember, in Genesis He hung the earth on nothing & it's still turning today! Listen Na'aman.. Was a great man 2 Kings 5; 1, But God was about to make him an exceptional one. Whenever he does that he permits us to get into predicaments without human solutions. What he wants us to have extraordinary influence. He often permits extraordinary affliction (ouch). Before you can be exceptional you must work to develop a faith that believes God for the impossible & trusts what he says, regardless of the pain or the odds. (Tony's situation at present, parole, again Bobs words of doom & gloom! Not receiving them!!)

God calling.

Do not fear. Remember how I faced the devil in the wilderness & I conquered with. The word of God is living & active. sharper than any double edged sword it penetrates even to dividing soul & spirit, Joints & marrow; it judges the thoughts and attitudes of the heart. Hebrews 4; 12 Andrew's opening to July prayer letter from Garth. Praise God!! "The sword of the spirit" You too have your quick answer for every fear, faith & confidence in me. Say it out aloud. Spoken word has power. Look on every fear not as weakness but as a very real temptation to be attacked & over thrown.

Rita: Wednesday 2/7/03.

Oh my precious the agony & the ecstasy, got a card & a letter today, words to read over & over again, but the agony of being able to write to you to help you through this troubled time is almost more than I can bear. Part of me just wants to 'sod it' & write anyway, any cost! But no my love must not give them any more fuel for their fire. Oh to be free to talk write & visit!! Hold on my love I draw strength from you as you do from me. You're right my heart beats in you, when I sleep you sleep. Has there ever been such a love as ours? It has certainly got stronger since we've been parted. Nothing will come between us my precious. Sr Mary rang this morning to make sure I was OK & to let me know the whole force of the R.C. nuns are praying & lighting candles even a novena too she said (9 days!) so my love we are covered on all sides. As I spoke with Mary & she asked if I'd heard from you, tears come into my eyes & a great weight in my heart. I feel so much pain for you & your life at present. How I long to reassure you my love. Then I prayed & put you completely in God's care. Rest in his love my sweetheart & you will feel mine automatically. Last Sunday coming out of church the most beautiful rose bush got my attention. I walked over to it & touched a rose & smelled its perfume & just like you with the plant on the piano, I was filled with warmth & felt you with me & peace from God that indeed passes all understanding. He is with us xxx.

Just had a chat with your mum, haven't spoken to her since her birthday. I tried to keep it light & we laughed a lot, she worries, not just about you but she has me now! & I don't want to add to her burden so I reassured her best I could, I am fine & our love is worth much more than a Job! It's for life & we will get through this my love. All my worries of finances, mortgage etc. wouldn't worry me at all if it was just me but my responsibility to Ben & Lucy... But God knows all these things & I put my trust in him. If it were just me I'd not bother! Would be visiting you as soon as the VO arrived...

But it's not just me ...& I can't wait till it's "we." I love you. Graham Rev rang me last night. He hadn't heard. I told him what I've been told & nothing more. He said I wasn't to worry about you, as there was more to you than meets the eye! How true is that my love?

339

But we obviously came to the conclusion from different standpoint! Mandy told me of the "green pen" & it won't photocopy. I laughed! How clever you are my love. I just wish there was some way I could contact you but I'm working on it & if it works it will be a very pleasant surprise for you xxx.
****

Repeated attempts to find out what's going on falls on stony ground. A meeting with the Board of Visitors, an organisation in place to deal with complaints by prisoners of the abuse of rules, results in a big fat zero. One month since my relocation. No phone calls and no visits from my beautiful Rita. I write to her using an address where my love letters are forwarded to her. I use a highlighter pen in vivid green just so the jail has to copy by hand all my letters. Photocopies don't pick up the ink on highlighters so all they get is a blank sheet of paper when they try to photocopy it. Why bother? Well why not? It's all just a game and you have to let them know that you know. On the phone to my mother I say what I want them to hear. Disinformation is still a good distraction for my long fast from my beloved Rita. The pain is killing my soul but feeding my love.

I fill my day with education. When I came in the obligatory test for literacy & numeracy was given to me and about ten others. Someone thinks education is the way to stop crime. Shame they don't think like that in the schools. Being an old hand at jail thinking and thanks to the guy sitting at my desk. I know education is better than working in some mind-numbing workshop. So you flunk the test and get fast-tracked to the learning zone. My illiterate friend told me to be careful not to guess because you can get forty percent right and that's a pass. In failing I open the door to computer skills and to creative writing. Preston has no badminton courts so old Betsy gets a rest. Without my typewriter the computer room is a must for my writing. While printing is out of bounds I am given my own disk to save my work. Creative writing means we get to watch a film then read the book. Just fine for keeping my head down. Fight club film is a struggle to watch but the book is a non- event for me. I once read a book that said no book deserves to be read. If it doesn't hold you after the first chapter you can close it, so that's what fight club gets from me. Film 1, book zero. Next is the film Shawshank Redemption. Great film with great acting. The book is called Rita Haywood and The Shawshank Redemption. The book is better than the film for me. Rambo book for sure. Style of writing is something you can't get from someone else it has to be unique. Sometimes too much knowledge is a bad thing. If you've got this far reading my story I thank you.

****

Rita: Thursday 3/7/03.

Joy at getting another card for my collection! Good news about Shelley. Funny how 'news' travels & it already spread to Shelley's home town! What has she heard! But if she's like you she won't be shocked! I just wonder how much 'news' or just the malicious rumours that I've heard. I decided to keep this diary as I so miss writing to my love; we got to know each other so well over the six months, yes almost six months. Half a year. How did we survive? I know one thing my love even though I was not really aware of it, I was under a tremulous strain, only when it all came down & I'd got over the shock, I realised how much strain I'd been under. Not a way we would have chosen my love, but it happened & as you say all part of God's plan for us. Pain but necessary!

This last couple of days I've had feelings of anger, deep anger! How dare they make something bad &

shameful of our beautiful love? We did not choose to fall in love it happened & I thank God with all my being for bringing us together at last! The anger has gone that's only destructive & negative, been replaced by peace. He is in control. My deepest pain is for you my darling & that I can't contact you. But feel you know I am with you every minute of every day when I sleep you are there in my arms when I awake you are there & I kiss you my love. Life without you in it would be no life at all xxx.

So down this afternoon. Lost, despair. I long for you so much & I can't see any time soon I can't bear this feeling. Such a longing in my heart to hold you. Tried to get on & do things but I can't. I'm too sad. Are you feeling down too my love? I know in my heart that we will be together, but time seems endless today. No end in sight for the pain I feel. Your music hasn't helped, I feel worse.

Two hours later & I feel better. I went for a long walk, cried en route got things in perspective again. Made a meal, drank plenty of wine (I know it's not the answer but it helps me for now) then when alone again I need your words, the words & cards since all this happened, you made me smile & you made me thank God once again.

I'm pleased your passions are aroused my love. I've been funny in that department my sweet. Only once have I had those feelings & you were needed. Soon my sweet. What have you done to me? Washed away all the pain & made me feel like woman again. All for you xxx.

Even in these times of financial & emotional uncertainty I wouldn't swap what we have for anything, Good night. God bless my love xxx.

Rita: Saturday 5/7/03.

I went to Preston today on the train that was to be a bit nearer to you! Ridiculous.

Rita: Saturday 2/8/03.

New day new freedom. Yesterday Ben's birthday & the day after my abuse, I was close to the edge couldn't eat, felt sick all the time an ache in the back of my head. That lots of alcohol & cigarettes did not improve. Got up after bad alcohol induced sleep & felt like crap. Made myself eat, hard but did it. Exercise, prayer, thoughts. If only I could speak with you my darling, if only I could hear you I know you would have the right words for me. Pain ,pain, pain.

Gradually it dawned on me, you are here with me I closed my eyes & felt your love, my heart full, your words let go of the past, look to us, look to the future, let go...

What a peace I felt. I do not want to go back to work for HM Prison service! "Don't worry about a thing, cause every little thing gonna be al'right Bob Marley on the radio. You or what?

Rita: Wednesday 6/8/03

It's been more than a week since I heard anything from you or about you. Pain. Mandy had no word & no mail for me. Sometimes I feel lost from you in the big outside world & you. Where are you? It's only with an act of will I pause & pray & feel you once again in my heart xxx.

I love you so much xxx.

I have just been & posted a letter to gov. Lomas Am I meant to contact him? Do I care? No. I will tell you one day my love how painful these two and a half hours were, it would have been less so if they'd just pulled my fingernails out that is only physical pain, my heart was abused every word we have ever spoken on the phone was placed before me in huge files & even one played out loud, shame? Embarrassment? No! An invasion of our love, words of love between us that was the worst pain of all my darling, but I kept on to the end...

343

Why write? Well he could have made it much worse; he did try to spare my embarrassment but of course had to 'prove' their case of inappropriate behaviour. All the time we tried my love meant nothing to them, falling in love with a prisoner, staying with his family... Guilty I'm afraid my love. So the wheels are now in motion for a formal investigation which will take a minimum of 3 months! Of no concern now my darling now I have let the past go. He did; off tape of course, express sympathy with my situation... So I wrote him a letter to thank him for that & to point out that I did not choose to fall in love & did my utmost to keep my integrity - enough for us but not them.

Rita: Sunday 10/8/03.

I am lost in the big outside world! What to do? I haven't heard from you for nine days! Lost indeed...On Tuesday it will be eight weeks 61 days since our world fell apart, it seems forever... I've been trying to get a reply from my request for contact with you via my union rep via governor...Endless & the pain goes on... just to see you, just to talk with you. Oh my heart aches so bad. Yesterday as I walked around all I could see were couples, holding hands, young, old everywhere. Why not us? Will it one day happen? It seems like a distant dream just now.

Your mum rang me last night from Alan's. I talked so positive about us being there together in November. It has to be; hasn't it? November even seems forever from where I am now. Beyond? No. Lucy's gone away again & It's terrible on my own, too much time to fill, battle to do anything but sit or lie on my bed & think of you & 'us'. What 'us'? Yes I'm down baby & that's why I'll write it here & not to you, you have enough to cope with in there. When & where will you move? Wish it were Kirkham because I am determined I'll visit with you. & Haverigg is a long way from here. Just to see

*you! Is it too much to ask after all the pain &
heartache? Endless. What does the future hold? I know
that God holds our future in his hands & I do trust him
& only his plan is the right one, I know that but today is
hard rain indeed. Must do something, this is no good
sat here...*
****

The 6th of August and I'm taken to the block to be
interviewed by the governor of Garth prison. In the
underground dungeon what is the ones of A. wing. I'm
led into an office where a small guy and a young girl,
smelling of sweet perfume, are sat behind the only
desk. The light from the overhead bulb reflects like a
mirror from his shining head. One other chair on my
side of the desk awaits my derrière. I've seen this guy in
Garth but never spoken to him. He was a floating figure
I passed on the wing and in the corridors of crime. I had
no idea he was a governor. On the desk, being operated
by the young girl is a police station style tape machine.
Black with its red buttons, dual cassette doors open
mouthed waiting for the tapes.

"Take a seat please." I don't wait for his first
question.

"First thing is no recording. And second what rule
have I infringed? If there is to be any action taken
against me I want my lawyer here."

"If you don't want the tape on that's fine it's just
easier for me. You haven't infringed any rule; you aren't
the focus of the investigation."

"So what do you want from me?"

"Rita Carroll has told us that she and you have a
relationship that is deemed to be inappropriate in hers
and your position."

"So why do you need me to give you bullets for
your gun? Do whatever you're going to do and keep me
out of it. You want me to nail down the lid. Well ask

345

your questions and lose the only one in Garth that understands what prison is and what prisoners are all about."

"OK does your brother own a flower shop?"

"That's nothing to do with you or whether Rita did any wrong."

"Do you smoke?"

"Nothing to do with this inquiry."

"When you were on the phone to your mother you spoke to a woman and someone in the background called out 'Rita', who was that?"

"You tell me."

"We know from Rita what we need to know, I can play the tapes for you if you like. She says she loves you and you love her. She says she spent time at your mother's home in Whitehaven."

"Just what is it you are saying we have done?"

"She has had an inappropriate relationship with a prisoner, you have done nothing. This rule isn't for prisoners it's for staff."

"OK so what does that mean? If you think we were sexually involved you're wrong. I know that's what it comes down to."

"If Rita treated you any different to the rest of the prisoners that would be inappropriate. She spent time at your mother's home and you spoke on the phone."

"This interview is over. You do what you have to and we'll get on with our lives." I get up and leave.

The result of Rita's 'inappropriate behaviour' comes down to her resignation. Love will overcome all with the added benefit of visits.

Preston is a local jail and they don't want me taking up a cell that could be better used for remand prisoners. I need to start my cat C campaign all over again. With a new jail and a new governor I could stand a good chance of success. Maybe this is a Rita's gambit. The

346

aim is still to get to Haverigg prison. My personal officer is the first target. He's not only my personal officer; he has about ten others who demand his attention. I have a slight edge on the others. When I came from Garth he was one of the screws who with a nod and a wink sniggered. I asked him if he knew Rita; of cause he did. She had worked there.

"Yes she worked here in the chapel for years." He says.

"And did she in all the time you knew her do anything wrong? Did she sleep around with half the jail? Bring in drugs or did she just do her job? And do it well? She was the only one who the prison let loose on the drug wing without officers being there." I'm riled.

"I never had anything but high regard for Rita she..."I can't hold back.

"Then why do you think she would have sex with a prisoner in a prison cell? Or do you think we had sex in the chapel?"

"It's what's going round. She wouldn't be the first and if it's offered on a plate who can blame you."

"You must live a boring life if that's what excites your day."

"I don't believe Rita would do what they're saying. She was always a ray of light when she was here."

"So you can tell the people who snigger about things they know nothing about; how wrong they are," I say.

"Well?" He doesn't know what to say or where to look.

"I can't believe she did anything wrong." He's back-peddling. Embarrassed after being challenged by someone who wasn't, as he thought, just after a quick encounter to bring sexual relief. He's more embarrassed when he finds out he's my personal officer. Coyness I can exploit. He has to plan my progress. Without cat C status I'm in a cul-de-sac. All things back to mundane daily grind. Time has come to see the movements' officer. This guy can send me on to Haverigg or down south to a bigger dump and miles away from Rita. I have to convince this screw I'm just what Haverigg needs.

The affect of drugs in Preston is pandemic. Every day drug projectiles bounce off the yard walls. If you're not paying attention while you're walking round the yard an orange may hit you on the head. The orange skin is stuffed with drugs. Or maybe a phone. This is the first time I've come across mobile phones in jail. Come to think of it I've never seen a modern phone that fits inside a hollowed out jaffa. If Rita had brought me one into Garth we wouldn't be in trouble for talking on the jail phone. Just goes to show, if you're going to break one rule you might as well break them all. It's difficult to find anyone who I can hold an intelligent conversation with. The chaplain is The Painted Lady from Garth. She can't believe I didn't make a move on her and she says as much. I'm taken aback. She is not only married but not my type. She just wants the juicy tit-bits. No meaningful, challenging stimulus from her. Forget the screws. No gym. Food down to a pre packed sandwich for lunch. Visits from my mother are good but she has to take two trains and stand on the street till they let her into the prison. She's my only regular visitor along with my youngest son. What he thinks I don't know. Time to move on.

My relentless toil over the last two years could be at an end when I come out of this office.

"Take a seat. You came here from Garth and you're serving 12 years for attempted murder." He looks over the top of his glasses. "You've served five years?" More of a surprised statement than a question.

"This is my sixth year and my parole year so a cat C would be good. It could help me get out."

"Have you had all your reports done Tony?"

"Yes November 11th is my EDR (earliest date of release)

"Well I can't see why we can't send you to a cat C prison." Yes; what a result I just have to get him to recommend Haverigg now. But before I can compose myself he continues. "Where do you want to go?" without sounding too enthusiastic I say. "Well Haverigg is close to my home town and my mother has a long way to come down here. She's travelled all over England in the last six years; it would be great if I could get to Haverigg."

"Okay but there's a waiting list for Haverigg it might take a week or two."

"I've waited nearly six years, two court cases, four categorisation review denials a medical operation and a sexual immorality accusation. I can do another two weeks."

"Your file is clean. Why has it taken so much to get to a cat C?"

"I have a great gift of upsetting people. Governors mostly."

"Not one nicking in over five years I would say that's a record. It would be in here I know that."

"Keep me-self to me-self and just want to do me jail but that's not enough for them. I was told when I got the twelve years 'you just do what you can and the governor will see you do the rest.' And they don't want me to have it easy."

"Over a hundred drug tests and not one positive result?"

"More, I stopped counting at a hundred and fifty. I don't keep the certificates any more. They don't get it. This shit is easy for me I don't do drugs and I don't let people get to me. It's not an achievement for me. It's normal life. I haven't had a cigarette all week. It's not an achievement; I don't smoke. Do you understand what I'm saying?"

"In prison it's not normal. Everyone is on drugs. Everyone is doing things they shouldn't be doing. We don't get many who aren't so I suppose we don't see the ones who live within the rules."

"You know there's no statutory law against murder? It's called Common Law. No one had to sit down and decide murder was wrong; it's obvious to any sane person. We, as human beings know right from wrong we don't keep to rules we do what's right. What credit should you get for just doing what's right?"

"Not everyone thinks like that though. Most think rules are made to be broken."

"If I keep prison-made rules but they don't keep their own rules what does that say to me? Why should I play their game? Prisoners see the prison behaving unjustly so they justify their own bad behaviour."

"Interesting but some people just think they can do what they like regardless of others around them. They will never keep to the rules," he says.

"True, think about this and I'll let you get on with your work. Without the Law or rules there would be no wrongdoing. Let me put it this way because I'm a Christian. Without God telling Adam not to eat from the tree in the Garden of Eden, man wouldn't have fallen from grace. Same with the Ten Commandments. They didn't stop sin they made what was being done sin. They showed the ones doing wrong what wrong was. As if they didn't know anyway. There's no reward for doing what's right, just punishment for doing wrong."

"You a philosopher then?"

"No I'm not; philosophy has no place for God. Jean-Paul Sartre said: 'Life has no meaning the moment you lose the illusion of being eternal.' We are all eternal beings the only question is where will we spend eternity?"

"Well for now you'll spend the next year or two in HMP Haverigg. Keep doing what you're doing and I can't see why you shouldn't get your parole."

"That would be a reward then for doing good?" he hasn't got my point. However, he has got the power to send me to Haverigg.

Every day new prisoners arrive. Some of them from police stations, others from prisons. A name I know from long ago comes onto our wing. He's a friend of a guy I met in Durham. One of the Strangeway rioters back in the nineties over ten years ago now. When I asked him what he was back inside for he told me he wasn't back in, he was still in. He got ten years for the roof-top occupation of Manchester's local prison. To be served after he had finished his five years for drugs; the crime he was in for in the first place.

"If you watch the news footage I was the one in the yellow waterproof coat. I was next to last off the roof," he tells me.

"Who was last?"

"Taylor was. He said if I didn't get off he would chuck us off. We was shafted mate, they changed the law just for us. No time off or parole for prison mutiny. That's what they called it." Taylor was the guy I met in Durham.

"How come you're in here?"

"I was kicked out of Haverigg mate. I can't do with cat C jails mate they're too petty, you can't move without them sitting on you."

"I'm waiting to go there what's the score?"

"It's great if you keep your head down and get onto R4. At first it's a bit basic but after a week you move from R1 to R2. R1's single cells. But the rest of the jail's billets."

"Visits?"

"A joke mate you could get an Uzi in through the visits." Not exactly what I was thinking about.

To top it all the parole board representative has come to write her report. 'Independent Witness' as they call her. All she wants to talk about is why I was moved from Garth and do I think I'm rehabilitated. What coursework have I done and, of cause, how do I feel about the victim? I feel like a bandsman on the Titanic. Playing in the face of inevitable doom. She never says she thinks I might be innocent.

****

Rita: Tuesday 12/8/03.

Must be a memorable day for us in our days. I hear tell you've seen your independent witness. You were prayed for. I got my "Without You" letter, my heart, my soul moved. You say it so well I feel. You feel. Pain. No word from Gillie. Clean, clean. Your mum coming for lunch on Thursday. June for tea. Lovely hundreds of butterflies inspired me to run to post box with Keswick postcard. Sent with such love, such pain we feel. Only 5 minutes walk.

Just been with misty, good dog. Brisk walk fresh air feeling you every step, will we walk here soon? This winter. Please God every day feelings for you. More intense. Will you be here this winter? Will you touch me? Will you? Hold me? Will you kiss me? So intense, so much love. Is it the same? Is it worse? Will it end? Will we be as any other couple in love? But one day my love, one day...

Rita: Saturday 16/8/03.

Another week in my dear sweetheart, kept busy all week, Lucy been away, back today. Twelve weeks you write. Can we wait? Well I was thinking, we've done 12 weeks yes 3 months apart now & although it's been agonising for both of us we've done it. Hoped for a

352

letter this morning as I know one is on the way, Disappointed, have to wait till Monday now but it's something to look forward to & I'm thinking you'll get a move soon. I hope to Kirkham as it's near here & I am determined to visit you. Haven't had a reply from governor Lomas. Rep on the case. Wednesday was a bad day. I got your letter & saw your agony between the lines.... Pain in my heart & soul... Had arranged to go to Walt & Val's at Heysham, worked very hard till 8.30 at night... Needed it to take my mind off things. It's good I have people, sensible people on the same planet! To talk to, this brings home the pain of your situation so much. Oh my darling you can talk forever to me & yes, just with your eyes you say so much. Mine will also speak to you forever my love I just can't wait & once we are married my sweet we will never be parted promise xxx.

Had a good day with your mum on Thursday, so good to bring her to my humble home but so full of love & happiness. Just missing one thing my love & that's you. So pleased she met my son as well, great.

****

Prison isn't that big of a world even with over 85 thousand people locked up. Often two opposing factions end up in the same jail. Just like in Durham when witnesses in my case ended up having to face me. Now a drug dealer who promised he would 'do me in' has turned up here. Back in '95 I was sitting in the court at Whitehaven waiting for a fare when he and ten homie-boys of his made the threat.

I was a taxi driver back then. My brother had an altercation with this guy who lived over the road. I was called on the taxi radio to help. When I got there the drug dealer with his minions had smashed the window of my brother's car. For no reason that was personal. Just wanton vandalism from people who thought they were untouchable. My sister-in-law had phoned the police by the time I arrived so we waited for the plod to send the cavalry. When I went out to lock the taxi two thugs from the drug house, came bouncing over the fence heading for me.

"Ya needn't think ya can blame us for that mate." They were now coming down the garden path towards the front door. Inside were my sister-in-law and her grandchild, a baby in arms.

"No one has said anything yet and I'm not your mate I was standing on the doorstep looking out for the police car. Another tall figure lunged through the middle of the first two with a misdirected punch. When I tried to make a strategic retreat into the house I found the door had been locked. With my back to the wall and nowhere to go I had to fight. In no time two more and a pit-bull were all trying to take a piece of me. As I bent forward to avoid an incoming punch I saw it, the short wooden shaft and the glint of metal. It turned out to be a ball-pain hammer. I managed to escape into the house just before the police car pulled up outside. One old copper came up the path and knocked on the door. Bernie it was and the irony is he was the first on the scene at Swindles' when he was cut up. Well the night turned into one in the police cells for the house full of young thugs. The hospital was the first stop for most of them. I was asked to identify them. Just lock up the ones that are bleeding I told them; so that's what they did, five of them.

I was asked the next morning to make a statement but told the police to let them out I had nothing to say. I would like to say at this point I was a law-abiding, hard- working member of society. The plastic gangsters couldn't lose face so the big wheel made a show of puffing out his chest in front of his homie-boys in the court waiting room. My mate Craig was amazed when I answered with 'okay thanks for letting me know'. He couldn't believe I just took it. That night someone poured petrol on the windows and doors of the plastic gangster's house and set it alight. I was arrested for it. No charges were brought. The others were the ones in the house when someone shot it up with a sawn-off shotgun. I was arrested for that as well. No evidence. No charges yet again. Now he's here. I wonder if he still wants to kill me!

The reason he's turned up here is interesting. Hiding from the ones who he turned Q.E. on is what I'm told. When the swoop came for his turn to pay the price for his drug dealing he took the witness box and gave what is called Queen's Evidence (Q.E.). Now he has to move around to avoid retribution. He has no time for me, a small part of his past.

Preston phones are inside wooden kiosks, top half plastic glass and the bottom a solid panel. The phone box cuts out the din of the prison mayhem, whilst keeping the user in full view. With my head resting on my arm as it lays on the phone box window a strange sight, even for prison, enters my vista. Bright blue suede, pointed- toe ankle boots. The wearer is a stocky guy wearing a dapper theatrical two piece with glitter on the lapels. Straight from the police cells dressed as he was when he left the club he worked at as a Tom Jones tribute act. Unfortunately for TJ he was stopped, breathalysed and failed. Not for the first time. Now he knows how the guy from the song 'Green Green Grass of Home' feels.

****

Rita Sunday 17/8/03.

Posted a hand written letter today, pondered at the risk... Did it anyway, Hey! What more can they do? Ask me if I care now. Work? What is that? I wanted you to get my letter of ordinary things. Places & times for you and me my baby. I wanted you to get that letter tomorrow so I got a stamp off my neighbour; the good couple next door, not the weird one on the other side. If I post it before church it will be on its way to you my darling at noon, anyhow, I want you to get it tomorrow because I will be getting two letters tomorrow Oh I can't wait. Such joy, such pleasure. Such anticipation I'm feeling good today my love, I have so much to look forward to I feel so blessed. Whatever it takes however long it is now, we have our future to look forward to. Unspeakable pleasures. I laugh out loud even on my own I feel you squeezing my butt cheeks & I tell you to behave am I mad? If so then give me more you are with me my precious. How are you today? Went to a wild church this morning. Girls have stayed all day & got a lift home. Good stuff. June been for tea. Got a new barbecue marinade, great sticky chicken, I love you so much.

Monday 18/8/03.

So very happy today. The utter joy I feel in getting two envelopes this morning, a card, a letter & some poems! So happy -it doesn't take much my darling & I've read them over & over again. Lovely. The letter written day before your mums visit & the card after the visit. You always have been able to speak straight to my heart & always exactly what I need to hear. That's been the hardest my love of cause I miss your hugs & kisses that goes without saying! But your words I need so much. Not long now my precious & at least we'll be able to speak.

I feel as soon as you're moved from Preston, the heat will be off you & why should they care who you speak to, or indeed who comes to visit you? I'm past caring now, they will do with me as they see fit & that will be months down the line... now is when I need your words of love & reassurance & vice versa my love. I need to tell you how much I love you. I posted you a card yesterday, the rose & I sprayed it with my perfume, will the fragrance last? Will it travel through the stench of prison to reach your senses? I hope so my love, yet again hand written. I hope you got my letter yesterday, my day of joy & happiness so you could feel that joy with my words to you - hope you get that card today so you will get another boost. Off to Doctors this morning to get a sick note (stress!) so I can spend some days with my wonderful friend Monique. Luv ya.

****

Moving day and this time I get to pack my own property. There are no empty seats on the van and all of us are going to Haverigg. The fresh sea air fills every cell of my body when I step from the van and take that first breath. As soon as my feet touch the Cumbrian soil I become a cat C prisoner. Reception is just the same as any prison. R1 is first to house me and the others who came from Preston. Two landings with open walkways for the twos. Steel prefabs built years ago as a temporary solution to overcrowding. They aren't the ideal style of accommodation but I know it's just for a week or two. After waiting this long I can rough it for a week. All my property made it through reception and the cells are all single.

Apart from life sentence prisoners I'm on the list of big sentences. Categorisation C prisons are wary of big sentences they're used to roundabout criminals who serve six month and before their bed's cold are back. The doctor is the first outing for me. The medical centre is just that, right in the centre of the jail. The old wooden hut sitting on a concrete base is my first taste of cat C freedom. When the wing officer tells me to go to the medical hut I take up position at the wing door. Standing there waiting for a screw to let me out I'm thinking about who's in here that I'll know.

"What you standing there for lad?" asks the screw on his way out.

"I have to go see the doc guv," I tell him.

"Well get yourself over there then and stop hanging around here." The unlocked door that I'm waiting for someone to unlock slams behind him. It's the first time in any prison I've moved around without an escort. It's a strange feeling walking alone across grass. The first gate in a fence that reaches high into the misty Cumbrian morning air is wide open. I haven't a clue where this hut is and I don't really care right now. People thronging to and fro fill the concrete paths that criss-cross the site. Black donkey jackets with blue plastic across the shoulders are the uniform that sets the cons apart from the screws. One thing common to all jails is the queue. The medical hatch always has the longest queue. Haverigg is the same. The hut finds me rather than me finding it. First time again for me is hearing dialect that is so close to my old town I can't help asking the lad.

"Where you from mate?" He turns round.

"Cleater Moor pal what 'bout you? Trevor's me name." I don't know him and he doesn't know who I am. I've been in jail longer than he's been on solid food.

"I'm from Whitehaven." The long exile has softened my Cumbrian crack or he would know by my accent.

"Do you know any of the Woodhouse lads? There's a few in here." He then starts to rhyme off all the mugs I don't want to meet up with. All friends of the drug dealer I've just left behind in Preston. Unlike him I don't have a problem. I definitely don't need to hide from them. But I wouldn't recognise most of them even if I was talking to one of them now.

"No mate I don't know them but they may know me..." The penny drops and so does his jaw. "Are you Tony Crowe?" He blurts out. Half the queue turns to look at me. Silence. News of my coming preceded my arrival.

"Yep that's me mate," he seems lost for words so I help him out, "do I know you?"

"No. It's all round the jail you were coming in. Are you on R1? Do ya want any one given a message pal? I'm on R3 me like if ya need ought like I'll sort it. Like weed or a phone. Have ya got a phone? One and a half will git ya a phone." I like the sound of a phone.

"I don't do drugs mate but a phone sounds good. One and a half what?"

"Hundred and fifty pounds pal. That's the going rate with a charger. Wait till ya come off R1 and I'll sort ya pal."

"What's the work here like?"

"Working outside's the best jobs but you have to be close to your release date." That reminds me. I'm on my parole year and a phone would just be the excuse they need to stamp 'denied' on my parole file. The doc is just the same as any other. Tick in a box to fulfil a Home Office requirement. The week on R1 is taken up with induction, or meet the jail. Chaplain Barry calls on me. I don't think he knows yet who I am. He will know soon enough I have no doubt. A friend in the stores kits me out with new gear. A friend I've never seen before in my life. I don't want to be cynical but the thought of me being a man who might start up a drugs outlet in the jail might influence friendships. They'll be disappointed if that's what they think.

Even though it's late summer the weather rolling in off the sea to the west and down the mountains to the east is unpredictable. Haverigg is an old RAF base. The hill, or Marilyn to give it its proper title, behind the prison, Black Combe, housed a beacon signalling system in the Second World War. Being the highest point for miles it was the ideal spot.

Some of the old buildings are still used today. It's a collection of wooden huts. The wooden huts of R4 are called chalets. They aren't relics of the war. They were bought from somewhere north of Lapland. Old oil field workers' accommodation. The library is a hut, the chapel is a hut and the education is lots of huts. The only brick built building is the block. It wouldn't do to have a wooden segregation unit.

****

Rita Tuesday 26/8/03.

Well my precious your mum rang at 9 am this morning to say you were at last on the move! One step closer my love to me being able to visit even though it's H/R not Kirkham. I'll be there!! I've had a busy week been at Monique's since Wednesday- Came back Sunday, long drive but so good to see her & of course she has met you so we can talk better, only she from my friends and family! Special! Just like her!. Yesterday being bank holiday, went to B/Pool & for once it didn't rain, had a good day you certainly see the sights there, as I was sat watching, you were with me my love and I laughed out loud more than once. Ate enough grease yesterday to keep a seal pup warm. It's obligatory at B/Pool is it not? Fell out with my beloved son on my return... he need to get some respect back around here! Lucy being a darling & that week at camp I feel she has really got back on track with The Lord, great. So much so she got out of bed at 8am, got ready (long job) & caught two buses to get to church. I wasn't here. That is great & I'm really so happy for her. Son being a right pain. But hey! Can't have everything. I love you so much my love, your card was somewhat rude you know I can't write such stuff to you. But I can talk & show you, can't wait. xxx.

****

R1 soon give me up to the call of R2. Ten rooms in a dorm each with a key for the occupant to use. Robbers use a spoon. The main door is locked at bang-up but we can move inside the hut between rooms. This is just what Garth told the judge when I lost in my effort to force their hand in my cat C judicial review. Old and scruffy with stinking beds and broken cupboards is what they are. When a room becomes empty the others relocate anything that's in better condition than their own furnishings. New jail with new daily drudge. After breakfast in the dining hut the fog horn sounds for work to start. For some reason that I haven't worked out yet everybody runs to the dining halls. I've never been in a jail where speed is a priority. From breakfast till night-time bang up, apart from the lunch time and tea time count to see if anyone is missing, we are unlocked. Free to move between dorms. It's a hive of activity with a micro crime-driven industry going on all around. Every evening a guy comes in the dorm peddling his goods with the cry of 'Get your pills and powders here' then he reads out the menu of today's offers. No screws anywhere to be seen, just cameras. Then there are the spies in our midst, slags who try to curry favour at the expense of a fellow con. A drug debt that can't be paid can be wiped out if the creditor is shipped out. The debt goes with him. That's why Haverigg has a high turnover.

With no wall it's a dally delivery of parcels raining down into the compound. The rain that takes my drought away comes from clouds rolling in off the sea. As the cold drops fall every one runs for shelter. I stay seated on the wooden bench outside the hut. Soon I'm alone. Just me and the cool refreshing water washing my face. For five years I've never felt the rain on my face. Never been able to sit watching the rain bounce off the roof. Listen to it rushing down the tin gutters.

Smell the rain. I didn't know rain had a smell till now. The screws can never know why I'm sitting in the pouring rain smiling as I look up into the sky. No one who hasn't experienced loss of freedom to walk in the rain can ever know why I'm not taking shelter.

Visiting time is a popular time for dealers to top up their stock. The screws walk the jail fence with dogs just before and just after the visits in an effort to thwart the efforts of the delivery boys. When they've travelled a long way for the visit they just want to get off home when it's over. The contraband business in here is big money with no police. If you get nailed it's just a ship-out. The local cons ask me when I'll be getting my first parcel. No shortage of willing workers to do the leg-work. They don't believe I want nothing to do with it all. But that doesn't stop the rumours reaching the ears of security. I know they think I'll be running the whole jail soon.

****

Rita Friday 29/8/03.

Down, Down, Down. I don't know why these last two days are so bad. Is it because you are further away? Can't be, I know you're in a better place, I'm writing giving you my home address & your mum will give you my phone number, hopefully on her visit with you today. Why so down? Its agony & I feel I can't come out of the gloom. I just want to cry... I'm afraid when you do get to ring me that is just what I'll do. I have not because I don't want you to worry about me, but I know in my heart you do already! Oh to be together, will it be soon my darling? I don't feel I can bear this much longer. Pain & gloom. Oh dear I've been reading your words about my joy & light & happiness, if you could see me now! No I will be OK I am most of the time... Not right now though... I've been ringing your mum every night, so close to tears. Does she know I'm not coping at present? I don't want her to worry; she is so happy that we will be together... One day. But when? It's endless just now. I love you xxx. Need to make myself eat again. I was great with Monique & really enjoyed eating; sounds mad I know but it's no pleasure when you have to make yourself eat & every mouthful is a chore! Oh my darling I need to feel safe in your arms I need to hear your reassurance, you make my fears disappear, I need your arms around me so badly... I must do something I'm off for a shower... Be better later?? xxx.

Saturday 30/8/03 3.30 am.

Oh my love to speak to you last night! To hear your voice. I cried & cried after... I fell asleep on the sofa & didn't wake up till 12.45! It must have been the relief; I don't know. Went up to bed around 2am thankfully only me at home. Tried to sleep but your face is inside my head. I keep seeing your face. Had to get up as there is no way I can sleep. So I'm up. Made myself a very large vodka tonic & I'm sitting here in my enormous dressing gown that reminds me of other phone conversations with you. No regrets my love. I love you. People can say & think what they will. I love you & I trust you. Never before have I felt that about a man. Scary, terrifying for me, who has always felt in control of a relationship, even though I've been hurt so badly in the past. I trust you. I don't know how it's going to work; I just know that it must. Your words from ages ago come to my mind. About 'destruct buttons' & all. Well you have access to that button my precious & I believe you when you say I have access to yours. Yours is safe with me my love, as I believe mine is safe with you. The vodka is kicking in so I'll say good night & God bless my love xxx.

****

A look at R4 is in order. With an invitation I get to go over there. If R2 is a flop house this is the Ritz. Pine beds with new mattresses, pillows, windows without bars, and get this; a shower inside the room. Two phones on every floor mean no waiting in line. Whenever you want to you can use them. Half the guys from Garth are in here including Brian the Buddhist, Taffy my welsh neighbour and little Gary. Only Eddy's missing from the old gang. The boys have it boxed off. They swim at the top of the pond with the best of everything. In two weeks I have the job of industrial cleaner. Not really a job, an educational course with qualifications at the end of it. Best of all a cushy number. From R2 I get a 'do not pass go', and head straight to R4. I've arrived. After so long fighting I'm where I want to be, all I need now is parole so I can start my new life with Rita.

Brian has a bit of a weed business going on. Gary has everything going on as usual. He's in great demand. His slight frame is the only attribute he needs to be a retriever of goods. The windows in R4 open just enough to let in fresh air but not enough to get out of. Gary however can slip out with room to spare. He's lowered down by his arms after dark to collect the parcels then retrieved in the same way, pockets bulging. A percentage of the booty going to him for a wage. The first thing I get Gary to pick up on his night time commando raid is a tin of pineapple chunks. I know it's not the normal illicit contraband but it's no different to Gary asking for a tin of corn beef in Garth when he could have asked for any kind of food he liked. I don't need a mobile phone, I can use the jail phone and if I need to talk without the jail listening I can borrow Brian's phone. Life is good. Visits are easy-going with holding and kissing not being a problem. The screws know who Rita is but she's never worked with them so apart from the smirks and school boy titters they leave us be. My mother only has a short trip from Whitehaven. She can hand the baton over to Rita now. Friends and family find time to visit. I've accumulated lots visits over the years and now I have enough saved up to have one visit a week, to the disapproval of the prison.

****

Thursday 3/9/03.

More abuse & agony of heart, tears, tears, tears for the past. Today has been a turning point. Only upwards from the pit now. Answered prayer, good Gov. who knew Si Mary well. No going back now! Max 3 months & need to have a job. Scary but freedom I know. My heart has been ripped out & man handled by 'people' I didn't choose. God is with me he holds the future in his hands & he will not let me go. No matter how scary things get. Keep calm now no more tears. I will see you next week & I know once I can look into your eyes & hear your words, all will be well my sweetheart. I will do nothing till then. I so longed for a letter from you today to give me strength. No letter. Reading abide in me. My arms are around you. No one said it would be fair, he promises to walk with me. Thank God. I must never put even you in his place in my life. He has brought our hearts together. Will he now let us fall? I don't think so. Reading Job in the depths of despair; 'I know my redeemer lives! Read Ecclesiastes 4 Two are better than one, strength together. Thank you Lord. I look a wreck. Miracle; cancellation at the hairdressers tomorrow. Now I just have to lay off the booze & eat some proper food. Will you notice my sweetheart? I so want to look my best for you. I love you, & you; & us are far more important than any job xxx...

Friday 12/9/03.

New place yet again. Such pure joy to see your face. Kiss your lips, hear you voice. How wonderful to have all the horror, worry, fear, pain behind us now. Very scary going into the prison. Many thoughts no keys, who will I see that knows me? Trembling by the time I had been rubbed down. But to see your face, your beautiful eyes, fell your arms around me. Oh that we would never forget. Time just flew by. Pure bliss 2nd visit, not as nervous. So much to talk about. So much left unsaid. Again we say; 'don't know how it's going to work out. Only know that it will so much to look forward to. I feel so safe with you I've never felt that with a man before. I've either been wary or in control. Do you understand me saying that? I have never felt a lot of things before & without you I never would have opened up enough to let anyone near. Of course I hadn't seen that but you had. To hear you say you were sad that I had never been loved before is a strange feeling. I don't feel sad about it because I didn't really know what I was missing. It was just how it is. & the times I had tried & given love... Well that's history & no doubt why subsequently would not let anyone near me. But you my precious are so close to me & I trust you not to hurt me & that was not an easy task for you or me. No going back now my love. I do feel a sense of excitement for the next phase of our journey. I'll have to travel without you in some places. Job centre. Oh no. I'll cope.

Wednesday 17/9/03.

Such peace such joy all day, from morning to evening. A knowledge deep inside. God is with me & an excitement for the future. How blessed to have had such a time. Days, weeks, months & only truly now enjoying this special time of an unlimited relationship with God. 'I have called you friends. John 15, v15. Word for today. Six days of thoughts on this one sentence, practice the presence of God is a skill a habit to be developed.

Wednesday 8/10/03.

Two visits with you prior to above. Two visits again till today. Decided not to visit tomorrow. Even though I desperately love to see you xxx. Much has happened since last entry still got the peace to say it's right even thought the niggles try to get in & rob me. Much happened with A & J need to meet with them. Got Fraser to announce at area chapel meeting that I was going to resign. Sr Mary aid he spoke very well (30th September) only today got concerned. Bob Mc C. rang & said he'd heard from H.Q. I'd resigned & to talk about my replacement. Not good, as well timed plans in disarray. Nor had he received the F5 & medical certificate I posted five days ago. Dismissal mentioned. Prayer time. Not done my Oswald Chambers Devotional Bible for a while. P 804 to kill or to heal. "Every art, every healing every good can be used for the opposite Reading was Ecc 3 v 1 - 22. It struck me as I prayed for my letter to be found by Bob, how the enemy is forever throwing niggles in. I prayed for & about many things this morning but my eyes filled with tears as I asked God that you be released in November & we will be together & before God. xxx. Got a call back from Bob 2 hours late to say they had found the letter & for some reason it had ended up at Wymott. Change of plans the - the well timed ones to get paid till end of November. I need to write a letter of resignation today & date it for 10th October. Which means my last day of prison employment is 10th November? Freedom on 11th November. Is that coincidence? I don't think so my love. 3 weeks less pay but... Went to Prison Fellowship group in Oswaldtwistle on Monday 6th. It was good to share of God's enduring faithfulness its 8 years since I last visited & about 15 y since we set it up. What a blessing again to be told most of them wouldn't be in P.F if it wasn't for hearing me speaking. Joyce said the same to me yesterday when I spent the day with her. In the end God's timing is perfect xxx.

****

Daz, a good friend, asks for a visiting order. It's good to see him. All the news of whose doing what and who's climbed to the top of the criminal world I was once a part of. News of family, Dawn divorced and now living with someone else. He tells me who from Whitehaven is in here, he knows more about the ones in here than I do and I live with them. He points them out on the visits. One request for a V.O. takes me by surprise. Dawn asks if she could see me. So much for the clean break with no contact, I still have her Dear John letter. The letter I asked her not to send. Just stop coming to visit, I told her and I'll know we have come to the end. But she sent it anyway. Now she wants to visit; three years later. The year of my parole. In three months time I could be a free man. Is that what has driven her to request this visit? The person she knew died in Long Lartin. We have nowhere to go now. Rita is my life now and when I get out. Still, Dawn deserves respect. I send her a V.O. for a visit, that's what she wants. It's strange to see her after all this time walking into the visiting room with her mate Susan. With the small talk out of the way and the story of her failed marriage covered it only leaves the new man in her life to discuss.

"He asked me to marry him," she tells me.

"Great and what do you think? Is he a better prospect than the last deadbeat you wed? How could you marry him Dawn?"

"I know, don't tell me. It was the biggest mistake of my life."

368

"He beat you up and was a piss-head Dawn. How could you not know that before?"

"I know."

"What are you asking me Dawn? Who's this new guy? Is he good with the kids? And does he love you Dawn? Don't just marry him so you're not on your own."

"I need to know if we have any chance of getting back together when you get out."

"You can't do that, Dawn. You have to make the decision for yourself not because of what I'm doing."

"I just need to know what my options are. Before I make any decisions."

"I can't be a part of this Dawn. It's up to you to do what's right for you now. Look, we have no chance of getting back together. I'm not the same person who left on that November morning seven years ago. You can't marry him just because I'm not an option Dawn."

"I just needed to know Tony. Now I can move on."

"Rita's my life now," she lifts her head.

"Yeah what's that about? She's a vicar isn't she?"

"Not really she worked in the chapel but she's not a vicar and if she was so what?"

"Right well now I can decide what to do. Now I know where I stand. Just wanted to ask that's all. I'll be off then look after yourself, right and I'll be seeing ya." The visiting time isn't over but the visit is for Dawn. The shine in her eyes from holding back the tears is about to give away her sorrow.

"Dawn be happy and if he's a good guy marry him. You look fantastic." We embrace for the final time. Her head turned to one side. Breaking away she walks to the door. Never looking back. Her hand wiping a tear from the corner of her eye. Susan comforting her with a reassuring arm around her shoulder.

Fall from Haverigg

The creative writing I enjoyed in Preston continues here. We meet in the education hut twice a week. Poets come and read their work such as the Wordsworth poet in residence. We enter into national writing competitions, short stories for some, poems for others. Journalists come under the heading of writers; I know it sounds mad but they do. I tend to see them more as wolves. We have the joy of being able to have some of our work evaluated by a local wolf, of the press. They can't all be just out for the big story come what may. Can they? She can't have been a journalist long, her youth wouldn't allow it. Sweet young thing with a warm smile. Pen and pad resting under her hands resting on her crossed legs. Briefcase standing by the side of her seat. A lilac stiletto swings on the toes of her crossed leg. Our chairs arranged in a horseshoe shape facing her. The teacher sits at the back of the hut behind us. The guys are fighting for the front seats. They live in the hope of her uncrossing her legs with abandoned regard for modesty. That Sharon Stone moment from Basic Instinct. Dressing in such a provocative style when coming into a prison full of men is at best naive. The hour passes in a mere flash of time. To the disappointment of the guys Sharon doesn't show up. The hope was kept alive till the bitter end though. As she wriggled in the wooden seat her skirt rode up another inch, revealing just a little more soft skin. Every eager eye knew she had to at some point move that sweet thigh from on top of the other. It was not to be, she reached down to her briefcase and put it on her lap, just as she flicked the swinging shoe back into place her foot hit the floor. The only erotic moments came from the writings of frustrated men. One by one we give her our work. The bundle is secreted away into her briefcase and the lid shut. The professional writer will be back to tell us how we compare to the Pulitzer Prize winning writers of the outside world.

Chapel is Wednesday nights for the outside groups to spend an hour with us. Music with a cup of tea and biscuits. Just like Garth. Tonight the area chaplain has come to give us a talk on the unity of Christ. This is the chaplain who Rita would say is her spiritual leader when she worked as a reader in the prison service. The same chaplain who turned his back on her when she needed him the most. Now he tells us about the unity of Christ and the Church. One body and one family. The bride of Christ. I've never been good at keeping my opinions to myself and now isn't the time to change. When introduced to Brian, the purple chested chubby chap smiled and shook my hand. The old guy is how I would imagine Santa without his red suit. His white beard trimmed short not to obscure his plastic collar of office. The religious garb of man's understanding.

"Pleased to meet you," he says.

"Tony's my name and you're Brian aren't you?" before he can answer I continue with my retort. "I think you know my fiancée." The trap baited I'm waiting for his question.

"Who would that be?" There it is.

"Rita's her name. You know her. It's the woman you turned your back on when the world was against her. She asked you to help and you did nothing. Rita Carroll one of the 'Family of Christ' you've just told us about," he gulps the tea from the cup in his hand and looks for an escape from my condemnation.

"How is she? It was a sad day for us all when...." He's fighting for words as he backs away, reaching for the table behind him with the now empty cup.

"Why did you throw her to the wolves? The unity of the church is a joke. The only organisation that shoot their wounded. If you really want to know how she is why don't you contact her and ask?" He's slipping away from me. A worm trying to escape the hook, not worth pursuing.

"Tell Rita I wish her all the best and give her my regards," he finishes with.

Someone once told me that I might be the only bible some people will ever see. If Bishop Brian were the only bible I had ever saw maybe I would be disillusioned with it all. Still I shouldn't be surprised at people's actions any more. Rita has a new job now. She works in the call centre for the job seekers inquiry line. Not the job she will spend the rest of her working life doing but for now it's an income. People are what she does and I'm sure people will be what she will do in the future. I couldn't help but ask her on the last visit if she was sure this was what she really wanted. She was surprised. But I just couldn't believe she had gone through so much and not lost heart. Her life has been turned on its head. Even friends from the prison have turned their backs on her. 'Friends', I say. What friend would abandon you when you need them the most? At a meeting of trustees, for one of the charities Rita works with, one of them, a fellow Christian chaplain, said to the chairman he couldn't believe Rita was there. The charity has nothing to do with the prison. Do they think she should hideaway in shame? He is also a member of the body of Christ. A joke is what it is. They were told by the prison not to associate with her.

Her commitment to us is one hundred per cent. I know that. I just can't help thinking, what I have done to this woman's life. A woman I love. That's the only glue that can hold us together. Without love the slings and arrows of life would have ended our union long ago. The past is in the past. We have to look to the future. What can they do to us now?

Words that have now come back to bite us. The young woman journalist found my story fascinating. Not the story I gave her to cast her professional eye over. She has written a story in her local rag about the chaplain and the prisoner. The Lancashire Evening News' front page is taken up with the vicar who is defrocked. Brian gives the church's position. The prison gives its 'a spokes man said' comments. None of which is flattering to us. What they don't know they make up. Creative writing indeed. Innuendo from the defrocked heading to the full stop at the end of the story. The archives yield photos of Rita from her time as a Thailand prisoner. Twenty- five years ago and it comes alive for her again through some career hungry tart. Just another storm in our tempestuous sea of confusion.

No news about my parole. Two months till my date and nothing yet. I don't think I want to know. I have no faith in the answer. Now the newspapers have ran this story I feel the chance has slipped further from my grip. Time has slowed to a day by day week. All my mates want me to ask what's going on but I can't. It's one of them questions you want to ask but know if the answer is 'no' you'll be devastated. It's a bit like Schrödinger's cat. As long as you don't know any different it's both yes and no. Only once you've been told does it become one or the other. Once the cat's out of the bag you can't put it back and what it is; it is. This was never my plan. I was never going to have so much to get out for. The only thing waiting for me was a bullet from a police marksman. The conclusion of my revengeful rampage. Just as the Judge said so long ago, 'The Best Made Plans of Mice and Men'. My plans are not your plans, I read. My plans are for you to be prosperous. I read.

Rita is the plan God has for me. A better plan than mine. My question is; if it's God's plan for my life why does it have to be so hard? Is there not another way? An easier way? Then I get the answer. If something costs nothing it's worth nothing. If something is too easy to get it's not worth fighting to keep.

Rita's birthday. Today, 13th October. Apart from that it's a normal working day for me. I'll phone her tonight and talk into the small hours with her. I'm settled in now winding down to the freedom cat C jail life. The jails up until now have been overtly oppressive so it's easy to fall into the illusion of freedom. The eyes are still watching us. People who don't understand that soon hear the words of doom filling their cell, or room. 'Pack your kit, you're moving.' The ship-outs are phenomenal. It's like the screws are on a mission to see who can ship-out the most cons in a month. Any one on R4 who's lasted more than six months is a suspected informer. Don't get caught holding a smoking gun is the game. There's always a gopher that'll carry contraband and not only the cell, but the whole jail is a hiding place.

The afternoon work session in the cleaning workshop lets the cat out of the bag. I'm compelled, with less than a month left till my parole date and every one saying I should know by now, to ask if I can go to the office and find out if the letter has come from the parole board. Without lifting her head my boss says.

"Your answer is here, you never got it." She tosses me a letter from the in-box on her desk. Not even lifting her head to look at me.

"When did you get this?" I don't know what else to say.

"This morning I think," still writing on something more important than my freedom.

"Well I would have liked to have it this morning. I've been waiting for it for months."

"Well you've got it now. And what difference would it have made." The letter says, I regret to inform you that your application for parole on this occasion as been denied.

Great day to tell me. How do I tell Rita on her birthday I'm not coming home to her? I can't do that. I need time to get used to the news. Not one nicking. Not one drugs test failed. What do they want from me? I played their game and they just laugh in my face. There's no reward for doing what's right only punishment for doing what's wrong. Now where do I go from here? Next year I can ask them again. Without anything changing what chance do I have? Six years ago in Durham jail I was told I had to start my campaign with rule breaking and hell-raising. I didn't believe it back then. Now it's turning out to be true. You can't get better if at first you give your best.

When I was a school boy, about fourteen years old, I was chosen from all the schools in Whitehaven to fill a slot in an Outward Bound course. The venue was The Lake District on the shore side of Ulswater. I was heading down a road of ruin at the time and I think my teacher arranged this to turn me from that road. I arrived at the school the day after all the others. They came from all over the country. I was the local boy. The only Cumbrian in the centre. The typical Lake District style, sandstone, slate roof building was an old weekend country residence at one time. The rooms were converted into dorms. There were five boys to a room. Each a team with a name taken from somewhere in the lakes. We were Bathenthwaite, named after the only true lake. I arrived about 3 o'clock. The place was empty, apart from one instructor who greeted me with a sense of urgency. Throwing my bag into my home for the next month, he headed off. I followed wondering what the hurry was. Out in the grounds, hidden in the trees of a small wooded area, was an assault course that wouldn't be out of place at a military academy. High up in the trees were rope bridges, zip-lines and a platform where the skill of stopping a rock climber falling to his death was honed. A steel, concrete-filled oil drum was the climber on the end of a rope. It was hoisted up by five boys pulling on the rope down on the ground then it was dropped. The young lad's job on the platform was to stop it. If he wasn't tied to the tree I'm sure the drum and the boy would both end up at the bottom. At ground level log walls to scramble over and wriggle under led through a route of pain to a clearing where the body was worked till no energy remained in it. Total exhaustion was the requirement. Speed was the ultimate goal. Something I didn't know back then.

I was timed for the first round. Not for speed over the entire course but for repetitions. For one minute I had to hang from an over head steel bar and pull myself up touching my chin on the bar. Press-ups, squats with a barbell made of concrete across my shoulders, stepping up and down onto a log for a minute. All the time the instructor, an ex- RAF officer, screaming at me to do more. I did my best and at the end I was done in. I couldn't stand. I couldn't speak. This was to be the norm every day for the whole month. First thing in the morning we had to line up naked on the jetty and one by one, on command, we jumped into the lake. The February mornings were cruel to a young boy's manhood.

We had to do the assault course every day. And get faster while completing the number of repetitions achieved on that first day. I should have learned from then that when you are expected to improve over time you need to start by keeping something back. It bit me back then and it's bitten me again. I gave my all back on that assault course and I've given my all over the last six years. I can't do any better so why do I even try?

That Outward Bound month taught me many things one of which was how to disarm the authority in a position to punish me. The lake side dip was also the punishment dealt out for rebellious behaviour. After falling foul of the freezing plunge once too often I suggested a plan to my fellow plungers. This morning when we all went for the character building dip we would ask if we could do it again. Once you're cold and wet once more doesn't matter. Our entire dorm re-joined the back of the line for another go, then another, until the instructor put an end to our joy. It stopped the plunge in the lake punishments. How can you be punished with something you enjoy doing? That's why I gave the TV back to the S.O. in Garth. What's the point of taking it away if I didn't want it in the beginning? When I think back to that month I realise it was the last step before ending up in a reform school or worse. All the boys were a bit wayward. Fights weren't uncommon. Another reason for the plunge into the lake. I only had one occasion where I couldn't talk my way out of the situation. Out on manoeuvres, you could say, camped in Ennerdale valley. One lad who set himself up as an expert in the art of Kung Fu lost, misplaced or had his plastic mug stolen. I was the suspect. He lost a yellow mug and I had a yellow mug. Case closed. He wouldn't relent even when a mate of mine told him I had a yellow mug before he lost his. I was terrified. This lad was Bruce Lee to me. He was Goliath towering over me like the fells that were surrounding us. He made his move and I jumped straight up crashing my fist down into his face. His nose cracked on impact, liberating bright red blood. He hit the grass before my feet returned to earth. The instructors were all staying in the hostel down the road and didn't witness the fight. Well the punch I should say. The only thought in my head was if he doesn't go down I'm finished and with that I hit him. With all my might I hit him. One of the boys ran to the hostel and brought help. The hospital said he had a broken nose and a cracked cheek. His story to the instructors was he fell and hit his face on a rock. I never saw him again. He was sent home to London. I was the daddy from then on and I never had any more bother. A lesson I used when the six would-be assassins in Durham threatened me. The ones who are the loudest aren't the biggest threat.

At the end of the month we all got presented with an Outward Bound badge. It was the prize to show we had the zeal and determination to endure the course. Rock climbing, camping, orienteering and boating on the lakes we did it all. We got awarded points for the dorm that were the best. Our dorm won the most points and we were given a big cake on the last day to celebrate. Then it all went wrong. On the first day we, no not 'we', everyone but me signed a contract, or an agreement if you like, not to drink alcohol or smoke. I didn't smoke anyway so no problem for me. I did drink and on a trip out to Buttermere I had a beer. Someone told on us and our dorm's victory was short- lived. The winner's cake was taken back and our badges were stripped. My protests of 'I signed nothing' were met with 'you can sign now to say you haven't drunk or smoked'. I wouldn't do it. Even winning we lost over rules I didn't know about. Some things never change. I get the points for staying out of trouble, passing drug tests, keeping rules. And now my reward is a big fat zero. Parole denied. Time off for good behaviour it used to be called.

Two days after Rita's birthday I tell her I'm not coming home. A low point in our young relationship. How can I keep going? Beaten and battered emotionally one voice resonates in my head. The bible says 'I will never leave you.' Any thoughts of giving up on God remind me of one verse. Jesus asked Peter "Will you leave me also?" Peter said "Where would we go?" Right now that's what I think; 'where else is there to go?'

****

Rita Wednesday 15/10/03.

Devastation, shock, numb. Have we got it wrong? Was not the timing right? I was convinced it was, but God doesn't get times wrong. Do I know you at all? I don't think I do now. Forgive me. After all we've been through. Nothing I could say to you today, or you me. Empty is what I feel. At least I know now I need a job or two now. The roof or the leaking shower won't wait. Even if we have too. Same thing again. 'They' don't take into consideration all that you tried to do. Be honest. Is it so bad? Of course once again 'their' standards are not ours. So we will have to pick ourselves up & get on with it. I thought for once I wouldn't have to do it alone. I so need your arms around me. Sitting with my head on your chest today almost brought me to tears. But I couldn't do that to you. Because I know what it cost you to go through all the parole procedure. All for what? Why did we hang on at Garth? Pain again my darling. What to say to loved ones now? Hold on, hold on. God will not desert us now. There is always a reason. Even if we can't see it now. Trust, he has promised Hope, Future. Hang in there. He will comfort those who mourn xxx.

****

No more bothering about rules and regulations. One year till my next parole refusal and another till they can't hold me any longer. Head down and look to that day.

Haverigg isn't the heaven on earth I imagined it would be. All day the screws are watching out for the slightest infringement. I know now why so many end up back in cat B. Preston. The inmates are the biggest problem. Looking for points from the screws. Time to talk to the love of my life on my own phone. Out of earshot of those who have no right to listen in. Gary is sent out on a mission. Picking up my first packet. Good old Daz is my deliverer. Using Brian's phone we guide Daz to the right spot on the other side of the fence. Scrambling over ploughed fields with deep ditches in the dark Daz comes a cropper. Head over heels he ends up at the bottom of a water filled trench. Drenched with muddy sludge he fights on toward the fence. The room light is our signal. If the light's on he can throw the booty. A flash on and off shows Daz where we are. When Daz says job done, Gary is lowered out of the window into the darkness. In no time he's back at the window.

"Away man pull us back up." He reaches up. His fingertips just peeping over the window frame.

"Did ya get the packet?" Brian asks him. He's not for lifting him up if he's not got it.

"Wey aye man, lift us back in man." He doesn't want to be out longer than needed.

"Did you have any problem finding it?"

"No man it nearly hit me on the heed." He pulls the heavily padded packet from inside his coat and passes it over. Ripping the bubble-rap off I get to the prize. A Nokia mobile phone.

"How do I switch it on?" I have to ask.

"The silver button. There on the top." Brian points it out.

"I've never seen a mobile phone till now. How am I supposed to know?" The small screen comes alive with the melody and logo of Nokia. "How do I send a message? Come on show me how to use it."

"You've never seen a phone before? I can't believe it. Give it here," Gary takes it and starts pressing buttons while telling me how it works. "You have to have it on silent so it doesn't ring and the screws hear it." This is advice for Gary who's been in jail for over sixteen years so I know he's never seen a phone outside prison.

"Last mobile I had was as big as a house brick. And you couldn't send messages on it. If it's on silent how do I know when someone's ringing?"

"It'll vibrate man. Text messages ya want. Keep it down ya pants so if they search ya they don't find it. And take the sim out when you stash it."

"The sim? You lost me again. What's the sim?" Gary flips the back of the phone off and there under the battery he removes a small card with a gold strip on it.

"That's ya sim Tony. Don't let them get this," he holds the small card up, "all the information's on here."

"What if someone sends a text and the sim's in me pocket? How do I get it?"

"When ya put it back in you'll get the text."

"How can it get into the card when it's in me pocket? That's mad."

"It doesn't go into the card in ya pocket man, „he smiles.

"Well where is it till I put the card back into the phone?"

"I don't know. Just put the card in and all the texts will come man. You ask some questions you do."

"I can't believe they just float around waiting for me to put the card back in. They must be somewhere."

"They're in the text waiting room. How do I know where they are? Just don't let them get the sim." He puts the phone back together and hands it to me.

"One last thing, how do I get money on it so I can use it? It's got a tenner on it now Daz said but how do I put money on when that's used up?"

"Ya need a top up man. Get someone outside to buy a top up card and text you the number; then you put the number in t' phone and the credit is put on the sim."

"I can't believe ya can get a hundred and fifty quid for this," I examine the small grey plastic box in my hand, "why don't they get one over the wall like I just did?"

"Ya need someone on the out who knows what they're doing man. And if ya have to come from a long way off its hard work man."

The first text of my life is to Rita. How good it is to be able to send messages whenever I feel like telling her how much I miss her. Time passes and early morning rushes in. The only thing occupying my evening is my new found magic box. To say 'good night' as I lay my head on the pillow. To wake in the morning to the message from Rita wishing me a blessed day with kisses is priceless. I still use the jail phone so as not to flag any warnings in the admin dept. If I stop using the jail phone they'll know I must have a mobile. The problem with my plan is Rita. Once again she slips up on the phone. She talks about what we've been texting and what we've been saying on the mobile phone. Rita's criminal mind is missing. Mine isn't, it's just been sleeping. Now is the time of the great awakening. Phones are not drugs so why not go into the phone business? Supply and demand. Playing their game has got me nowhere.

The three-handed deal works just as well for phones as it does for drugs. No one gets to know who's who. I never come into the game as a player. Just how I like it. First Brian the Buddhist finds the buyer. Daz delivers the packet. Gary goes commando under cover of darkness retrieving it. The money is paid by their people on the out to my people. The screws are kept busy trying to find them, which is good for business. With Gary's wage he sets himself up in a little dealing of commodities. Brian smokes the commodities. Looking for that elusive enlightenment and nirvana. The only problem with all that that I can see is you don't know if you've ever done enough. I can't do any more, according to the bible. Jesus did it all for me. I'll stick with God who did what I could never have done. He paid the price for me so I don't have to. Now that's what I call enlightenment.

The phone needs to be small so I can hide it. The smallest phone on the market is a Panasonic. The size of a matchbox I can hide it in my cell. When I have to hide it on my body I can. The charger is now larger than the phone. With my universal took kit, namely a set of adapted nail clippers, I can open the back of my Hi Fi. The headphone socket is an ideal place to tap off three volts to charge any phone. With some rewiring inside my boom-box the charger's ready. The plug to the phone and a phono plug from an old set of earphones is all I need now. Easy to hide in the Hi Fi or my typewriter. The phone fits nicely into the finger of one of Gary's rubber gloves. The waste water trap under the wash hand basin is just right for hiding it through the day. Why does Gary have rubber gloves, you ask? He gets them from the workshop. Industrial Cleaning. Gary's an old hand. Excuse the pun. Seventeen years in prison kills any memory of what a woman feels like. He makes what he calls a 'Juicy Lucy'. I've never had one off him but without going into too much detail it's a latex rubber glove filled with warm water and tied in a way, that's the clever bit, so it feels like a woman. The men use it for sexual relief. And on that note I'll leave it.

The billet is a safe place to smoke drugs and go about your business without any interference from screws. Too safe it seems. But in appearance only. Covertly we are under the watchful eye of the security screws. Spies are in every billet. Cons that at the price of a fellow inmate seek to win favour. The reality is they will be found out and in jail you can't hide forever. R4 is my billet and just before lunch unlock the muffty screws storm the building. We're ordered to stand by our doors. Outside on the corridor. Cell by cell the drug dog climbs all over the bed. Every cell is searched by two screws. It's no coincidence. Last night one of our number had a delivery over the fence. With access to the whole building the cell isn't the best hiding place. The dog finds nothing. Height will always beat the dog. If it can't get to up spot it; it can't find it.

There are more dogs to worry about though. One screw takes a chair from the last cell to the end of the corridor. At the top of the stairs, by the phone, there's a hatch giving access into the roof space. With the chair as a step the screw, using his stick, pops open the hatch cover. Reaching into the darkness whilst wobbling the chair, making it chatter on the wooden floor. He searches for what he knows is up there. His enthusiasm gives him away. More and more manic he become as he works his way round the periphery. Triumphantly clutching an oz of cannabis resin wrapped in cling film he jumps down, sending the chair flying. The ensuing huddle can only be described a scurry of screws. Without another word to us they all tramp down the stairs and out the door, slamming it behind them. The eggs are never all in one basket and sometimes it's good to let them find a small thing to hide a bigger thing. It's a game. Tomorrow the whole billet will be drug tested for sure. That's just how it is. My phone is safe in its hiding place.

Christmas is coming again. This is the first one when I won't be sending the greetings for the season to the police. I've been set free from that. I will send a card to Kevin, and to Rita. With the relaxed regime this year should be the best yet. For prison that is. Even with the petty rules they don't bother me and I don't bother them. Life is more of a slumber these days. I keep my head down. Don't get noticed by the security dept. and float by like a ghost ship in a fog. The chapel isn't a great institution of biblical learning. The turnover in here is rapid. No one has time to take on any long term commitments. If they don't go because their time is up and the day of freedom has arrived, they fall foul of the security zealots. More men are shipped out than let out.

Lock down for lunch and the cry 'DOOR' rings out. Too soon for lunch means it's a spin or worse it's a snatch squad. They always come at lunch time for the removal of a prisoner. The only thing I've noticed to be standard in every prison is the lunch time snatch squad. There's no drug dog. Is the first clue. There are four screws. Another clue. Who have they set their sights on? The thunder of jack boots climbing the wooden stairs is another clue. Someone on the second floor. My floor.

"Stand by your doors" The S.O. orders our landing. With ID cards hanging on a string around our necks we stand on the corridor while they inspect each one. Maybe someone is missing. At the lock down we get counted. If the number's wrong we have a roll call. The screws don't waste much time examining the ID on their way to me.

"Crowe CP3703?" he asks as he checks the blue folder in his hand.

"Yeah. What's the problem?"

"Pack your kit son you're moving." This can only be a bad move.

"Moving where to? It's Christmas in two weeks," still looking down at my file he says.

"Just pack your stuff we'll be back in five minutes."

"Bags?" The screw at the back of the bunch, a brute of a man whose face tells a tale of how he's lost more fights than he's won, bent nose, thick eyebrows and a notch out of his left ear. He hands to me, over the heads of the rest, three black bin bags.

"We'll be back in five minutes. Be ready," he says. Off they go leaving me to retrieve my phone from the sink trap. Hiding it in a new no-go area, down my pants in my crotch. The block is where I think I'm off to. Gary thinks in this game of snakes and ladders, I'm going back to square one. Or rather R 1. Reminds me of Super Mario. The game boy that burned my head out in Durham. All computer games work the same. When you fail you can't practice till you overcome the point you've reached. No it's always back to the beginning. To start all over again. Life's sometimes the same. It took the Israelites forty years to complete a seven day journey when they left Egypt. Once more round the mountain.

The tin, two-storey sheds where I was when I first came in, where everyone starts off, is my once more round the mountain. Demanding an explanation is futile. Let's just see where I end up. Bags bulging fit to burst. Two screws front and two behind. The march across the camp takes me to R1. From the Ritz to the Pits. Gary was right. Just in time for lunch. The default meal of the day. My menu choice is one thing I can't pack into the black bags. It stays with my old room in

R4. Here I get whatever they give me. Unless that is I'm of a religion that dictates what I can and can't eat. I'm not. My God says you can eat what you like. The prison says, 'and you can eat it in your toilet'.

The cell is tin. The walls are riveted plates of steel. The floor is the same and the roof. All painted prison blue. Shipping containers would be more comfortable. My wooden pine bed is replaced by a standard issue prison bed. No TV. Bars on the small slit windows. A tin toilet and sink. One small table and one broken chair. No mention of my transgression. There are three standards of privileges, basic, standard and enhanced. All R4 prisoners are enhanced. This is basic, if ever there was a definition for basic this is it. Bang up. Only open for feeding and showers, in the communal shower. My room with its shower is gone. Back to my music and my writing. Education classes have stopped. Work has stopped. Free movement around the camp has gone. Christmas is cancelled. A document is posted under my door. It says I am being investigated for unacceptable activity around the prison. No other explanation. A week or maybe two weeks is what I'm told then I'll be moved back into the prison. R2 first then work my way back to R4.

I feel my world has collapsed in on me and I don't want anything to do with the screws or the prison. Time to hibernate. I'm a new believer in God and I still don't know how to trust God with all things in my life. Even though I said I would hand over my life to Him way back in Long Lartin. I'm hanging on to the rudder. Every ship's captain needs a pilot-skipper to guide the ship into port. It works like this. The captain steers the ship but the pilot tells him where the danger lies under the water and out of sight. I still don't listen to the pilot of my life.

Christmas morning and all I want to do is talk to my beloved Rita. Waiting for the door to open is so painful. I have to get to one of the three phones before the lunch time rush. My phone can only come out after the evening lock-down. Forgoing prison's answer to Christmas dinner I'm single-mindedly heading for the phone. The ring tone frustrates my eager anticipation. I need to hear Rita's sweet voice with its encouraging words of hope. A pregnant pause, then the click of the recording equipment. She's there. In her world. A world I can't see in my mind's eye. Is her phone in the hall? On a table in the living room? In the kitchen? What's she wearing? I've never been to her home. My imagination is blank. Her beauty fills the void as soon as she speaks.

Christmas lunch is being readied for her household and she has left at a critical point to answer my need. The gravy is in between becoming one lump or two. Or the crowning glory to the festive meal. To switch off the heat could bring disaster. To stop stirring now is sure ruin of the rue. But here she is forsaking all for me. And not for the first time. The cacophony of stainless steel kitchen implements, doling out food on to stainless steel trays, is punctuated by the shouts of a screw. So much so I can no longer filter it out. I'm the cynosure of his world. In my enthusiasm I have fallen foul of prison protocol. On my feet are flip-flops. The overzealous new kid, eagle-eyed screw is drawing my attention to my inappropriate attire. This is not a problem for using the phone. However, for the collecting of food it's an absolute no-no. Closer and closer he invades my space pouring out his wrath.

"You can't collect food wearing them," pointing to my feet.

"I'm not collecting food, I'm on the phone." I keep talking not wanting to waste a second of this joy.

"Well you'll have to go back to your cell and change them."

"Do you mind? I'm on the phone," I defiantly turn my back on him. Time is up anyway. My two minutes of stolen time is over. The screw is standing at my door calling my name so he can move on down the landing. Hanging up the phone. Cutting off the only contact I can have on this Christmas day. I head back to my tin box.

"Where's your dinner?" The turn-key screw asks.

"I've got the wrong footwear on," I wave a foot at him.

"Get some shoes on and I'll come back for ya son."

"Shut the door I've had all the nourishment I need for this day. It's just another day in 'parasite;' one of many." That distinct sound of the door slamming followed by the bolt hitting its keep can't rob my joy. A tin of tuna, sweet corn and cheap mayonnaise serving my nutritional needs. Until my next visit I have to live off that phone call.

The heating in the cell consists of one water pipe running through the cell. My cell is at the end of the pipe. It comes in from next door, runs along the outside wall under the bed. Most of the heat that's made it to my cell escapes through the wall. One day is like a week. Hot drinking water before bang up in a jug that keeps it warm for about half an hour. Six cells at a time unlock for meals. Sure is back to the beginning. Visits are my only respite. With saved up visiting orders I have a visit every week. For three weeks I'm watched and poked. At night screws creep along the landing. Jack boots replaced with trainers. Listening for signs of illegal phones. Spying through the pin hole in the Judas flap on the door. My anti- surveillance, or rather early warning device, is one I learned of in Long Lartin. Fill the mop bucket with water and make a long mast that will float on the water. Rolled up news paper in a small plastic bottle will do. Stand the bucket near the door and when a screw walks down the iron walkway the mast sways from side to side. Reminds me of sailing ships rocking on the swell. The only thing missing is the chink chink of the halyard as it slaps against the mast. Works a treat. Have you heard it said a week is a long time in this technological age? Haverigg is moving with the times. Their newest tool in the fight against prisoners using phones is a tracker. Or scanner that finds phone signals. I know because last night they put it outside my cell. When the screws had all gone for the night I put the sim card into my phone and called Rita. We talked all night. Love and laughter blotted out the cold jail cell. Christmas behind me for another year this was going to be a getting to know each other time. Ready for when I can love Rita in the real world. I fall asleep content, even though I had to pile all the clothes I owned onto the bed in an attempt to stay warm. The weight was breath taking.

Before the breakfast unlock the hit squad converged on my bed in a flash. No time to wake before the screws were stripping back layer after layer of substitute bedding. Speed and surprise working in their favour. On the stripping back of the last sheet my phone spilled on to the floor with a condemning rattle. Two screws dived to secure it fearing it may somehow elude their grasp. My protestation of the degrading way they swooped was lost in the jubilation of the moment. The air in the cell was sucked out like a back draft when, as quick as they came in, they left. The door slammed. The footsteps dissipated. Silence returned. My first nicking in six years is on its way and I don't care. No reward for doing good just punishment for breaking the rules. Maybe it's time to move on. This jail has lost its appeal. I wanted to come here for visits from Whitehaven to be easier. Now my visits are from Rita. Blackburn. I have to sleep under the bed with the hot pipe inside the covers to keep warm. I'm slipping away from sanity. I need to change things. In times of trial we all turn to God. Time to take him out of his box. The 'God box' people put him in when things are going good.

"Why am I having such a bad time?" I ask him. "If you have my best interests at heart why do I have to live like this in a cold cell? What have you brought me here for when it's so bad?" I take the time to read my bible looking for answers. It says God has a plan for my life and all things work for good to those who are in Christ. It makes me think I can't be in Christ then! What possible good could come from my suffering? That small still voice we often call our conscience screamed inside my heart. It's my inner man, my spirit.

"You are in the wrong place." Well that's just what I've been saying.

"I didn't send you here. You insisted on coming here. I closed all the doors but you kicked them open. You went to court in London. You fought for years to come here and now you blame me? You are where you wanted to be." It's true I was single-minded in my endeavour. I never asked God if it was the right place for me. I wanted my own way and now I have it. I need to trust more in what God has in mind for me and not what I think is best. Didn't I say I would do whatever he told me to do back in that cell when I first made a commitment to follow him? Then as time goes by back he goes into his man-made box. His 'God-box', only to be taken out when things go wrong. Without him in my life how can it ever go right way? I've messed up again.

The seg unit welcomes me into its cold, brick-walled teeth. To my surprise little Gary's in the next cell. There's only four so they don't like to tie them up when R1 is just as good a place to punish naughty boys. His crime? A phone found in his cell, or room as they like to call them on R4. Being a lifer he can only be given block time. A week is the normal retribution required by the jail.

The governor reprimands me for having my phone.

"I will assume you brought the phone with you from Preston. I know you had access through a member of prison staff in Garth." She thinks Rita gave it to me in Garth. She knows that's not the case but it's a let off for her prison.

"Assumptions are often wrong. Rita did nothing against security whatever you may have been told." What's the point of my retort? They don't understand.

"As you're on R1 and basic regime I'm going to leave you there for another two weeks to see how you get on. Then you can move on back through the prison." She marks my file with its first nicking report.

"I have one foot out the door so why not just get me out of your dump of a jail? Send me somewhere where I'm not treated like a six-week shoplifter."

"You are here and here is where you'll stay. You're going nowhere," I know that's not how it works here.

"Really? You think so do you? I think I'm already earmarked for a ship-out."

"I'm the number one governor and I'm telling you you're not going anywhere." I've overstayed my welcome here and she knows it really.

"We'll see." Even in this low security jail the adjudication is conducted in the segregation unit with two brutish goons standing over me. Once over I'm sent on my way, unescorted, back to R1. The security gates are all wide open for movements, work and such. The gate from the block, the gate I have to get through, is locked. A screw arrives just at the same time as my disgruntled self. It just happens to be the worst screw on the whole camp. His weather ravaged face is peeping out of his greatcoat-pulled-up-collar. Red-nosed, not from the biting Atlantic wind, but from too much drink. If he were an animated Disney animal he'd be a weasel.

"Where you been then son?" The nicking sheet protruding from my pocket takes his eye.

"Just open the gate. It's nothing to do with you." The gate's locked but he feels it necessary to block my way with his skinny frame.

"Been on a nicking son?" Rhetorical question, "what's that for then?" Could be just the wrong time to piss me off. One sure way of getting out of a jail is to be a threat to the smooth running of the well-oiled wheels.

"What's your name," then I look for his identification number. The number supporting epaulette of his uniform is hidden under his coat.

"What do you want to know for?" He pulls his collar even higher lest his secret identity be revealed.

"I know who you are and I know you live in Millom. Do you know where I'm from?" My turn for a question needing no answer. "Whitehaven, just up the road from here I tell him.

"What you saying?" He knows what I'm saying without hearing the words.

"I hope you can sleep at nights. You take your job too serious. It could be the death of you if you're not careful."

"Are you threatening me?" He reaches for the lock with his big brass key.

"I'm not one of your boys who you can push around. I'm not taking grief from a turn-key dog like you. Just open the gate."

Slipping back into my old life still bothers me when I calm down. But I'm working on it. Trouble is it works so well. Even though I know I should not be who other people make me to be. I will be who I am and not change because of others. Working on it. The first step is; I know I shouldn't change who I really am.

"I can nick you for that." His quivering voice betrays his integrity.

"You do that. I don't give a hill of beans what you do." Altercation over I'm on my way back to my ice cave.

In one hour like clockwork. New to R1 and the roundabout of cyberspace is Gary. Well if anyone will end up where he started its Gary. In Garth he was caught with a video player in his cell and an adult movie. He had a false back in his locker and the video was hidden behind it. He hired them out on the wing. Along, no doubt, with a 'Juicy Lucy'. When the governor asked him why he had it he told him it was for education. Gary didn't know the tape had gone missing and the governor didn't know anything about it. The screw was left to explain the content of the tape. 'It was of a pornographic nature sir and we destroyed it.' At which the governor said to Gary, 'I thought you said it was educational?' Quick as the best blagger who ever stood on that spot Gary retorted with, 'well Gov it certainly taught me a thing or two.' The grin of the screws let loose a titter. Life sentence prisoners can't lose time. They don't have any to lose. Ninety-nine years is their sentence and it never gets any less. We, on the other hand, get days added to our release date. Days in the block for lifers are all they can do, or remove his telly for a week. Just fresh from the block he's with me now.

Gary has a new phone for me and he takes the cell over the landing where he can see my door from the small gap in the door jam. No more spy scanners at my door without me knowing about it. Through the day I have to farm out my phone so they can't find it again. Gary is here one day before he's spun. Three screws looking for phones. The toilet brush holder is the best Gary can do in this sparsely furnished abode. Body search first reveals small raps of pot hidden in his pants pocket. The screw pull them out and looking at Gary's disappointment quickly he puts them back, making sure his brethren didn't see them. Not so with the phone. First place investigated is the bog brush stash. Bang to rights. The phone drops out. We are what are known as, on top. The screw tells me I have more phones than BT. There's no point in sending Gary back down the snake. He's already on the first square of this mad house.

"Pack your kit you're moving kid." I'm told.

After my encounter with the screw at the gate I'm for the off; so much for the number one governor and 'you're going nowhere,' at my nicking. No governor can override security and security won't take a chance on the health and well-being of one of their own men. The weasel has come through as I knew he would. The definition of a screw I was once told is a bunch of bananas; they come in bunches and they're all yellow. Question is where will I end up now? I have to trust God more and let him take me where he wants me to be. It's not natural to me to stop swimming and float along. The odds are I'll return to Preston. I've met tons of Haverigg returns in there. And I thought how mad are they? They get to the relaxed, comfort; one could say serene, R4 and can't keep out of trouble long enough to enjoy it. How we know best when we know nothing of where someone has come from.

Preston greats me once more on my epic adventure. A dog on one of those retractable leads I am. They press the button and I'm pulled back here. The last time I was here my cell in the rafters, under a tin-clad roof, was so hot the bread turned to toast. Anticipating another long summer as a guest of governor White, who just happens to be the fellow in the life of Miss, governor at Haverigg. Not married. Sort of long time courting. That long they refer to each other as 'my partner.' I can never understand the term partner used in a loving relationship. I'm old school. Girlfriend for me is followed by fiancée then wife. Partner is someone who you enter into a business arrangement with. It doesn't suggest a loving committed union. Or am I just too much in the past? Leave me where I am please. I digress.

After the rigmarole of settling in once more, my domicile is C wing; cell four on the twos, keeping well away from that tin topped Turkish steam bath they call a roof. My companion, Preston being two beds to a cell jail, is a young kid who loves his car. Deep blue with chrome oozing off every light-catching accessory. Hot hatch I think they call them. German engineering designed to beguile young men. Most times luring them to their death. Named by Hitler, 'the People's Car', a VW Golf GTI. He has a photo of it on the wall next to his bed and he says its 'phat,' which, he tells me, means great. Never tell your woman she's 'phat' however great she is, I tell him. He's just too young for me to live with. He's a nice enough kid but I like my own company these days. Over the landing is a rare thing in here. A single cell. Number forty is on the end and full. Time to work on the landing screw; see if I can't talk him round to my way of thinking. The car loving kid is an Asian. He ticked the Muslim box for religion when he came in.

"I'm a bad Muslim," he says.

"Why do you think you're a bad Muslim?"

"I don't go to pray. Five time a day I should pray. And I drink alcohol."

"You don't have a beard either. Would that make you bad?"

"Go easy mate I don't shave yet," he laughs.

"Well what do you do that makes you a Muslim?"

"What do you mean like? I's a Muslim. Me whole family's Muslim. I was born one. Like you's a Christian."

"I wasn't born a Christian." That's confused him.

"What did you use to be? Before you was a Christian?"

"I wasn't born anything other than a baby. You can't be born a religion. I became a Christian when I accepted Jesus as my Lord and Saviour."

"What do you have to do as a Christian then to be a good 'un?"

"There isn't anything we can do to win God's favour. He already loves me one hundred per cent. He can't love me anymore."

"How do people know you're a Christian then?"

"Do I live like the rest on here?"

"What do ya mean mate?" Confusion floods his face.

"Do I do drugs? Fight? Scheme and rob other cons?"

"No you do nothing. You just keep ya self to ya self like," a light comes on in his brain, "so you have to be good all the time to be a Christian? I think I get it but we have to be good so Allah will show mercy on us." Just when I thought he was getting it.

"How good is good enough for you to win in the end," I ask him.

"I don't know. That's up to Allah."

"Well I'm not being good to be a Christian. I'm trying to live a good life because I'm a Christian. I don't have to do anything really; I live this way because I don't want to live that other way. My God will still love me however I live. I have accepted Jesus as my

Saviour. That means He did the good living in my place and he did the dying on the cross in my place. So He did it all. I don't have to do much. He told me just to tell people who he is and what he did for them. So me telling you is what He told me to do."

"That's it? Sounds too easy."

"It is easy but lots of people will go to hell in unbelief. I know my God will welcome me into his kingdom when the time comes. Do you?"

"No we don't know till we get to stand before him."

"Good luck I'll stay with my Jesus."

Lunch time another nail in young Mohamed's coffin is the food he brings back. Quiche with ham and eggs. Convinced it must be turkey meat in his pie he wolfs the lot. I haven't the heart to tell him and if living as a bad Muslim he's happy a bit of ham won't make it any worse for him.

My single cell

The guy living in my cell over the landing has gone. Time to make my move for a single cell. If you're not fast you're last and I've already missed the opportunity. The screws are moving a guy from the reception wing into my single. I say mine because I've laid claim to it. The new occupant barricades himself in as soon as the door closes. It's his great plan of action to get a ship out. Again my request falls on a deaf ear. All for the work of moving two cards on two cell doors and changing the paperwork in the wing office. Instead of bringing a new boy on to the wing and only doing one cell move. It's that easy a reason to refuse my request. This guy lasts the night. At the morning unlock he's bouncing round the floor of the cell like dried rice on a snare drum being beaten by Keith Moon on acid. He's an epileptic with a history of fitting violently, ruling him out for a single cell. The wing screw opens my door.

"Pack your bags you're moving into forty," I reckon he's plumbing for a safe bet. Having failed with the last two pick-of-the-day cons. I don't need telling twice. Dragging my property bags round the landing, with a little help from me young pal Mohamed the pork-eating Muslim. I can't help thinking what kind of god he has. His god never inspires him or communicates with him. Five times a day he says he has to pray. The same chanting words at the same time. I spend many a time just talking with my God. I can speak without words to him and he answers me. He speaks straight into my heart. When I asked my young friend if Allah had ever spoken to him, he couldn't in his wildest imagination understand what I was asking. His mission is to please his god. A god who never lets him know if he is pleased or not. I've planted the seed and now it's up to The Spirit to water it.

The book for my inspiration in the creative writing class is The Commitments by Roddy Doyle. Reading it in my new cell each evening. Preston still has no electric in most cells, this one included. My radio from Durham was handed out so until my mother can send me a small battery powered transistor radio I have my books to read. Having seen the film taken from the book I can see and hear the characters created in the mind of Doyle. That Dublin twang with the dry Irish humour. Not many books make me laugh out loud. My neighbour shouts me from his window. He wants to know what I'm laughing at. I can just see him flicking through the radio stations looking for the channel I'm finding so amusing.

"I'm reading a book mate I tell him. A silence comes back. "It's funny, you've maybe seen the film it's called The Commitments."

"Don't think so mate who's in it?" I can't resist naming a character from the book.

"Joey The Lips Fagan. And Jimmy Rabbit." Silence then, "don't know them mate. What else were they in?"

"They're not actors' mate they're the characters," I read him some of the book from my window.

"What's it about? I'll have it after you pal if ya don't mind?"

"No, I'll finish it tonight and let you have it in the morning," I give him the plot. "Two friends. Derek Scully and 'Outspan' Foster get together to form a band, but soon realise that they don't know enough about the music business to get much further than their small neighbourhood in the North side of Dublin. To solve this problem, they recruit a friend they'd had from school, Jimmy Rabbit Jr, to be their manager. He accepts graciously, but only if he can make fundamental changes to the group, the first being the sacking of the third and mutually disliked, member - their synth player. After this, Rabbit gets rid of their name, making them "The Commitments", (all the good 60's bands started with a 'the') and, most importantly, forming them from another synth-pop group to the face of what he thinks will be the Dublin-Soul revolution. ("Yes, lads. You'll be playing Dublin Soul!")

Not wanting to give the whole book away I leave him hungry for the rest.

"Sounds like my kind of book pal. I'll let ya get on with it and see ya in the morning."

Getting back to the story removes me from my cell and transports me into a small Dublin night club where a bunch of individual musicians play. The singers sing soul music made famous by the legends. The end comes when the individuality pulls the union apart. Having knocked on the door of success they leave just as its opening. A lesson in life we all need to learn.

Roddy Doyle's writing keeps me laughing with his witty collection. 'The Van' centres on Jimmy's father, same Irish humour but I've never seen the film. The basis of the story is that Jimmy Rabbit Sr. has been laid off from his job and has no money. His friend, Brendan 'Bimbo' Reeves also gets laid off and gets a redundancy cheque. With this cheque the two friends decide to purchase a 'chipper' or fish and chip van. Jimmy and Bimbo's friendship gets strained, because Jimmy starts to believe that Bimbo and his wife Maggie are planning the work behind his back.

The writing style of Roddy Doyle is one of great comedy prose with live, believable and funny people of everyday life. Then I find a book called, The Woman Who Walked into Doors'. Powerful and gripping with a completely different style. Far from laughing whilst drinking the words off the pages of this book, I'm moved by Doyle's ability. Showing her life through her eyes brings me to tears. The hurt and heart ache; trapped. Hopeless and living in perpetual misery. The novel tells the struggle and survival of an abused wife named Paula Spencer. It is narrated by the victim. The title comes from an incident narrated in the book, where Paula's husband asks her how she received a bruise he was responsible for, and she replies that she "walked into a door Until now I've never picked up a book and read it all the way through. I guess I've never had the time or the interest. When Rita gave me the complete works of John Steinbeck in Garth. I was overwhelmed by its size and put off by the first thing I saw. The title hit me right at the heart of the injustice I felt. 'The Best Laid Plans of Mice and Men' was what the Judge said before he condemned me to twelve years incarceration. The same words were looking at me from the tome in my hand.

Poems opened my literary eye. Bob Dylan has got to be one, if not the greatest, poet of the twentieth century. Words can be powerful used in the right way. The power of life and death is in the tongue, the bible says. In this cell I write. With a pencil I pour out nonsense on to white sheets of A4. Not filtering my thoughts. Putting down random words in blocks of ten. Words that become a poem, a sonnet or a limerick. The green fluff that comes from nowhere is a curiosity that invokes my pencil. One thing a writer should do is write. All I write doesn't always make sense but so what! The first thing I wrote way back when was a ballad. 'The Quad'. My pencil never left the page from start to finish. When I read what I'd written I thought I must have read it somewhere else first. I wonder what would have been different in my life if somewhere some teacher had taught me just one thing. I wonder if I was given the gift of seeing words the right way round and letters in the right order what my road would have led to. Why did no one know why I found words difficult? Only now in jail do they want to know what my IQ is. If schools did their job right maybe prisons wouldn't have to do it for them. Not limited by words, the test says I'm well over the average of one hundred; ironic. When I left school I went to be a welder at Sellafield Nuclear Plant. The aptitude test was a doddle, passed with time to spare. Then I was asked to fill in the application form and right there was when I lost that chance. A smaller marine engineering firm in Workington were taking on apprentice welders. A friend of my dad's got me an interview. All was going well till he slid the form across the table and I froze. Couldn't even write my address. I had learned to weld at school and at home I had my own equipment. I would make wrought iron gates and car trailers. Once I made a kiddie fairground ride for another friend of my dad's. I was never asked to weld on the interviews. Just write my name, address and maybe why I wanted to work for the company. Something I couldn't do if my life depended on it. When I was a diver I had to go to Strathclyde University to pass some exams. Two days of lecturers then the written test. I was thirty years old. Old enough to know what I needed to do. Fudging it was over. I told the examiner I was word illiterate. Although I could read I couldn't write. I was allowed to dictate my answers to someone who wrote them down on the exam paper. I passed with 100 % correct. So if you find a mistake in my words don't condemn me. Now you know where I've come from.

Not all the books I've read have been as interesting as Mr Doyle's. The Fight Club stole my attention for one chapter. I read the second to give it a chance before I closed it for good. I was once told no book deserves to be read. It has to earn the right to turn every page. The

403

Alchemist by Paulo Coelho was a page turner for me. The profound message in the story is a life lesson for all who are looking for something in their life. When Paulo told his parents he wanted to be a writer they had him committed to a mental institution. His first book bombed. The Alchemist had a first print run of nine hundred. He was dropped by the publisher. Today that book from its humble beginnings has sold 30 million copies translated into 71 different languages. Paulo was told the book will never sell and he would make more money on the stock exchange. He has over 30 books to his name and he's not a poor man. Like The Chronicles of Narnia by C. S. Lewis there is a hidden biblical message. A message that has been read by one hundred million people in the case of Lewis's best known book. My first book is Words of A Demented Prisoner and there are eight copies. The ones I made in Garth and gave to the chosen few.

Real life lurks ready to pounce on the other side of my blue door. My son has managed to get himself locked up. Shelley his sister only knows he was lifted by the police and has never been seen since. A good deduction is he will be a guest of the YOI Lancaster Farms. Working on this assumption I ask the S.O. to inquire as to his status. The prison computer will find any prisoner in any prison. I know because we would use the one in Durham when the screws ran to an alarm call. They left the office with the computer logged on.

Sure enough Dom is in The Farms. At the morning unlock I make my request at the application's desk for an inter prison phone call. Then wait. All day I wait. I wait with calm composure knowing the wheels of jail turn slowly. The SO knows me from Garth. He's the one who threw my file in the air at my review. He moved here when he was on the cliff edge of a mental breakdown. Not wanting ripples in his serene mental

404

pond, let alone tempestuous waves, I'm sure I'll get my call.

Nothing. The day is coming to a close and after five o' clock the chance will have gone. Another application and a long wait not knowing if he's OK. Not being able to tell his sister I've found him and he's doing fine. Time to act. Unlock for food. Four o'clock. First the count to see all prisoners are correct. Flap opens. Face fills the glass slit. Flashing a shaft of light into the dusty atmosphere for a second. I boot the door and call him back.

"What do you want?" he asks.

"I want my phone call that I've waited all day for."

"What phone call is that then Crowe?"

"The call I made an app for this morning at breakfast. An inter-prison call to my son in The Farms," I know he knows what I'm talking about.

"The Farms don't do inter-prison calls. They won't permit it."

"It's a prison and do you really need me to quote rules to you? Just get the S.O. and let's sort it before the end of office hours," more and more I'm winding up. The tried and tested method of getting their attention is oozing into my mouth.

"Alan isn't on now. He's gone of shift and its feeding time so we're too busy right now may be you can sort it for tomorrow. Put an app in at breakfast." Well that's lit the fuse. He goes to close the flap.

"Just a minute. I haven't finished. The next time you open this door it had better be to take me to the phone or the block and if it's the latter bring your best men. The first one through this door will lose his face. You can only come in one at a time and I will take the first one." I turn my back to the sound of the flap being sucked back into position by the magnetic catch. I

405

really do not like having to do this. It's not my language. It's theirs. They understand it all too well.

No battle clad block warriors this time. Just the wing SO who wants to feed the wing with no fuss.

"What's your problem?" He looks down searching for a barricade behind my door.

"I want my phone call today," I don't get up from my chair.

"The Farms don't do them. Maybe..." Here I go butting in again.

"It's a prison. Don't be telling me they don't do them. I need to know my son is in there and he's OK. He was taken off the street and no one knows where he is or if he's OK. I need to talk to him. And today. If I don't get to talk to him on the phone I want an inter-prison visit and as I'm the higher category they will have to bring him here. Now why don't you go and tell them that?" I know they won't want the hassle of bringing him here.

"I'll ask them again for you. But I don't think they'll permit it. It's not their policy." Again the flap closes shut. The call goes out, 'all away on the ones. The two are correct. Ready on the threes.' In five minutes they'll start opening up. I have to make my stand if they don't sort my phone call out. On the landing I can hear the muffled chatter of the screws. They're standing at their stations ready to let loose the one hundred and twenty men. Six cells at a time waiting for the S.O. to give the command to open up. First he has to deal with the disgruntled occupant of forty on the twos. That's me. Time is running out. At five o' clock I'll have lost the chance. How hard can it be to let me have a phone call that I'm allowed to have according to their rules? The iron stairs rattle with the sound of feet. This is the S.O. or the block hit squad. At the flap comes the face of the S.O, two screws standing behind him, one a wing screw the other the wing P.O, one step down from a governor.

"I've phoned The Farms and they'll let you talk to your son. They don't usually do it but I told them you were worried about him." Now he's doing me a favour? I don't care what he needs to justify the craziness of prison I want to talk with my beloved son and know he's OK.

"That's very good of you now open the door and let's get it done before they change their minds," happy it's safe to do so he unlocks the door.

"The wing office phone is ready for you. They've gone to get your son. You can only have a minute or two. We need to feed the wing."

"Don't let me stop the smooth running of the wing. You've had all day to sort this, I did put in an app this morning and no one told me till I collared the officer doing the count it wasn't happening. Turns out he was wrong." The phone in the wing office is waiting and on the other end is my son. Satisfied he's fit and well, even though he complains vehemently. He says he's the victim of discrimination by the local police. It's his doing that they know his name and he thinks now that he's trying to live a better life they should forget the old Dom and give the new one a chance. Life's not like that. When you do good no one remembers but when you do bad they never forget. The PO oversees my call. No recordings are taken on this phone. When I hang up he says, "there now what was all the fuss over? You only needed to ask; that wasn't difficult now was it?" Rhetorical question. A worm on a hook waiting for me to strike like a frustrated salmon. I have my victory so don't need to engage in niceties with this overweight, over- bearing and overwhelmingly arrogant jobs-worth.

"You can get your food if you like", he says as I walk out the door. I have to collect my mug and water jug. Seeing me walk back to my cell confuses him. My stay on this occasion is short. I feel like a dog on one of those retractable leads. Whenever Preston pushes the button I end up back here; reeled back in.

My cat C. status is still with me and the allocations officer has a place in Wymott prison with my name on it. I can't help thinking it would have been easier to have sent me there from Garth in the first place! The journey reminds me of the time I went to Garth from Long Lartin. All be it shorter with less trepidation. It's the same spring morning with the hedgerow bursting into bloom. Steam rises from the fields. That morning dew liberated by the warmth of the sun. Baby lambs dotted like mushrooms break up the green patchwork landscape. The aroma I can imagine from the time of sitting in the rain at Haverigg. I can just hear the grass growing as it stretches skyward.

Wymott opens its door devouring the van and its occupants. The door lowers snuffing out the light of the morning sun, trapping us in the air-lock. In five minutes the inner door rattles open. Slowly yawning; sucking in the stale jail air. The reception waiting room already holds new recruits. Two rooms keep the rule 45 prisoners and the normal location prisoners apart. Rule 45 being vulnerable prisoners Or VPs for shot. That's what the jail calls sex offenders. I would say it's the rest of society who are vulnerable. These are the predators that prey on young kids and old people. This jail has the main VP population in the North West. Ten of us new boys are waiting to be processed. Unlike Haverigg this is a closed cat C prison. Cells not dorms. Walls not fences. Locked doors and escorted around the grounds whenever we move. Visits are a far cry from the easy going Haverigg. All my property is allowed. Six bags including my matching plate and mug. White porcelain decorated with bright red cherries, courtesy of my beloved Rita. My hi-fi is reinstated for my musical delectation. Own clothing apart from visits means no jail rags. Waiting for my fellow cons to pass through the process gives me time to get to know who's came from where. Most like me have come from local jails. Short term prisoners who are from the area. No VPs, or so we all thought. Peter has come from Lancaster Farm and he knows my son. Now he's twenty-one he's not a young offender any more. Jail from now on. Just another institution for the boy. Y.O.I. (Young Offender Institution) is a hard life where if you don't fight and gain respect from the others you become a victim. It really is worse than any prison. Peter has been fighting from twelve years old. If not with his drunken father who would beat him, from being shunted from institution to institution. Being well built and with the height advantage over most kids his age, he's well equipped to be a victor rather than a victim. He's last to be dealt with before we head off onto our wing. And the only one who the door closes behind as he's asked some interesting questions.

"Do you want to go on the VP wing son?" We can all hear these incriminating questions.

"No why would I? I'm not a nonce mate," Peter says.

"Well we just noticed on your pre-cons you have a conviction for assaulting a minor. Child assault you could be vulnerable on normal location?" the screw informs him.

"I've never been done for kiddie fiddling mate. I don't know where you've got that from but it's a load of crap mate," Peter's defence instinct is kicking in. Half the men already have him condemned.

"Says here you assaulted a kid of fourteen..." Peter butts in mid sentence.

"I was done for a fight when I was fourteen. He was a kid but so was I and it was just a fight mate. Two kids fighting that's all. I can't believe this."

"He's right, says here it was a section 18 wounding. Nothing to do with sex offending," the officer on the computer says.

Still someone in the waiting room says. "Do you believe that or do you think he's a nonce?"

"Did you not hear the screw mate? It's a load of bollocks. The kid's Okay", says another. This is the very thing that gets people stabbed. If it's on your file it's got to be true. Mine says I'm a driving instructor instead of a diving instructor. But that mistake wouldn't get me put into hospital with a face full of scolding water. Peter's would. The friendly attitude doesn't extend onto the wing where I'm met by one of them jobs worth screws who think prisoners have too much of everything except time to serve. My six bags are my responsibility and if I can't carry them I shouldn't have them, he thinks, out loud. Dragging them along while complaining under my breath at the lack of help, or a trolley for ease, delights the screw. It makes his day when my cherry patterned mug, a gift from Rita, falls out of the bag and shatters into a mosaic of shards at the wing gate. One good thing comes from my mishap. A young guy, who must be a wing cleaner, picks up two of my bags and takes then up the iron stairs to the second landing. The cell next to his is where I'll live. TV and clean walls; better still white porcelain toilet and wash hand basin, also clean. For a jail it looks OK. Two landings with four phones. Snooker table on the ones, two pool tables and a table tennis table folded up and standing next to the food serving hatch. This is just making ready to dish out lunch. White clad cons are waiting for the food trolleys arriving from the kitchens. Two guys are stealing five minutes on the phones while the screws are busy dealing with us. Wymott jail, could be any jail. Same cells. Same blue doors. Same everything. Induction for the first week and a job in the metalwork shop making the doors and gates that everyday incarcerate me. Ironic? The prisoners fashion their own fetters. On offer is education. Not the creative writing that I enjoyed in Preston and Haverigg. The access to a computer means I can use the disc I made in Preston to continue my writing. The course on offer is European Computer Driving Licence. I sign up with no hesitation. The next love of my mundane life is the gym. A badminton court is waiting for me. First the beep test to see if I won't drop down dead with the exertion. Four beeps is the minimum for attendance to the gym. A breeze for me, who for the last five years has every day done some form of fitness work. The gym is full of new fish. Some just off the streets; some, like me old hands at jail. When the first beep sounds we all set off jogging across the hall. Then the second beep all the way to the required minimum fourth beep. My signal to stop, to the dismay of the ultra competitive screw who is urging everyone on.

"Why have you stopped? You're not even warmed up yet," he says to me as I walk toward the showers.

"I did the beep test so I could attend the gym and play badminton. Four beeps is the requirement why would I do more than I have to?" I say.

"Do you not want to know how far you can go? You could get to twelve beeps."

"And what do I get? A night out on the town or maybe a month of changing two sheets a week instead of only one. I've done enough to get what I need. There's no point in doing more. I have nothing to prove to myself or to anyone else thanks. First in the shower will do for me

"You look fit why not give it a go?"

"Like I said I have nothing to prove. If you need to know how fit I am badminton's me game I'll see you on the court if you like."

411

"It's a date. Are you any good?"

"I can hit it back to you. After four years of playing every day I would say I'm a fair to middling player."

"Can't wait to see what you've got."

"Tony's me name see you on Friday." At that I leave the rest of the guys bouncing off the walls in an effort to beat the next beep. One by one they drop to the floor. Gasping, gulping air, bright red spent salmon flapping having given their all. At the point of breathing their last. Ten beeps and only two left; they fight it out. Now it's a race between two men, who have to be number one gym-head. Stumbling on the sweat-soaked wooden floor they both touch the wall for the twelve and final beep. Now it's a sprint to the end. Never mind the beep; these two are competing against each other. Their reach is the decider. Fingertips only now separate the fitness fanatics. At the end there can only be one winner. The gym screw calls the victor and with it, an end to the session.

Walking back to the wing, through the caged walkways, we meet a prisoner with a red kite towering above his shoulders, perched on his leather clad arm. A killing machine if you're an intruder who has managed to find his way into the space only prisoners should inhabit. We are to be witnesses of the unbalanced power of the skilled Hunter. A pigeon franticly searching for an exit stands no chance of escape. The kite's wings spread, casting a black cloud on the concrete pathway. With a whoosh the killer swoops on the intruder. Its talons like a vice; grips the unworthy victim in mid flight. Dropping down to the floor. Clocking the quarry beneath its wings. The grey body motionless. Life is ended in a second.

Wymott's a strange prison for me. Relaxed rules on the outside but in reality the prison is stealthily very much austere. To keep my enhanced prisoner status I

412

have to be tested for drugs weekly. Yet the visits are the worst I've had the unfortunate pleasure of experiencing. Even the sweets from their own shop have to be eaten out of a clear plastic bag. No holding each other. One kiss at the start and one at the end. That's the extent of personal contact. Although it's a cat C prison there's a steel wall surrounding the jail. The jail is notorious for housing prisoners who are on the numbers. Prisoners who will be attacked by others who put their crime in the box labelled 'decent criminals'. Sex offenders need protecting when the children and the old, or women, are not their focus of interest. Wymott is the champion of protecting them, like Peter who wasn't one in the end.

The chapel is run by a woman who I would say doesn't own a bible. Heavily pregnant which makes her just a little bigger round the waist and with a congregation of two she doesn't light my spiritual fire. The Roman Catholic mass is run by a friend of Rita's. Sister Mary has a sign on her office wall that reads 'How much can I do and still get to heaven'. An avid follower of the horses she is the supercritical Irish Nun. The joy of the Lord flows from her face and I need to see that joy every Sunday. So I forego my C of E. label and slip into the world of rosary and purgatory. I know little of Christianity, even less about the strange practices of Rome. I was once engaged to be married to a Roman Catholic girl so I do know something of what they believe. And I did work in Garth where I rang the bell to call into the host Jesus. I don't need to question the differences in the doctoring and the bible. What would be the point to that? We sing songs and worship the same God.

My pal in the next cell in from Blackburn. His wife has no transport so I arrange for her to come and visit with Rita. He helped me when I came in and struggled

413

with my bags. He has a phone but no charger. My re-jigged Hi Fi is just what he needs to charge his phone. For this symbiotic relationship I get to use his phone to talk to Rita. Until he is joined on the wing by his fellow brethren all is fine. The Asian Muslim living next door was just a mate who sat in my cell and drank tea. Now I'm invisible to him. I can hear his kinsmen telling him to stop, 'having it' with me. When he comes on the landing he dives into his cell so he doesn't have to talk to me. I can see a new side to him. When I was his mate and no one else would show him any friendship we were fine but now he has his Muslim pals I'm the worst thing he could touch. Well so be it. I'm happy to keep myself to myself.

Racism is one-sided sometimes. I was once told you can't be black and racist. We are all one race, the human race. The job of serving food is one of the good jobs, especially if you go to the gym and need all the extra food you can get. Coming back from the gym and my badminton session, a black guy is pitching his case for the cushy number. The officer is a young woman who is wearing too much make up and not enough skirt for being in a prison full of men who have been deprived of femininity for years.

"Miss, Miss," he shouts after her as she wiggles her way up the iron stairs. Her thin white blouse is transparent. The delicate lace garment under it shows off her breasts in their best light. The whiff of woman floats along behind her.

"What can I do for you?" stopping half way up and turning round. After a slow long undressing gaze the guy says, "I can't help noticing there are no black Muslims working as servers. Muslim food needs to me served by a Muslim Miss." Worried she was offending some human rights nonsense she succumbs to his behest without hesitation.

"Are you a Muslim? Would you like to do it?"

"I am yeah, and I would like it Miss."

"I'll do the paperwork and you can start in the morning at breakfast." Smiling at his successful ploy he wonders off to give the good news to his brethren. I can't help but have some fun with the teasing lace baring beauty.

"Excuse me Miss but I can't help noticing there are no gay servers giving out food! Is it because this prison is sexist?"

"I don't know. Is there no gays?" She's lost for an answer.

"Well I can help you out I'm homosexual and I don't mind working with heterosexuals or black Muslims. Perfect for the job so you won't be seen to be sexist Miss." Before she can answer I mince passed her on the stairs and head off tossing my laundry bag into the open door of the laundry room. My smile is bigger than the black guy's. It really is that crazy.

The next day when I go to retrieve my gym kit from the laundry the door is locked and I need it for the afternoon badminton session. Who's wafting along the landing but Miss Lipstick and Suspenders.

"Miss, can you open the door? I need my washing."

"Where's the laundry orderly?"

"I've no idea but my bag is just there Miss, on the clean side. So just open the door and I'll be off."

"How do I know it's yours?"

"Well why would I want someone else's washing?"

"Okay but I've heard all about you."

"Really what have you heard?" She looks me up and down; undressing me with her lustful eye. I don't take my eyes off her face.

"You're not gay."

"I don't know; I'm always happy and full of joy. Does that not make me gay?"

"You're the prisoner from Garth who was caught with the chaplain. If I let you in I can't come inside with you."

"I wasn't 'caught' with anyone and I wouldn't worry about coming in with me. You have nothing to worry about; you're not my type Miss. I don't pay for it." She turns the key in the door and stands back. Key still in the lock; connecting her by chain to the now open door. My last comment missing its mark.

It would seem our tale of love is now a tale of frustrated sex. Not enough for the whole prison service to turn our love into a sordid affair. The reporter I met in Haverigg has printed her version of it in the local rag. The Lancashire Evening Post is running the story as news. A bit late for news but there we have it. It must be a slow news day and we fill a blank page. How many people will see it in the centre pages of a local second rate rag? More than I think. Rita is the main target of the story. Her past is dredged up. Old photos along with the old story of Bangkok headline the story. Then there's the always ever anonymous 'a prison spokesman says.' More lies that paint a newspaper selling fantasy. The advice Rita gets from her friends is to take legal action against the reporter. As with Job in the bible I can't help thinking that's bad advice. That's like trying to shout down the guy on stage when he has the mike and you don't. Nothing is what we'll do and it'll die.

Like a virus left to its own devices and given the right conditions the story grows. The next week reporters from the national press have taken an interest. Rita's home is besieged. Her children are ambushed as they leave for school. This being Rita's second experience with the over- zealous press she warns the children to say nothing. A difficult request for Rita's son Ben but one he heeds. When nothing is forthcoming the net is widened. Friends and neighbours are interrogated. With the cheque book of shame in hand all the papers make a bid for our true story of the 'unfrocking of a chaplain'. The only one we give a thought to is The Sunday Times. But if it doesn't glorify God why would we do it? Certainly not for the money. And the money went up every time Rita said no to the offer. No we'll let them print whatever they want and ride out the storm. Sunday is the day they'll print their story. Not our story but the story as written by their creative writing wolf. Each trying to out write the other. Each one looking for that one edge that'll sell more copies than their opposition. We are ready for whatever is to come.

An unexpected visit to my cell comes in the shape of Sister Mary. Seeing how I'm not a Roman Catholic her visit is a surprise.

"Hello Sister what can I do for you? Would you like a cup of tea?" she's standing in the doorway with her key still in the lock.

"No thank ya I can't stay long. Just been talking with Cormac Murphy O'Connor bout Rita and yourself."

"And who's he then Sister?"

"Oh away with ya he's Archbishop of Westminster. You know who he is!"

"And you've talked to him about Rita? What on earth about?"

"The papers. The story they'll be printing on you's two this Sunday." Her Irish gets thicker the more excited she gets.

"We'll thank you sister but what's he got to do with it?"

"Well he's just got off the phone and he says t' tell ya the story's been stopped."

"What? They aren't going to run it?" I don't understand what she's telling me really.

417

"No they aren't. I've rang Rita and she asked me to let you know."

"Well that's amazing sister. Would you thank him from us? He must have some pull to stop it going out by all the press."

"He has friends in very high places." She raises her eyes skyward. I don't know what to say so I let her go without another word from me.

"I'll be seeing ya on Sunday. Praise God." She closes the door and I reflect on what just went on. All the church Rita is a part of did nothing. The help came from an unexpected direction. Just when we look for help in the obvious place God uses the unusual place, just so you know it's from Him and not from men.

There is still a fly in the soup. The eager young reporter from The Lancashire Evening News, sells her story to my town's local paper, spreading the virus farther. A step too far for the big boys to ignore any longer. Two weeks after the hand of God stopped the story it goes viral. It brings back to mind the onslaught I received at the same hands back in Durham after my injustice verdict. Rita's now dragged into my world of unwanted press attention. Brian The Buddhist's wise words would be 'will it all matter in two hundred years?' Today's news is tomorrow's fish and chip paper. Well it was before the health and safety brigade banned its use for the wrapping of such. As bad as it is we stand together giving each other strength to weather the storm. Maybe we should have took the money and told our true story. Time will tell. Those who know us know the truth of our love and the honour we keep for each other. We will one day be together and we will be free from sleaze.

With one week till I finish my European Computer Driving Licence my new cat D. status is approved. My short stay is coming to an end. Not too soon for me;

this jail is a drudge. One thing holds me here. I have to finish my education course. I've just two more classes to complete to win my academic document of computer competence. HMP Kirkham is waiting. The van comes once a week on a Wednesday. My class is on Mondays. I can go on this week's van or finish the course. I need to get out of here. However, with nothing but my skills to earn a living when I get out I need all the help I can get. With my head overriding my heart I watch the Kirkham van drive out of Wymott with an empty seat. My seat. Will next week's van still have a seat with my name on it? If there's no room in Kirkham I'll have to stay here till they again have a place for me. This week's visit with Rita lifts my spirits. She says all the right things as we endure the austerity of visits Wymott style. That's our last time of no holding and little kissing. The next visit is in the open, naturally lit, friendly environment of HMP Kirkham.

HMP Kirkham

The transport from Wymott is a coach. No handcuffs, one screw. He's the driver, an old guy working out his pension. Who would want to escape from here? If you do you've escaped but if you walk off the site when you get there you've absconded. What's the difference? About 18 months in jail is the difference. Still all are not blessed with common-sense. At the traffic lights in the centre of Leyland one of our unhappy bunch makes his way to the front. He asks the old guy driving to open the door. Without a word he complies. With the sound of compressed air forcing the piston out the door lets in cold fresh air. At the same time it lets out the young guy who just can't resist the urge. May be he knows someone is waiting for him at the other end and that he'll be given that ever-lasting smile. He hops off and the door closes behind him. The old driver turns his head and asks.

"Any more for this stop or are we all going all the way?" No one says a word. Most can't believe the old guy just opened the door and let him off the bus. I understand. Why would he try to stop him? He'll be back. He just escaped but if he'd waited till he got to the jail and then skipped off he would have just absconded. That would have given him less jail when he's captured.

Without knowing we enter the grounds of HMP Kirkham. No wall. No fence. No bars and no cells. Huts like Haverigg with rooms housing one prisoner in each. I can finish off in here. It's a retirement home for screws. There are more gardeners in here than screws. It's a working agricultural market garden. Flowers and vegetables are the income of the jail. Prisoners are the workforce. The gym has the best badminton courts I've seen so far and the screw's an old pal from Garth. First time he sees me he wants me to work in the gym. That's not for me in such an easy jail. It's spring time and the time Kirkham plants seeds. I can work in the greenhouse were the warmth of the early season sun is magnified. If all goes well I'll be here till I'm released next year. Seven years ago 2005 seemed to be a time somewhere in the infinity of a lifetime. Now it's next year. My year. The end of my long fight. A fight where my opponent has been me! My anger and resentment against the people who lied and put me in here was poison. A poison that I was drinking in the hope it would kill them. Now I'm drinking in the love of a woman with a joy that unless you've been there words wouldn't do justice. Visits are between Rita and me. We're alone in the midst of a crowded room. Holding and kissing with a passion never known before. Planning our wedding. Our life. Our first date. Our first day together. That first night of unfettered romance between two lovers. Nothing can slow down time as it races toward that date. The old pals from Garth are here. All except Eddy who was given his parole just before Christmas. Mr Blue Suede Shoes is here better known as T.J. The suit and shoes have been swapped for blue work-wear and black boots. Tom Jones in a donkey jacket. I think it's more surreal than when I saw him in Preston. The Wednesday night chapel get-together, common to all jails, is no different here. Tonight the entertainment is to be our very own TJ. The interest is overwhelming, not a seat to be had in the theatre of God's house. I can't help thinking it's a full house for the wrong reasons. T.J. makes a living as a tribute act. Respect for his skills is not apparent here. Linda, the chaplain, gives the big build up competing with the cacophony, whoops and howls congregation. A venue even Johnny Cash would think twice about facing. With the full catalogue complete, despite the constant requests for a song he wasn't singing, some not even from Tom's collection, T.J. raps the evening up with 'Green Green Grass of Home'. The dream of a man on his way to his death on death row. How we dream of our green green grass of home. Instead of the green grass of Kirkham where if you walk on it instead of the path you hear that familiar shout 'get off the grass!' The ducks are the only ones with the freedom to defile the green grass of Kirkham. The saying here is; 'if you hit a screw you get seven days taken off your remission. If you kick a duck you get fourteen days. Two screws are worth one duck'. Not only prisoners from the past are here. The gym screw has moved on closer to his end term and too has governor Brown. I saw him heading over to the admin building when I was heading over to the post office for my letters of love. We work to our day of freedom and so it would seem, do they. It's enough to give you Stockholm syndrome. Back in Preston I said to a nasty screw, who was swearing and screaming at a fellow prisoner outside the chapel, giving profanity its true meaning, "I think I have Stockholm syndrome." My satire was completely lost on the ignorant putz. He asked me, 'do you need a doctor?' I told him, 'I think I'll get over it with a bit of help from people like you'. I'm not the only one who governor Brown influenced with his common-sense interpretation of prison rules. Rita holds him in high regard. He saw her waiting in the visits and took the time to talk to her. When they had finished he told her it would all turn out right for us and this was the best chance I would have at getting out. He wished us all the best and was sincere. If only my parole rested on his shoulders instead of a faceless bureaucrat in London who only knows what is written in my prison file. Pointless as it is, the automatic parole process has started. Nothing is in my favour. Even less than last year. But I can see the finish line creeping closer. A year of badminton and picking tomatoes for twelve pounds a week isn't that bad and next year I'll start my reintroduction to the outside world. A world of DVD players and flat-screen TVs. Phones without boxes and doors without locks. Worthy opponents are thin on the grown. Brian the Buddhist just won't play me now. He plays little Gary who he thinks with his six-foot Buddha-resembling frame he can bully. Size isn't a good indicator of dominance. Gary has been in the toughest of jails. In Frankland maximum security jail he hit the gym, everyone does at some time, at four foot ten and about forty kg he was never going to be a contender for any muscle man competition. Even with the smuggled- in steroids Gary only reached a record weight of sixty kg, with the attitude of a two hundred kg meat-head. He punched above his weight. Literally, Gary threw all his bulk into a punch that connected with its intended target only to snap his own arm. That ended Gary's ambition to be king of the weights and turned him on to short tennis. They play half hour of tennis and argue for the other half hour over line calls. While waiting for my challenger to show face I warm up. Hitting the birdie against the gym wall. Waiting on the tennis court for the same reason is Ted.

"Do you want me to hit some back to you Ted?" I ask him. Warming up on the tennis court will do me.

"No you're okay mate," I can't weigh up where he's from. He has an educated tone in his indistinguishable ascent.

"Do you know how to play badminton Ted?" Maybe he can hit a few back to me!

"I can play a game till our partners come if you like," he says.

"First to twenty-one and I'll let you serve first," I can't take the mick or he'll never play me again. He beats me twenty-one to nil. Before I know what went on Ted is thanking me for the game and walking to his court where his mate's ready for him. After the session, having gotten over the shock, I ask Ted, „how come you play so well and only play tennis?"

"I was an under twenty-ones international when I was a younger man. Now I'm getting on towards fifty I take it easy on the tennis courts."

"You can't just stuff me and then not give me a chance of a re-match."

"When do you come to the gym Tony?"

"Every day; I miss evening meal sometimes to get a court." We would take turns missing out on the prison rush for feed to secure a court.

"OK you get the court on Fridays and I'll play you."

Back to winning one point at a time. My game is coming on leaps and bounds. A month it takes to win my first game by one point. Faster, sharper and fitter I am. Ted is the only one who I can get a game off. He wins most of our Friday evening duals. But to be the best you have to beat the best. Even if it is a postmaster who fiddled the books out of a few thousand pounds. When I came here I commented on the expensive looking cars on the car park.

"The officers must be on good money here. Those cars are top of the range." There were cars not out of place on a corporate forecourt.

"They aren't officer's cars. Them are the prisoners," the old guy driving told me.

"Why would you park your car here when you're inside doing your jail?" I asked him.

"Weekend cons son; that building over there," pointing at an accommodation block at the other end of the line of posh motors, "is the weekend jail. They come in after five and for the weekend to do their time. Then they can keep their job on. You'll see after five

424

this car park will be full." Weekend jail! I couldn't get me head round it. Ted lost his job in a small town post office so no weekend jollies for him. A phone is the only thing I have to do with the outside world. Unlike Haverigg the jail has kinda given up on them. I don't know anyone who hasn't got one. One guy even runs an unlocking and repair service from his room. A Japanese Liverpudlian phone expert right on the door step. After my Friday night workout with Ted I join the guys who are sitting outside the hut drinking some orange juice laced with vodka. The screw's office is right next door, one of which stops to comment on the warm evening and the relaxing time the guys are enjoying. When he goes I say to Gary, "can you hear a sort of buzzing, rattling noise?"

"Why I man it's ya phone ringing. Where's it at?"

"In with me badminton bat on the table." I reach over for the bat to unzip the cover.

"I can't believe he never heard it. And you were keeping him talking man. I just wanted to get rid. You're mad mate," he says as he takes another swig of his screwdriver. An appropriate drink under the circumstances.

"I wouldn't want to scupper me chances of parole by getting a nicking. Give us a go on that drink Gary."

"A way and see what Brian's got for us."

"I don't need any drugs," I tell him.

"Why no man I know that. It's a pineapple. A real one. He doesn't know what to do with it."

"How 'bout eating it?" Gary laughs and we head off inside before the screw comes back to find the rattling noise. The pineapple is a strange thing to smuggle into a jail but jail's a strange place. It tastes better than the tinned stuff I had in Haverigg. Just the thing to cool me down after a gym session on a warm evening. Brian is a low-fat vegetarian according to his ID card. You have to show it when you collect your food. They have dining halls here where you sit and eat together. No eating in your toilet here. Brian is nether low fat nor a vegetarian when it comes to weekend breakfast. The full Monty is what he goes for. One thing stands between him and black pudding with fried bread. A screw who knows everybody and where they should eat. Often Barry is pulled at the last step before the bacon hits the plate. Sending him all the way over the camp to the veggie canteen. Oh the price we have to pay for our beliefs. He never misses the coffee and biscuit Wednesday nights in the chapel ether. He says Jesus would have been a good Buddhist he was even reincarnated, according to his understanding of the resurrection. Two old women are this week's turn. A bit different to T.J.s rock roof-raising Delilah. These two old dears have been coming here for years. Unlike T.J.'s night our numbers are depleted. Chocolate Hob Nobs make the low number a good thing for Brian. The small talk turns to the ladies long association with Prison Fellowship. The very same organisation my lovely Rita was instrumental in starting up in the UK.

"You may know a good friend of Tony's," Brian says to one of the old dears who's drinking her tea from a small bone china cup.

"I wouldn't have thought so, who is it?" she asks, not ever thinking we would have a mutual friend.

"Rita Nightingale," he hits her with. Spluttering in disbelief she says, "I heard Rita speaking when she came to our church. Oh you don't know Rita Nightingale. You're teasing me."

"No not really. Rita is my fiancée. We'll be married when I get out."

"Get away from here you're pulling my leg." Its right out of her box and when I ask Linda to back me up she's like a rabbit court in headlights. I have to pinch

426

myself every time I think of Rita and me living together as man and wife. So I can understand this poor woman's amazement. Linda has the job of writing the report for my parole application. I wonder what she really thinks. Her official stand is bog standard. She could be talking about anyone. Just a name change would do for most prisoners. She could have it on a file where only the name needs entering into the blank space.

My day out

The day out is the goal of most prisoners here. When you've jumped through all the hoops you can ask for a day out. You have to name a person who will take you and a place where you would like to spend the day. It has to be Preston or Blackpool. This week is the week when I have jumped through my last hoop. And Saturday is to be my first day out. Seven years without being in the world is coming to an end. Eight o'clock in the morning I, along with a horde of others, wait for the nine o'clock release. Breakfast is served in the waiting room but no one's taking the time to eat it. My stomach won't accept anything but butterflies. Some have been going out for months. Some are going out for four days and others for a week. How can you go home for a week then come back? Seems crazy to me. Rita is on the car park. Sitting in her car looking eagerly for her man. Kisses over we set off for Preston, my chosen destination. Rita knows what it's like to walk out into a world that for so long has been denied. A senses overload is inevitable. Even the speed of the car is faster than the jail-house stroll I've lived with so long. Rita was put outside the main gate of The Little Tiger in Bangkok where she had to make her own way.

Our first stop is a railway carriage cafe where we eat breakfast. The seaside town of Lytham St Anne's is sedate, slow and relaxing. Guss Lives here. A Wednesday night visitor to Garth and a great guy who played guitar and sang gospel songs. He always gave a message with his music. Now I'm here eating breakfast with the woman of my dreams. I don't know if we are alone. For so long I've only saw Rita sitting over the table. A requirement of the day-out is signing on at the local police station. My police station is Preston and the time is a strict twelve noon. After than you are reported

428

as absconded and an arrest warrant is implemented. My first day out isn't going to be my last and at the stick of noon I'm signing my name on my license at the front desk. The day is one of newness. New to me. Where Rita lives. What her children look like. What the world looks like now. What a pub dinner tastes like. We stop on the way back at a very nice pub close to the jail. Brian and Gary need to know all the details of my trip into the 'normal' world. I say to them.

"It was great but it's good to be back to normality."

"This is not the normal world Tony," Brian says, "that is. You'll have to get used to it." It was so alien. How can that be normal? I felt like a fish out of water. Without Rita I wouldn't have gotten through it. In two weeks I can do it again. Then more and more days out till I get one week. I become a weekend con without the posh car on the car park. I might get to go to Rita's for Christmas. A stark contrast from last Christmas. Now that's a prayer I would love to have answered.

"Crowe. You're wanted in the office." The shout from the billet door floods the corridor of my hut. When I come out of my room the messenger is nowhere to be seen. The administration runner is a con who delivers anything that the screw tells him to. This time it's for me to go see what the answer to my requested next day out is.

"You sent for me gov? Crowe," I identify myself to the old guy sitting behind his paper filled desk, his head in a cloud of cigarette smoke. Without looking up he hands me a letter.

"Here you are read that son. And sign to say I've given it to you, there." He hands another A4 form to me for my mark.

"What is it?" I ask him.

"Read it son," he lifts his head sits back and tacks a toke on his cigarette, "you're going home son."

"Your application for early release on parole is granted...." I'm out of there with my unbelievable letter from the Home Office. I need to phone Rita. No waiting in the phone line. My phone is in my pocket and the room is where I'll phone her.

"Brian get on the door kid I've got to make a call. Give me a shout if you see a screw coming our way."

"What's going on? What did the office want? Have they turned down your day release? I told you not to go into any pubs never mind the one down the road. A screw must have seen you." As I press the call button that reads Rita; I hand him the letter.

"Just get the door Brian." Off he heads reading the letter as he goes, telling everyone in the billet on the way.

"Hello my darling is it Okay to talk? I thought you were phoning tonight. I'm just at work now," she says.

"I've been given my parole. I'm coming home. Can you believe that? I'll be home for Christmas. Two more months and I'll be out for good not just for the day," Rita can't get a word in.

"Door," Brian shouts."Tony man a screw's heading right for this billet," he shouts out.

"I've got to go I'll phone you later. Love you."

"God is good. He can make a way where there is no way. Love you so much." I press the end-call button and stash the phone. Brian comes back from his door watch.

"Go on mate you're going home."

"I can't believe I'll be home for Christmas Brian. Let's go an' tell Gary," I reach for me letter.

"Have you read all of this letter mate? It's your second application for parole isn't it?"

"Don't tell me there's something I've misread Brian. Give it here."

"It says right here 'immediate release'. That's tomorrow morning pal not November. You don't have to wait two month. You're going home in the morning my son."

"You are kidding right? They can't do that. They can't just put me out without giving me more notice than half a day."

"No you're out of here in the morning and I'll have your PlayStation." Opportunist Buddhist

"Get on that door I need to tell Rita." The screw's gone past.

"Rita they are going to let me out in the morning I can't believe they're going to put me out without any time to get ready."

"I'm in the probation office building. I'll go next door and ask them what's' going on." Rita's new job is resettlement of offenders. I know. How mad is that? The result of her investigations is no one knows I'm getting out and the people who will keep their eye on me aren't ready for such a dangerous criminal to hit the streets of their town. A multi agency planning strategy (M.A.P.S) meeting needs to be called and people need to be informed of my release. All this takes a week. A week that gives me time to get used to the idea of walking out of a world where I've become institutionalised. September 26th 2004. I walk out of HMP Kirkham and never look back. I'm carrying my property in two bags. The rest Rita took after her last visit. Her very last visit to any prison. The baggage I carried into prison I'm leaving behind. The hate, anger and pain. Is still in that chapel office of Garth. The new life with the new woman in my life along with my new spirit and renewed soul. You will never be free until your soul is healed from the hurt of your past. Rita's car is the only one I need to see on this glorious morning. Holding each other for what feels like an age along with a kiss never before experienced we are the last to drive away. Just as Rita said; God has made a way were there was no way. Against all the odds I'm free. No one, including me, ever thought I would be let out one year and two months early. My God is great. I can't wait to see the new life He has for Rita and me.

THE END
****

Kevin Joseph Commons Eulogy

He was my solicitor, but more than that he was my friend. He once told me if he wasn't a solicitor he would be in prison himself. I didn't ask why and he never told me any more than that. K. J. C. for me will always mean what the man behind the initials was.

The K is for the Kindness he showed to my mother and me when I was sentenced to 12 years imprisonment for a crime he knew I didn't commit. His genuine acts of Kindness to my Mother were the actions of more than just a lawyer to his client. When my sister died he was only too happy to represent the family in all matters. He stepped in and stopped the custody fight for my dead sister's young children, winning the day for my Mother. Kevin worked on the case pro bone for much of the time. He took time out from his busy work load to send my Mother flowers and champagne on her birthday when I was in prison. When the Jail stopped me from wearing my suit in court he thought nothing of going out and buying me a new one using his own money. When I sent Kevin the draft manuscript of my book A Murder of Crows, Salvation he told me I had gotten his eye colour wrong. I said they were blue and in fact they are green. I told him I have poetic licence and they should be blue to match his warm loving personality. Portly was the only other thing he pulled me on. Only because the girls in the office found it funny the boss was described as portly.

The J stands for; what else but Justice. Kevin stood up for justice where ever it was and would seek it out where ever it was hiding. How he kept his continence in the face of clear injustice is a credit to him. He told me he was one of the authors of The Bail Act, an act that was meant to free from prison people who were waiting for their court date. It was, still is, abused by the CPS. Justice he told me, 'was not served today' when he sat with me in a prison cell at Keswick after the police told lie after lie to obtain the committal to Carlisle Crown Court. Justice was what he was thinking about when he told me my plan to beat the police was wrong. I had a plan to fight lies with lies but Kevin told me you are better that them, you shouldn't lower yourself to their immoral standards. He was right. My plan was perfect, it would have closed the door on the lies told by the police and opened a door that meant I was no better than them. He wouldn't lie or cheat even when all around him justice was being attacked with great venom. When someone involved in my case went to him years after I was jailed and asked him to act for them in court he told them it would be a conflict of interest. How many lawyers would have just taken the job and the legal aid cheque?

The C stands for Collector. Kevin told me his love of old buses. A million miles away from crime and courts. He collected books and I was glad when only two months ago he told me he had retained, as he put it, a book I gave him in 2000. The book, Words of a Demented Prisoner is one of only eight printed. I know because I printed it and bound it in Garth prison. It's my words and I was that demented prisoner. After reading the poetry book Kevin sent to me a tome of a thesaurus along with an equally huge dictionary. I can't help thinking now of the times I had to carry them from jail to jail and cell to cell.

Now Kevin is collecting accolades for a life of servitude. From a community he choose as his own and a county he called home. From Carlisle to Barrow in Furness he is a household name. When the police brake down the door of a suspect the cry goes out "Call Kevin J Commons." A gentleman with integrity, how could he have been a lawyer? He was a friend who knows the

434

law. I hope he has been promoted from The Bar to a far off star. Sleep well my friend.

****

Thank you for finishing my book, I do hope you enjoyed the read. Why not contact me by one of the methods below Please remember that the worst day in your life is only twenty-four hours. God loves you and we love you be blessed.

If you liked this why not look at the other books from Tony and Rita.

Words of a Demented Prisoner by Tony Crowe.

The re-mastered best seller Freed For Life. No Going Back By Rita Nightingale.

Drop us a line now at:

Email: tony@ritanightingale.org

Email: rita@ritanightingale.org

Website: http://www.ritanightingale.org

Join us on Facebook or Twitter

www.ingramcontent.com/pod-product-compliance
Lightning Source LLC
Chambersburg PA
CBHW031040110426
42740CB00047B/754